Law and Employment

Discipline

Philip James has been a Senior Lecturer in Human Resource Management at Middlesex University Business School since 1989. Prior to taking up his current post he had lectured at the University of Birmingham and worked as a researcher and editor at Industrial Relations Services. He has researched and written widely in the field of human resource management and taught in the area on a wide variety of degree courses and management seminars. He is a member of the editorial advisory board of the *Human Resource Management Journal*.

David Lewis is Principal Lecturer in Law at Middlesex University Business School, where he has worked since 1973. He is a law graduate who also has a Diploma in Personnel Management and an MA in Industrial Relations. Apart from teaching on a wide range of degree courses and being a regular contributor to specialist commercial seminars, he has considerable experience as a consultant in employment law. He is currently a member of the editorial committee of the *Industrial Law Journal* and a Visiting Lecturer at the University of Wollongong, Australia. His highly successful *Essentials of Employment Law*, currently in its third edition, was first published by the Institute of Personnel Management in 1983.

Law and Employment series

General editor: Olga Aikin

The law relating to employment can seem labyrinthine – but with today's escalating number of legal claims, managers ignore it at their peril.

Managers must be able to construct sound yet flexible and progressive employment policies built on firm legal foundations. This important new series will enable them to meet the challenge. It forms a superbly practical and, above all, accessible source of reference on employment practice and the law.

The IPM has specially commissioned Olga Aikin – one of the country's foremost authorities on employment law, a qualified barrister and well known legal writer – to steer the project. The books have been written by leading employment law experts and human resource practitioners. Together they provide a unique combination of up-to-date legal guidance with in-depth advice on current employment issues.

Other titles in the series include:

Contracts
Olga Aikin

Industrial Tribunals
Roger Greenhalgh

Redundancy
Alan Fowler

Law and Employment series

Discipline

Philip James and David Lewis

Institute of Personnel Management

© Philip James and David Lewis 1992

All rights reserved. No part of this publication may be reproduced, stored in an information storage and retrieval system, or transmitted in any form or by any means, electronic, mechanical, photocopying, recording or otherwise, without the written permission of the Institute of Personnel Management, IPM House, 35 Camp Road, Wimbledon, London SW19 4UX

Typesetting by The Comp-Room, Aylesbury
and printed in Great Britain by
The Cromwell Press Ltd, Wiltshire

British Library Cataloguing in Publication Data

James, Philip
  Discipline. – (Law & Employment Series)
  I. Title II. Lewis, David III. Series
  344.10412598

ISBN 0-85292-485-2

The views expressed in the book are the authors' own, and may not necessarily reflect those of the IPM.

Contents

General editor's foreword	*page* vi
Preface	vii
Acknowledgements	viii
Abbreviations	ix
1 Introduction	1
2 Formulating disciplinary rules	4
3 Designing disciplinary procedures	26
4 Putting the rules and procedures into operation	62
5 Putting discipline into practice	81
6 The consequences of getting it wrong	110
Appendices	
1 Sample disciplinary rules	125
2 Sample disciplinary procedures	142
3 Sources of information and further reading	193
Bibliography	194
List of cases	196
List of statutes and regulations	198
Index	199

General editor's foreword

This series is essentially a user's guide to employment law and good employment practice. The objective is to provide managers, trade unionists and the employees themselves with a basic understanding of the legal rules and basic principles which affect the employment relationship. There is no intention of turning everyone into a lawyer, but today a little knowledge of employment law is far from dangerous and a fair amount can be a positive advantage.

In the past thirty years we have moved away from a situation in which the law relating to employment could be ignored, in which legal actions were few and far between, into one in which the number of legal claims is increasing and in which the law is becoming far more complex. But this does not mean that it is a matter for lawyers, or, even when lawyers are essential, that the decisions have to be left to them alone. Lawyers and consultants can only advise. Business decisions have to be made by managers; employees have to decide whether there is an advantage in suing. The law is rarely 100 per cent certain and the ultimate decision has to be made by the client.

The law is not enough. The purpose of the law is to set minima and devise means of dealing with the fall-back situation when the parties cannot reach a solution. Good employment relations demand far more than mere compliance with legal requirements. They require an understanding of the nature of the relationship between employer and employee and how the manager manages it.

This series is concerned not only with the practical application of the law but also with the problems and issues which arise before, during and after employment. For this reason it starts with the practical situation and explains the law relating to it, the pitfalls and advantages, and suggests approaches which may be helpful.

The authors are all experts in their fields and combine legal knowledge with practical expertise.

Olga Aikin

Preface

When this book was commissioned the authors hoped to utilise their knowledge and experience as polytechnic lecturers. Such has been the gestation period that prior to publication Middlesex Polytechnic was replaced by Middlesex University. As firm believers in the polytechnic concept the authors would therefore like to dedicate this work to the staff and students who contributed so much to the life of the polytechnic at Middlesex. We trust that university status will not result in the total loss of that distinctive flavour that the polytechnic gave to business education.

Finally, it is customary in such a preface for the authors to thank their partners for their unfailing support and encouragement. No doubt Angela and Jenny would agree that it would be wholly wrong for a book on discipline to depart from long established practice! We therefore wish to record both the assistance that they provided and the burdens that we have imposed upon them.

David Lewis
and
Phil James

Acknowledgements

A number of individuals and organisations have provided invaluable assistance in the preparation of this book, and the authors would like to express their gratitude to all those concerned. Special mention should be made of the help provided by the library staff at the IPM and Middlesex University, the access given by Industrial Relations Services, and Fiona Neathy in particular, to the company's survey material on disciplinary procedures, and those organisations which agreed to allow copies of their disciplinary rules and procedures to be reproduced. Finally, the authors wish to thank Maureen Spencer for her incisive comments on the first draft of the book, Anne Cordwent at the IPM for her efficient management of the project and Olga Aikin for her editorial comments and guidance.

Abbreviations

ACAS	Advisory, Conciliation and Arbitration Service
AHA	Area Health Authority
AIDS	Acquired Immune Deficiency Syndrome
BC	Borough Council
CBI	Confederation of British Industry
CC	County Council
CRE	Commission for Racial Equality
DC	District Council
DE	Department of Employment
EAT	Employment Appeal Tribunal
EC	European Community
EOC	Equal Opportunities Commission
EPA 1975	Employment Protection Act 1975
EPCA 1978	Employment Protection Consolidation Act 1978
HASAWA 1974	Health and Safety at Work, etc., Act 1974
HIV	Human Immunodeficiency Virus
HMSO	Her Majesty's Stationery Office
HSC	Health and Safety Executive
ICR	Industrial Cases Reports
IPM	Institute of Personnel Management
IRLR	Industrial Relations Law Reports
IRRR	Industrial Relations Review and Report
IRS	Industrial Relations Services
IT	Industrial Tribunal
LBC	London Borough Council
LTE	London Transport Executive
NFU	National Farmers Union
RHA	Regional Health Authority
SDA 1975	Sex Discrimination Act 1975
SRSC Regs 1977	Safety Representatives and Safety Committee Regulations 1977
TUC	Trades Union Congress
TULR(C)A 1992	Trade Union and Labour Relations (Consolidation) Act 1992
UCATT	Union of Construction, Allied Trades, and Technicians
WIRS	Workplace Industrial Relations Survey

This series has been produced for instruction and information. Whilst every care has been taken in the preparation of the books, they should not be used to provide precedents for drawing up contracts or policies. All terms should be carefully considered in the light of the prevailing law and the needs of the organisation. When in doubt, it is recommended that professional legal advice is sought.

Chapter 1
Introduction

Since the beginning of industrialisation employers have faced problems securing work-force compliance with organisational requirements concerning attendance and performance. Today is no different.

Research conducted in the mid-1980s suggests that in workplaces with twenty-five or more employees around nine employees per thousand are dismissed each year for reasons other than redundancy – a figure which suggests that a worker with a forty-year career has, on average, a 40 per cent chance of being dismissed at some stage for disciplinary reasons.[1] This figure moreover gives only a very partial indication of the scale of disciplinary action taken each year by employers. It takes no account for example, of situations where employees are encouraged to leave 'voluntarily' because they do not 'fit in'. It also takes no account of the widespread use of action short of dismissal.

Disciplinary action against workers therefore remains an important part of the human resource strategies used by employers to bring worker behaviour into line with that required. Its use, however, has potentially harmful as well as beneficial effects. Poor disciplinary practices can give rise to actions for breach of contract and complaints of unfair dismissal or sex and race discrimination. They can also cause damaging management-worker disputes and more generally have a harmful impact on worker commitment and motivation.

Careful consideration consequently needs to be given to the design and operation of disciplinary regimes. Inappropriate or poorly designed procedures, for example, can cause unnecessary delays in dealing with disciplinary issues and generate feelings of unfairness and injustice. In doing so they can undermine the benefits of other aspects of an organisation's human resource strategies. Current trends in disciplinary practice and human resource management more generally usefully highlight this point.

In recent years many employers have, in response to the more hostile and competitive economic environment confronting them, embarked on radical reviews of their existing human resource strategies in an attempt to improve labour recruitment, retention and utilisation. These reviews have frequently resulted in important changes being made to payment and reward systems, 'production technologies' and supervisory practices, and internal training and communication systems. Many of these changes have been aimed at securing greater commitment and flexibility from workers. That is, generating an environment in which workers can be trusted to carry out their responsibilities efficiently without the need for close monitoring and supervision.

At the same time many employers have felt compelled to adopt a more rigorous approach to the enforcement of work rules and standards as they struggle to cope with less favourable financial and product market conditions. This shift of approach is reflected in the statistics on unfair dismissal claims shown in Table 1. As can be seen, these show a steady rise in the number of complaints lodged with the Advisory, Conciliation and Arbitration Service (ACAS) during the past few years.

Table 1   Unfair dismissal cases received and dealt with by ACAS individual conciliation: IT1 and non-IT1

Cases	1988	1989	1990	1991
Received	36,340	37,234	37,564	39,234
Settled	23,582	24,438	22,516	13,321
Withdrawn	5,160	4,583	6,333	7,518
To industrial tribunal	6,479	5,894	6,376	8,051
Total completed	35,221	34,915	35,225	28,890

Source. ACAS annual reports, 1989 and 1991.

The net result of these two trends is that employers are frequently walking a delicate policy tightrope. On the one hand, competitive pressures are seen to necessitate a tougher approach to discipline. On the other, these same pressures are prompting many of them to adopt human resource initiatives which are dependent for their success on the achievement of a greater degree of trust and co-operation between managers and those they manage. It takes no great insight to see that the first of these strategies can, if mishandled, seriously undermine the second.

The process of designing and implementing disciplinary rules and procedures needs, then, to be handled sensitively, with due account being taken of the legal, economic and internal environments in which they are to operate. In other words, care must be taken to ensure that they will in practice do what they are supposed to do. That is, contribute as positively as possible to the wider objectives and goals of the employer.

This book is intended to help employers develop disciplinary procedures which will make such a contribution. More specifically, its purpose is to provide guidance on how to develop and implement disciplinary rules and procedures which will not only meet the legal obligations of organisations but contribute to the effective recruitment, retention and utilisation of their human resources. For this reason it does not, like many other texts, essentially treat the issues of discipline as an extension of unfair dismissal law. Rather the legal context is simply treated as one of a number of considerations which need to be taken into account when designing and applying management policies in respect of discipline at work.

The book is organised as follows. The next two chapters examine in detail the issues, both legal and organisational, that employers need to bear in mind when designing and formulating disciplinary rules and practices. Chapter 4 outlines the principles that should inform the management of discipline, while chapter 5 goes on to provide detailed guidance on how to handle a wide variety of disciplinary situations. The concluding chapter provides a brief summary of the legal liabilities that employers can incur if disciplinary matters are handled wrongly. Examples of disciplinary rules and procedures used by a number of organisations are given in two appendices.

Reference

1. P. K. EDWARDS and C. WHITSON 1989. 'Industrial discipline, the control of attendance and the subordination of labour: towards an integrated analysis', *Work, Employment and Society*, 3, 1 (1987), 1–28.

Chapter 2
Formulating disciplinary rules

Disciplinary rules are intended to let workers know the standards of conduct expected of them, and to provide managers with the necessary authority to carry out their managerial and supervisory tasks. To achieve these objectives they must be: as comprehensive and specific as possible in terms of content and effectively communicated to the work force. Due regard must also be had as to whether they are lawful and conducive to the maintenance of satisfactory management–worker relationships.

Ultimately it is management's responsibility to ensure that adequate disciplinary rules are developed, implemented and communicated effectively. Guidance on the steps necessary to fulfil this responsibility is provided in the ACAS Code of Practice on Disciplinary Practice and Procedures in Employment and the ACAS advisory handbook *Discipline at Work*.[1] The first of these is of particular significance, since it is admissible in evidence in unfair dismissal proceedings and, where considered relevant by a tribunal, must be taken into account when determining the fairness of a dismissal.[2] In contrast, the ACAS handbook, strictly speaking, has no legal status. However, in practice, industrial tribunals do attach importance to its guidance when considering unfair dismissal cases.

The ACAS code states that when drawing up rules the aim should be to 'specify clearly and concisely those necessary for the efficient and safe performance of work and for the maintenance of satisfactory relations within the work force and between employees and management' (paragraph 6). Obviously the rules that organisations deem necessary will differ as a result of variations in their operational requirements, internal structures and management and worker attitudes and relationships. This is acknowledged in the ACAS code, which states that 'the rules required will vary according to particular circumstances such as the type of work, working conditions and size of establishment' (paragraph 6).

The lawfulness of rules

Employers have considerable discretion as to the types of behaviour which they wish to make the subject of disciplinary rules. However, this discretion must be exercised reasonably and in accordance with statutory and common law obligations. Otherwise rule enforcement will be vulnerable to legal challenge via complaints of unfair dismissal, allegations of racial or sexual discrimination, or actions for breach of contract.

Particular care should be taken to avoid requirements that have a disproportionate effect on one sex or a particular racial group which cannot be justified on grounds other than those of sex, marital status or race. These will constitute indirect discrimination under the Sex Discrimination Act 1975 and the Race Relations Act 1976. For example, the ACAS advisory handbook draws attention to the dangers of imposing unjustifiable rules in relation to mobility of employment, language standards and the wearing of particular clothing or uniforms.

An EOC investigation into the Leeds Permanent Building Society usefully highlights the dangers of mobility clauses which have a disproportionate impact on one sex. In this case the EOC examined the practical implications of the society's requirement that staff at executive officer grade or above had to be mobile throughout the country. It found that in practice more men could comply with this requirement than women and that as a result the latter suffered a detriment with regard to promotion prospects. The EOC went on to conclude that the application of the clause was unjustifiable and unlawful.

The potential discriminatory effect of language requirements is similarly highlighted by British Rail's decision to review the selection test procedures used in respect of its train driver training course as part of a settlement of a claim by eight Asian guards that the tests used were racially biased. Prior to the settlement, the industrial tribunal had heard expert evidence that the verbal reasoning tests used as part of the selection procedure were not relevant to the job and put those who spoke English as a second language at a disadvantage because of the strict time controls incorporated into the tests.[3]

It should, however, be noted that Sikhs are exempt from the obligation under the Construction (Head Protection) Regulations 1989 to wear a safety helmet on a construction site.[4] Compliance with this exemption does not leave employers vulnerable to allegations of discrimination from other groups of employees who are required to wear such helmets. Similarly, under section 51 of the Sex Discrimination Act 1975 women may be lawfully excluded from certain types of work where it is necessary to comply with Part 1 of the Health and Safety at Work Act or statutory requirements intended to protect women as regards pregnancy or 'other circumstances giving rise to risks specifically affecting women'.

The subject matter of rules

Salamon has divided the actions which may lead to discipline being imposed into three broad categories:[5]

- Actions contrary to some general societal norms relating to personal behaviour (e.g. fighting, swearing, stealing or drunkenness).
- Actions contrary to specific rules derived from external legislation (e.g. health, safety or hygiene).
- Actions contrary to the managerially determined general work control system (e.g. timekeeping and work performance) or contrary to the concept of managerial authority and prerogative (e.g. failure to obey instructions or insubordination).

Clearly these categories of action are not mutually exclusive. For example, stealing and drunkenness can adversely affect work performance as well as being contrary to societal norms. Nevertheless the categories provide a useful framework to bear in mind when approaching the task of drawing up suitable rules for an organisation. They also highlight the fact that certain issues will almost invariably need to be covered by rules. Thus the ACAS advisory handbook *Discipline at Work* indicates that rules should normally cover the following issues: absence, health and safety (including alcohol consumption), misconduct, substandard work, the use of company facilities, timekeeping, holiday arrangements, and racial or sexual harassment. In relation to some of these issues the handbook provides some useful prompt questions that should be answered when drawing up the rules:

- *Timekeeping*
  Are employees required to 'clock in'?
  What rules apply to lateness?
- *Absence*
  Who authorises absence?
  Who approves holidays?
  Whom should employees notify when they are absent from work?
  When should notification of absence take place?
  When is a medical self-certificate sufficient?
  When will a doctor's certificate be necessary?
- *Health and safety*
  Are there special requirements regarding personal appearance or cleanliness, e.g. length of hair, jewellery, protective clothing?
  Are there special hazards?
  Are there non-smoking areas?
  Is alcohol prohibited?

- *The use of company facilities*
  Are private telephone calls permitted?
  Are employees allowed to be on company premises outside working hours?
  Is company equipment generally available for personal use?

The above are clearly only a sample of the wide range of topics typically covered by disciplinary rules. Others commonly covered include:

- Security (including the right to search employees).
- The use of personal vehicles on organisational business.
- Disclosure of confidential information.
- Availability for overtime working.
- Attendance at medical examinations.
- The claiming of travel and other expenses.
- The ownership of patents and inventions.
- The accepting of gifts or hospitality.
- Contact with the media.
- Undertaking public duties.
- Gambling.
- Fighting.
- The carrying out of cash collections.
- The misuse or theft of company property.
- Compliance with on-site traffic regulations.
- The sale of goods on work premises.
- Engagement in outside work.
- The posting of unauthorised notices.
- Disclosure of relationships with job applicants.

Inevitably organisations will vary considerably regarding the subjects which they wish to cover in rules and the way in which they choose to word the rules relating to those subjects, as the examples in Appendix 1 show. For example, rules relating to health and safety are likely to be considerably more detailed in a chemical plant handling hazardous substances than in an office. Similarly, retail operations may require more detailed rules covering theft and its investigation than other types of enterprise. The same applies to banks and other financial institutions.

Whatever their subject matter, rules should be phrased in clear and unambiguous terms and should leave employees in as little doubt as possible as to what types of behaviour are either expected or prohibited. Thus if the intention is to prohibit employees from consuming alcohol during working hours, then this should be stated directly rather than indirectly, for example by making reference to the use of alcohol on work premises. Such clarity helps avoid unnecessary arguments over the legitimacy of any relevant disciplinary action. It will also lessen the likelihood of subsequent dismissals being found to be unfair by industrial tribunals.

Ironically the issue which is most central to the employment relation, the specification of job duties and standards, is the area where clarity of this sort is arguably hardest to achieve. Opinions as to the approach which should be adopted in this area differ considerably. Some organisations, perhaps particularly in the public sector, prefer to produce relatively detailed job descriptions outlining the main tasks and responsibilities of staff. Others favour a more general approach towards the definition of what employees are expected to do. Both approaches have their advantages and disadvantages.

The use of detailed job descriptions has long been seen by many commentators as a sign of good personnel practice. Supporters of their use argue that such documents give potential and current employees a clear indication of what is expected of them, provide a sound basis for analytical job evaluation schemes, and help ensure that recruitment is carried out in a systematic and fair way. The EOC, for example, argues that well drafted job descriptions, by providing a yardstick against which selection decisions can be made, provide a valuable means of avoiding discriminatory recruitment practices.

Nevertheless, there have been a number of highly publicised examples of organisations choosing to avoid the use of detailed job descriptions and relying instead on very broad and general statements of employee duties and responsibilities. The adoption of this approach has attracted particular attention in the case of a number of greenfield site operations set up by Japanese companies in recent years – although its use is now increasingly spreading to existing brownfield sites as well.[6]

The desire to maximise labour flexibility and avoid the development of unnecessary job demarcations has been a major influence underlying the adoption of this 'minimalist' approach to job definition. Thus it is argued that detailed job descriptions, such as those prepared as part of job evaluation exercises, carry the danger that employees will eventually start resisting doing work which is not mentioned in such documents. This danger, it is argued, remains even if job descriptions make it clear that employees can be required to undertake other, non-specified tasks.

It is not possible to reach any general conclusions about which of these approaches regarding the definition of job responsibilities is best. Much depends on the environment within which they are to be used. The minimalist approach, for example, is likely to be more feasible where grading structures are relatively simple and hence there is less difficulty in defining the boundaries between grades. It is also likely to be more practical where worker commitment is high and there is a substantial degree of trust between managers and workers – a point which again highlights the importance of treating the issue of discipline

Formulating disciplinary rules

as an integral part of human resource management.

In the case of certain types of work it is admittedly possible to lay down quantitative measures of minimum performance. Sales personnel, data process operators and production workers are just some of the categories of worker for whom it may be possible to specify such standards. However, for many kinds of work 'objective' measures of this type are not available. As a result the evaluation of performance inevitably involves a considerable degree of subjectivity and hence scope for disagreements as to whether a given level of performance is satisfactory.

An increasing number of employers have attempted in recent years to minimise the extent of this subjectivity, or at least to systemise its application, through the adoption of formal performance appraisal systems – although there is considerable disagreement concerning whether appraisal should be used to evaluate past performance as opposed to identify training and development needs.[7] Where appraisal systems are employed in this way, appraisers are most commonly required to assess employee performance under a number of headings and also to indicate their overall standard of performance, utilising a standard scale. In some organisations the results of this process are directly linked with pay, for example by using them to determine the size of annual pay increases or the allocation of bonuses and additional increments. However, it should be noted that there is considerable disagreement regarding the desirability of developing a link of this kind.

The establishment of a clear link between pay and the results of appraisal effectively means that those who perform relatively badly are penalised financially, at least in relative terms. Such systems can therefore be seen to incorporate a form of implicit disciplinary action. However, a well designed appraisal system should not be primarily about the imposition of 'negative motivators'. Rather its purpose should be to identify the steps that need to be taken to improve existing performance.

In some cases the steps required may involve the provision of additional training and support, in others the commencement of formal disciplinary proceedings. Indeed, some performance appraisal systems explicitly require disciplinary action to be initiated where performance falls below a given level. If action of this type is envisaged, then it should be done through the disciplinary procedure not through the appraisal process. Under no circumstances should appraisal interviews be transformed into disciplinary hearings.

Where it is possible to specify quantitative measures of required performance, it does not follow that they should always be used. The motivational and disciplinary gains that could be obtained through their use need to be considered alongside the drawbacks associated with them. Several disadvantages merit specific mention here. One is the danger that the standards specified can easily be treated as maximums rather than minimums – a problem which will of course be compounded if the relevant standard is set too low in the first place! Another is the risk that workers will concentrate on the achievement of the specified target, particularly if it is seen as onerous, at the expense of other aspects of their job which, although not quantifiable, are equally important. Sales personnel, for example, may concentrate on the level of orders they obtain rather than the quality of after-sales service they provide. Similarly, production workers may concentrate on output at the expense of quality, or choose to ignore safety rules which conflict with the demands of production.

Drafting rules

The process of drawing up disciplinary rules cannot be carried out properly without a thorough knowledge of the working environment to which they relate. Since such knowledge is likely to be dispersed throughout an organisation, it follows that the process of formulating and revising rules should be subject to widespread discussion and consultation. Only in this way is it possible to ensure that the rules are not only comprehensive and realistic but seen as fair and reasonable.

The importance of such consultation and discussion is stressed in the ACAS code. In it ACAS notes that, to be fully effective, both disciplinary rules and procedures need to be accepted as reasonable by those who are to be covered by them and by those who operate them. It therefore goes on to recommend that management should aim to secure the involvement of employees and all levels of management when formulating new, or revising existing, rules and procedures.

Not all managers will view this approach with great sympathy. Some will see it as a waste of time and an unjustifiable interference with managerial prerogatives. On the other hand there seems little point in unilaterally determining rules and then finding that their application generates considerable ill-will and resistance among workers. Thus the potential value of workforce involvement in overcoming such problems should not be underestimated. It should also be noted that dismissals based on rules agreed with workforce representatives are less vulnerable to successful challenge before an industrial tribunal.

There is no one right way of trying to involve the work force in discussions over rule formulation, although it is obviously sensible to use or build on existing consultative or negotiating machinery, possibly through the establishment of a joint working party (see p. 55). Equally, there is no guarantee that there will be a positive outcome. It may be that management and workers simply have to differ on particular points.

It should also be borne in mind that trade unions are frequently hesitant about getting too closely involved in rule formulation because of fears

Formulating disciplinary rules

that it will undermine their role in representing members against whom disciplinary action is taken. In some organisations unions may additionally avoid entering discussions over rules because the outcome might undermine their existing controls over disciplinary matters and strengthen those of management. Nevertheless, unions are more willing to become involved in negotiations and/or consultation over rules than is commonly supposed, as the extract on work standards taken from the agreement concluded at IBC Vehicles (see below) illustrates.

In any consultative or negotiating process it is vital that management is willing to take all viewpoints seriously and to provide explanations where it is decided to reject a particular idea or suggestion. Sensitivity must also be shown to existing attitudes, practices and traditions in the organisation. Otherwise what appear to be desirable rules may in practice make matters worse rather than better, at least in the short run.

The findings of numerous research studies serve to emphasise the importance of this latter point and in doing so highlight the trade-offs which organisations inevitably have to consider when drafting disciplinary rules. A good example is Gouldner's classic 1950s study of management-worker relations in a gypsum mine in the United States. Gouldner shows how the decision of the mine's new owners to break with the 'indulgency pattern' which had previously characterised relationships at the mine and to replace it with a more authoritarian approach to discipline resulted in a wildcat strike and ultimately led workers to adopt a narrow bureaucratic orientation to their work and to the employing organisation.[8] A similar point emerges from a more recent study of a machine shop carried out by Terry.[9] Management concluded an agreement with the union which required workers to clean 'machine tools and associated equipment'. Workers subsequently adopted a narrow definition of this phrase and refused to continue the informal practice of cleaning the area around their machines, which had never been resented before.

IBC Vehicles, Luton: Extract from
management–union agreement

Standards of conduct

The rules set out below have been drawn up for the guidance and safety of all Employees. In establishing reasonable standards of conduct they contribute to the smooth and effective working of the Company. It is practically impossible to draw up a totally comprehensive list, but the following will be seen to conform with common sense and to fully illustrate the kind of behaviour expected by the Company.

Discipline

1.1. Employees must be prepared for work and at their place of work at the start and end of their normal working day/shift. The same will apply to lunch and other breaks.
1.2. Employees wishing to leave their place of work for any reason must obtain permission from their supervisor.
1.3. Employees must regularly and punctually attend for work and should not be absent or late except for unavoidable reasons. Where circumstances permit, prior approval for absence or lateness should be sought.
1.4. Employees must maintain the required standards of work both in quality and output.
1.5. Employees must carry out the proper instructions of supervision.
1.6. Employees must not sleep during working hours.
1.7. Employees must not be in the canteen during their working hours unless specifically authorised.
1.8 Employees must not defraud the Company or falsify Company documents.
1.9. Employees must not bring alcohol or any non-prescribed drug on to Company premises, nor must they be in an intoxicated or drugged condition whilst at work.
1.10. Employees must not undertake any form of personal business or work, including the sale of articles, whilst on Company premises.
1.11. Assault, fighting, disorderly conduct, indecent behaviour, offensive behaviour and sexual harassment are forbidden on Company premises. (Acts of sexual harassment include unwelcome and unsolicited sexual advances, sexual propositions, unnecessary physical contact, unnecessary and repeated sexual comments that affect individual's employment status, work performance, or the acceptability of the working environment.)
1.12. Employees must not bring any offensive weapon on to Company premises.
1.13. Gambling, betting and moneylending are forbidden on Company premises.
1.14. Employees must not smoke, eat or drink except in authorised areas. Doing so in production vehicles is particularly excluded.
1.15. Employees must not distribute letters or literature or post signs, posters or notices on Company premises without the permission of the Personnel Department.
1.16. Employees must not make money collections for any purpose without management permission.
1.17. Employees must not infringe Company policy covering the giving and receiving of gifts and gratuities.
1.18. Overalls must not be worn in the canteen.

Moreover it is not only non-managerial and supervisory staff who may react adversely to the introduction of new disciplinary rules. Managers

Formulating disciplinary rules

and supervisory personnel may also do so. New rules may be seen as unnecessary or potentially harmful to the co-operative relations they have built up with staff. Alternatively rules may be seen as too lax or inconsistent with other policy requirements. For example, new absenteeism controls may be resisted because they are too time-consuming or because they will cause disgruntlement among workers.[10]

This is not to say that workforce involvement in the development of disciplinary rules will completely avoid such problems. That would be to overstate the case. Unions may formally agree to rules, for example, because they feel they have no alternative rather than because the rules are seen to be acceptable. Similarly, the fact that a union has agreed to a new rule does not mean that the rule will be seen as acceptable by its members, as the Terry study demonstrates. All that is being suggested is that consultation and/or negotiation over rule formulation is likely to minimise the scale of the difficulties that may be experienced.

Disciplinary rules can therefore have costs as well as benefits associated with them. These costs and benefits, both short-term and long-term, need to be considered carefully when revisions of rules are proposed. This again raises the point made earlier about the need to consider how disciplinary rules will impact on other aspects of an organisation's operations. Such considerations may, for example, lead an organisation to avoid tightening disciplinary rules at a time when it is introducing new human resource strategies designed to encourage greater commitment and self-discipline on the part of workers for fear that the former may inhibit the latter.

Specifying offences and penalties

Disciplinary rules should make it clear that failure to meet the standards laid down can lead to disciplinary action. It is desirable to reinforce the point by giving an indication of the types of behaviour that will be viewed as constituting a disciplinary offence. This may be done in the rules themselves and/or by cross-reference to the disciplinary procedure. The extract from the procedure used at GEC Measurements, Leicester (see overleaf) provides a good example of how this can be done.

The ACAS Code of Practice states that 'employees should be made aware of the likely consequences of breaking rules' and in particular that 'they should be given a clear indication of the type of conduct which may warrant summary dismissal' (paragraph 8). The penalties for non-compliance can take a number of forms. The 1979 IPM survey, for example, asked responding organisations to indicate, in relation to four different types of staff, whether they used any of the following eleven sanctions when there were breaches of discipline:[11]

> **GEC measurements, Leicester: extract from disciplinary procedure**
>
> *Acts of misconduct*
>
> The following list is not intended to be comprehensive and merely serves to provide examples of misconduct which through the application of the above disciplinary procedure could lead to dismissal:
>
> - Persistent absence.
> - Persistent lateness.
> - Wilful or persistent bad workmanship or failure to meet company standards.
> - Refusal to obey reasonable and lawful management instructions.
> - Intentionally breaking company rules.
> - Discriminatory action against other employees.
> - Intentionally wasting or misusing time or materials.
> - Unauthorised absence.
> - Wilful or premeditated insubordination.
> - Horseplay.
> - On duty knowingly under the influence of drink or non-prescribed drugs.
> - Offensive language and/or behaviour.
> - Sexual harassment.
> - Intentionally endangering the health and safety of employees.

- Unrecorded oral warning.
- Recorded oral warning.
- Written warning.
- Final warning.
- Withholding increments, merit awards or bonus payments.
- Transfer to other work.
- Downgrading.
- Suspension on full or basic pay.
- Suspension without pay.
- Termination with notice.
- Summary dismissal.

The responses are detailed in Table 2. As can be seen, the most common non-dismissal sanctions reported were the various types of written and oral warning. Each of these was mentioned by at least 68 per cent of companies in relation to all the specified categories of staff. Suspension on full or basic pay was the next most commonly used sanction, mentioned by the majority of respondents for each type of worker. All but one of the remaining forms of penalty were mentioned by less than half the respondents. The exception was the use of suspension without pay, which was reported by more than half the companies for operatives but was rarely used for the other three grades of staff – particularly managerial personnel.

Table 2   Sanctions used in disciplinary cases (% companies)

Sanction	Operatives	Supervisory–technical	Clerical/secretarial	Managerial
Oral warning (unrecorded)	75	73	74	68
Oral warning (recorded)	86	81	83	75
Written warning	94	90	94	86
Final warning	90	87	90	83
Withholding increments, merit awards or bonus payments	15	23	22	25
Downgrading	27	30	25	30
Suspension on full or basic pay	68	64	61	55
Suspension without pay	53	32	30	15
Termination with notice	89	87	89	82
Summary dismissal	74	67	70	60

Source. IPM (1979).

In considering the penalties to be imposed for particular offences careful attention must be paid to their practicality and likely impact both on the individual concerned and on management–worker relations generally. For example, it is pointless providing for the options of demotion or transfer if there is little likelihood that suitable alternative jobs will be available without causing an unacceptable degree of disruption. Thought also needs to be given to whether such penalties are really going to help resolve the underlying problems that gave rise to the disciplinary action or whether it will simply move them to another part of the organisation. The advantages and disadvantages of fines and suspensions without pay similarly need to be weighed carefully. If it is considered desirable to provide formally for the use of these types of sanction, then they should be used as a discretionary alternative to dismissal, possibly in conjunction with a final written warning. Ideally some indication should also be given of the circumstances in which the discretion will be exercised. Otherwise they may appear to be applied in an arbitrary and inconsistent manner, which could have legal as well as industrial relations consequences. For example, some disciplinary procedures provide for transfer to other work to be used as an alternative to dismissal in cases of poor work performance, while others allow such transfers to be imposed only as an alternative to dismissal at the appeal stage (see Appendix 2).

Care must also be taken to ensure that the penalties specified can be lawfully imposed. Suspension without pay, demotion or transfer can be imposed only if contractual authority has been secured in advance or if an individual employee agrees to accept them. Similarly wage rises can be withheld only where employees do not have a contractual right to receive such a rise. Fines and other deductions can be imposed only in accordance with the provisions of the Wages Act 1986 (see p. 72).

The ACAS code states that 'except in cases of gross misconduct no employees should be dismissed for a first breach of discipline' (paragraph 10). Gross misconduct is not defined in the code, and organisations have discretion as to the types of behaviour they include under this heading. In betting shops, for example, the placing of bets by employees is regarded as gross misconduct.[12] However, such discretion must be exercised reasonably. Theft, fighting, malicious damage to company property, flagrant breaches of safety regulations, intoxication by drugs or alcohol, and serious cases of racial and sexual harassment are among the actions commonly treated as gross misconduct.

Every effort should be made to define gross misconduct as clearly and comprehensively as possible. Nevertheless, disciplinary situations will inevitably arise which it was not possible to foresee and hence are not covered by specific rules. Indeed, this point is acknowledged in the ACAS code (paragraph 6).

The absence of a relevant rule does not necessarily mean that an employee cannot be dismissed fairly for acts of gross misconduct. However, such dismissals will be upheld in only two types of situation: where a tribunal concludes that an employee should have been aware that the relevant conduct would be viewed gravely either because it was broadly comparable to other offences listed in organisational rules as constituting gross misconduct or because of its inherent nature. Thus in *C. A. Parsons & Co.* v. *McLoughlin* [1978][13] the EAT held that the dismissal of a shop steward for fighting was fair, notwithstanding that there was no express rule dealing with the issue. In doing so the tribunal observed that '. . . these days it ought not to be necessary for anybody, let alone a shop steward, to have in black-and-white in the form of a rule that a fight is something which is going to be regarded very gravely by management'.

It is consequently advisable to make it clear that the types of behaviour listed as constituting gross misconduct are intended to give only an indication of the forms of behaviour covered. The extract from the disciplinary

Formulating disciplinary rules

procedure at Weidmuller (Kipton Products) Ltd given below provides a good illustration of this approach. The value of a clause of this type must not however be overestimated. For example, in *Meyer Dunmore International* v. *Rogers* [1978][14] the EAT held a dismissal for fighting unfair even though there was a rule prohibiting 'any assault or violent act'. In reaching its decision the EAT observed that: 'If employers wish to have a rule that employees engaged in what could properly and sensibly be called fighting are going to be summarily dismissed, as far as we can see there is no reason why they should not have a rule'.

Dismissal should not be made an automatic penalty in relation to acts of gross misconduct, since unfair dismissal law still requires consideration to

---

Weidmuller (Kipton Products) Ltd: extract from disciplinary procedure

Gross misconduct

Examples of offences (not exhaustive) which *will normally result in summary dismissal* are:

- Gross neglect of duty.
- Grossly offensive behaviour.
- Gross neglect of safety rules.
- Deliberate damage to Company assets.
- Incitement to or use of physical violence towards anyone at all on Company premises or whilst on Company business.
- Fraudulent timekeeping.
- False and misleading statements, e.g.:
    (i) On application of employment or at medical examination.
    (ii) At accident investigation.
    (iii) During employment designed to harm the Company and/or other employees.
- Failure to obey instructions given by the Company (provided these are in accordance with accepted practices).
- Theft, incitement to steal or deliberately damaging property on Company premises.
- Bringing of firearms and/or misuse of offensive weapons on Company premises.
- Drunkenness during working hours.
- Accepting secret profit or bribe.
- Divulging confidential information.
- Allowing private interest or duty to conflict.
- Misuse of drugs.
- Clocking in or out for another person.
- Sleeping on duty.

be given to whether it is an appropriate sanction in the circumstances. Thus in *Taylor* v. *Parsons Peebles* (1981)[15] the employer dismissed Mr Taylor in accordance with its policy of dismissing any employee who deliberately struck another. The industrial tribunal which heard the case found the dismissal to be fair. The EAT, however, overruled the tribunal's decision on the grounds that no consideration had been given to whether dismissal was reasonable in the circumstances. In the Appeal Tribunal's view it was unreasonable because the company had not taken into account other relevant matters, such as the employee's long service and previous good conduct. Rules relating to gross misconduct should therefore be phrased to indicate that such conduct will 'probably' or 'likely' result in dismissal.

As to the penalties that can be imposed in respect of offences falling short of gross misconduct, organisations differ considerably regarding how much guidance they give. Some prefer to leave the issue completely open, while others provide relatively detailed guidelines. The latter approach is perhaps to be preferred, since it limits the scope for subsequent argument over the fairness of any disciplinary action taken.

Guidance on the potential penalties associated with particular types of offence can be given in several ways. One is to list the main types of offences and then draw up a table which outlines the potential penalties associated with them. The procedure used at Wiggins Teape provides a good illustration of this approach (see Appendix 2). Another approach is to indicate the types of misconduct which are associated with particular types of penalty. The disciplinary procedure of County Nat West, also reproduced in Appendix 2, provides an example of this alternative approach. By way of contrast, some organisations simply prefer to specify the types of offence which can result in the standard disciplinary procedure being short-circuited (see p. 38). Whichever approach is adopted however, care must be taken to ensure that managers are left with sufficient flexibility as to the precise penalty to be applied. Otherwise they may be forced into taking disciplinary action which is unreasonable in the circumstances of a particular case.

Communicating rules

Once disciplinary rules have been formulated all but the smallest employers are legally obliged to inform employees of them. Under section 1 of the EPCA 1978 employers are required to provide employees, within thirteen weeks of the commencement of their employment, with a written statement containing certain particulars of their terms and conditions of employment. If the organisation has more than twenty employees, this statement must contain a note which specifies any disciplinary rules applicable to the employee or makes reference to a reasonably accessible document where they are specified. Such a note must also be given, or at least be made available, where employers are exempt from the requirement to provide a statement of particulars under section 1 because the relevant terms and conditions of employment are contained in a written contract. In addition, employers are obliged to inform employees by means of a written statement of any subsequent changes made to the disciplinary rules within a month (section 4). This statement may either detail the changes concerned or refer to another document where they may be found, provided that employees have a reasonable opportunity of reading the document during the course of their employment.

The statement of written particulars provided under section 1 of the EPCA does not constitute a contract or even conclusive evidence of its terms. This therefore raises the important question of whether organisations should make it clear in letters of appointment that work rules form part of the contract of employment or alternatively whether they should rely on the status of rules as 'lawful orders'. The first approach has the advantage of spelling out the contractual obligations of employees clearly and reinforcing the notion that the employment relationship is characterised by mutual agreement between employer and employee. On the other hand, it does place limits on management's freedom of action, since any changes in the rules have to be agreed with employees, either directly or through their trade union.

One final point should be noted about the statement of particulars required under section 1 of the EPCA. This is that the statement does not need to contain details of any rules relating to health and safety. The rationale for this seems to be that such rules should be covered by the safety policy statements required under the HSWA 1974.

Section 2(3) of the 1974 Act requires every employer, except those who for the time being employ fewer than five employees, to:[16]

> Prepare and as often as may be appropriate revise a written statement of his general policy with respect to the health and safety at work of his employees, and the organisation and arrangements for the time being in force for carrying out that policy, and to bring the statement and any revision of it to the notice of all his employees.

No further details are given as to what should be included in this statement of policy or how it should be brought to the notice of employees, although official guidance has been published by the Health and Safety Commission. This guidance makes clear that it is acceptable for the statement to make reference to other documents containing more detailed information on such matters as working procedures and practices. Ideally a copy of the safety policy should be given to all employees and its contents explained as part of the induction process.

The same principles apply to the dissemination of disciplinary rules more generally. For example, the ACAS code states that every effort should be made to ensure that employees know and understand such rules and goes on to observe that this 'may be best achieved by giving every employee a copy of the rules and by explaining them orally. In the case of new employees this should form part of the induction programme' (paragraph 7). The ACAS advisory handbook also emphasises the importance of ensuring that rules are understood by young people with little experience of working life and by employees whose English is limited.

In larger organisations rules should be, and usually are, included in staff handbooks. Steps should also be taken to ensure that they are accessible during the working day. This may be done by posting copies on notice boards, ensuring that workers' representatives and line managers have copies, and making clear that they are available in the personnel department.

Organisations differ as to how they go about specifying rules in their staff handbooks. One approach is simply to list the obligations of employees regarding such matters as timekeeping, attendance and health and safety under the relevant sections of the handbook and then to list any remaining requirements under a separate section. The extract from John Laing's handbook (see overleaf) provides an illustration of this approach. Other employers prefer to produce a far more comprehensive list of rules which effectively summarise all the main obligations of employees (see Appendix 1). Whichever approach is adopted, however, it is advisable to include a catch-all clause which makes it clear that employees are expected to comply with reasonable instructions given by management and any formal organisational rules relating to their employment.

The importance of communicating rules effectively to employees cannot be overemphasised. Failure to do so may not only result in employees being unaware of the standards of performance expected of them, but may also increase the likelihood of disciplinary action being seen as unfair or unreasonable by both employees and industrial tribunals. For this reason management should not delegate the task of communication to trade unions by adopting a policy of agreeing rules with them and then assuming that the unions will convey them to their members. Tribunals have found dismissals in this type of situation to be unfair when they were not convinced that the unions had made members sufficiently aware of the rules that were alleged to have been broken.

The point is illustrated by the decision in *W. Brooks & Son* v. *Skinner* [1984].[17] In this case a storekeeper/loader who got so drunk at the company's Christmas party that he fell asleep and failed to turn up for the night shift was dismissed. Behaviour of this type following the Christmas party had been treated leniently in the past by setting the absence against holiday leave. However, this particular year management had agreed with the union beforehand that any employee engaging in such behaviour would be dismissed. A copy of the agreement had been shown to Mr Skinner. Nevertheless, the EAT upheld the industrial tribunal's finding of unfair dismissal on the grounds that the new rule had not been made sufficiently clear to him.

The implementation of rules

Workers should be given reasonable notice before new disciplinary rules come into operation. This is especially important where a new rule may cause hardship or discomfort, for example a ban on smoking. The same applies when it is decided to start enforcing an existing rule more rigorously. In both types of situation it is desirable to provide staff with an explanation of the change of policy to prevent it being seen as arbitrary or inconsistent. It must be emphasised that sudden shifts in disciplinary rules should be avoided for industrial relations as well as legal reasons. Employees may react to such changes in a hostile way and, even if they don't, a considerable amount of good will may be lost.

Once in operation rules must be applied consistently, otherwise any subsequent dismissal may be found to be unfair. They must also be applied in a reasonable and non-discriminatory manner. For example, disciplinary action for breaching a rule requiring workers to 'obey all reasonable orders' should not be countenanced if the employee was required to contravene a statutory health and safety requirement or to act in a discriminatory fashion. Not only is this unacceptable on moral grounds but it would leave the employer vulnerable to action for breach of contract and claims of unfair dismissal or race and sex discrimination. Thus in *Showboat Entertainments* v. *Owens* [1984][18] the dismissal of an employee because of his refusal to carry out an instruction to exclude blacks from the employer's premises was found to amount to unlawful discrimination under section 1(1)(a) of the RRA 1976.

Primary responsibility for enforcing disciplinary rules on a day-to-day basis will invariably rest with line managers. It is therefore important that they are adequately informed of their disciplinary responsibilities and given the skills and authority necessary to carry them out (see p. 57). Senior management must also demonstrate willingness to support managers on disciplinary issues, otherwise managers will see little point in taking their role seriously. The lack of such support is an all too common source of complaint among supervisors and junior managers.

Finally, the implementation of disciplinary rules should be monitored, so that any unsatisfactory features of the rules themselves or their operation can be identified – for example, unacceptable variations in the way in which they are enforced as between different departments,

John Laing group of companies: extract from staff handbook

Company rules

You are asked to observe certain rules while in our employment. The rules are made for our mutual benefit and you should raise with your manager any problem you experience with them.

Use of private cars. Before using a private car on company business, you must obtain written approval as a registered user, on the appropriate form available from Personnel Department.

Gifts. The company does not allow its employees to accept gifts from, or to make gifts to, anybody with whom it has or may have business connections.

Part-time jobs. We expect that an employee will be able to devote his full energies to his work. Should you wish to take on part-time employment (including lecturing) outside working hours you should discuss the matter with your manager.

Public duties. Should you wish to undertake public duties you should discuss the matter with your manager.

Publications. Staff intending to publish books, technical papers or articles which are concerned with the work of the company or its subsidiaries should first submit the draft to their manager for approval. Enquiries from the press, radio or television should be referred to the Public Relations Service.

Confidential information, inventions, patents and design works. In a competitive world any lively and expanding organisation seeks to keep ahead by originating and developing new ideas, techniques, equipment and materials. Those engaged on this work, and others who, in the course of their conduct of company business, are entrusted with information of a confidential nature, which may include patentable ideas, will expect that the company should take proper steps to safeguard the security of this information. Your attention is, therefore, drawn to the rules on confidential information, inventions, patents and design works printed on the facing page, which all employees are required to observe.

Safety regulations. We set considerable store by our reputation in accident prevention and we look to the staff to maintain this by strictly observing all safety regulations, not only in their own interest but also as an example to others. If your employment takes you on to construction sites or into factories and the nature of the work calls for the wearing of protective equipment, do not go without it. As required by the Health and Safety at Work, etc., Act 1974, an abstract of our Group safety policy is printed on p. 33 of this handbook.

Fire regulations. Strict fire regulations apply to all company premises, and it is your responsibility to read the fire instructions in your office, locate the fire alarm and emergency exits and also to take part in precautionary exercises.

General. On sites, in depots, factories and offices, rules may be published to meet varying conditions and the nature of the work. These rules will be posted on notice boards or circulated to individuals as appropriate.

Formulating disciplinary rules

or management–worker disagreements over their interpretation. Such monitoring can be conducted in a number of ways. For example, in the area of health and safety, inspections and audits can be carried out and accident figures and reports studied. More generally, useful information on the appropriateness of rules and their implementation can be obtained from such sources as formal disciplinary hearings, attitudes surveys, exit interviews, workers' representatives and simple observation.

Key points

- Disciplinary rules are intended to let workers know the standards of conduct expected of them and the consequences of not meeting them. Employers have considerable discretion in determining such rules, but this discretion must be exercised reasonably. Absence, health and safety at work, substandard work, the use of company facilities, time-keeping, holiday arrangements and racial or sexual harassment are among the topics normally covered by rules.
- Every effort should be made to ensure that rules are reasonable, realistic and as specific and comprehensive as possible. These objectives are best achieved by involving employees and all levels of management in their formulation. Where trade unions are recognised it is desirable for rules to be agreed with them. However, unions may prefer not to get involved in rule formulation to that extent. If such is the case, they should be given the opportunity to be consulted.
- The sanctions that may be imposed vary from oral and written warnings at one end of the spectrum to dismissal with or without notice at the other. Sanctions between the two extremes include fines, transfers and demotion, the withholding of pay rises and suspensions without pay. If these latter options are to be used, they should be used as a discretionary alternative to dismissal. Employers must ensure that they can impose them lawfully.
- In considering the sanctions to be used, employers must consider both their practicability and their acceptability in the workplace. Except in the case of gross misconduct, an employee should not be dismissed for a first offence. Behaviour which will be held to constitute gross misconduct should be listed in the rules. This list should be as comprehensive as possible. It is nevertheless advisable to make it clear that the list is intended to give only an indication of the types of offence that will be held to amount to gross misconduct. It is also important to make it clear that dismissal is a 'probable' rather than automatic outcome when an employee is found guilty of gross misconduct. Indeed, mechanistic approaches to the application of all penalties should be avoided as far as possible.

- It is vital that rules are communicated effectively to employees if the rules are to affect behaviour in the way intended and not lead to successful complaints of unfair dismissal. This is best done by giving copies to employees and explaining them during induction programmes. All but the smallest employers in any event have statutory obligations relating to the provision of disciplinary rules under the EPCA 1978 and the HSWA 1974. Under no circumstances should the communication of rules be delegated to trade unions.
- Employees should be given reasonable notice before new rules come into force or existing ones are more rigorously enforced. Explanations of such changes should also be provided. Sudden shifts in disciplinary policy should be avoided as far as possible for both legal and industrial relations reasons. Once they are in operation, rules must be applied in a reasonable, consistent and non-discriminatory manner.
- Line managers will invariably have primary responsibility for enforcing disciplinary rules on a day-to-day basis. The content and importance of rules must consequently be explained to them. The same applies to any proposed changes. They must also be provided with the skills and authority, including the backing of senior management, necessary to carry their responsibilities out. The implementation of rules should be monitored to identify any problems associated with their operation, such as too great variations in the way in which they are applied by managers in different departments.

References

1. ADVISORY, CONCILIATION AND ARBITRATION SERVICE, *Discipline at Work: the ACAS advisory handbook*, ACAS, 1990.
2. See section 6(11), Employment Protection Act 1975.
3. See *Equal Opportunities Review*, August 1991, p. 8.
4. Construction (Head Protection) Regulations 1989, SI 1989 No. 2209.
5. M. SALAMON. *Industrial Relations Theory and Practice*, Prentice-Hall, 1987.
6. See, e.g. P. WICKENS, *The Road to Nissan*, Macmillan, 1987.
7. See C. FLETCHER AND R. WILLIAMS, *Performance Appraisal and Career Development*. Hutchinson, 1985.
8. A. GOULDNER, *Wildcat Strike*, Harper, 1954.
9. M. TERRY, 'The inevitable growth of informality'. *British Journal of Industrial Relations*, 25 (1977), 76-90.
10. See M. MARCHINGTON and P. PARKER, *Changing Patterns of Employee Relations*, Harvester, 1990.
11. INSTITUTE OF PERSONNEL MANAGEMENT. *Disciplinary Procedures and Practice*, IPM, 1979.

12. *Ladbroke Racing* v. *Arnott* [1983] IRLR 154.
13. IRLR 65.
14. IRLR 167.
15. IRLR 119.
16. See Employers' Health and Safety Policy (Exception) Regulations, SI 1985 No. 1584.
17. IRLR 379.
18. IRLR 7.

Chapter 3
Designing disciplinary procedures

Disciplinary procedures lay down the procedural mechanisms through which the behaviour of employees can be brought into line with that expected of them. The process of formulating such procedures requires considerable thought and care if they are to perform this function both efficiently and lawfully.

The ACAS Code of Practice on disciplinary practice and procedures provides a fundamental starting point when considering the preparation, revision and implementation of disciplinary procedures. The code emphasises that procedures should be viewed primarily not as a means of imposing sanctions but as a way of encouraging improvements in individual conduct. Paragraph 10 of the code goes on to suggest that procedures should:

- Be in writing.
- Specify to whom they apply.
- Provide for matters to be dealt with quickly.
- Indicate the disciplinary actions which may be taken.
- Specify the levels of management which have the authority to take various forms of disciplinary action, ensuring that immediate superiors do not normally have the power to dismiss without reference to senior management.
- Provide for individuals to be informed of the complaints against them and to be given an opportunity to state their case before decisions are reached.
- Give individuals the right to be accompanied by a trade union representative or by a fellow employee of their choice.
- Ensure that, except for gross misconduct, no employee is dismissed for a first breach of discipline.
- Ensure that disciplinary action is not taken until the case has been carefully investigated.
- Ensure that individuals are given an explanation for any penalty imposed.
- Provide a right of appeal and specify the procedure to be followed.

These principles more or less reflect the rules of natural justice, so the importance of bearing them in mind when drafting disciplinary procedures cannot be overemphasised. Failure to build them into procedures will considerably increase the likelihood of subsequent dismissals being ruled unfair (see Chapter 6). Nevertheless, they must be applied in a way which accords with the structure and culture of the particular organisation.

The issues that need to be considered when formulating disciplinary procedures can usefully be discussed under the following headings:

- The coverage of procedures (in terms of organisational level, workers and subject matter).
- The specification of offences and penalties.
- The provision of informal counselling.
- The location of managerial responsibility for discipline.
- The handling of appeals.
- Third-party intervention.
- The representation of employees.
- The processes of procedure drafting and implementation.

The coverage of the procedures

Organisational level

A crucial issue to be resolved in multi-establishment enterprises is the level at which procedures are to apply. A number of options are possible. They range from the workplace, through intermediate levels (such as divisions and business centres or units) to the whole organisation. Examples can be found of procedures operating at each of these levels. However, recent years have seen a growing number of organisations decentralising their procedural arrangements, most notably to the workplace level.

Workplace-based procedures have a number of advantages. In particular, they enable procedures to be more locally based and hence more responsive to local precedents and sensitivities, they involve fewer levels of decision-making, and they reinforce local management responsibility for disciplinary matters. On the other hand, decentralisation carries the risk of issues being mishandled by inexperienced managers and union representatives. Such people may have little understanding of the relevant procedural and legal requirements or the broader industrial relations environment within which decisions have to be made.

Conclusions about the level at which disciplinary procedures are to be formulated and operated should be reached only after careful deliberation. The scale and variety of an undertaking's activities, the extent to which management is centralised or decentralised, the degree and nature of trade union organisation, and the levels at which other personnel issues are dealt with, are among the important factors to be borne in mind. For example, decentralised procedures are likely to be attractive where there are a number of different workplaces all of which employ significant numbers of workers and have well staffed personnel departments. They are likely to be less appealing if the organisation consists of a large number of small establishments where personnel issues fall within the remit of a non-specialist line manager. Similarly, decentralisation is more likely to be favoured by companies whose activities are spread across a wide range of different industries than by those which operate in one type of market and whose operations are characterised by relatively little variation in work activities or management structures. Decentralised collective bargaining arrangements are also likely to be seen as conducive to the devolution of responsibility for disciplinary matters.

Obviously no hard-and-fast rules can be laid down concerning the organisational coverage of procedures. However, it is worth noting that the majority of workplaces with twenty-five or more employees seem to be covered by procedures which apply to more than one workplace. Thus the 1980 Workplace Industrial Relations Survey (WIRS) found that only 20 per cent of procedures applied solely to an individual workplace. The remainder either also applied to other parts of the parent organisation or operated on an industry-wide basis. Indeed, virtually all procedures in the public sector operated at one of these two levels.[1]

Multi-site procedures do not necessarily provide for managers from outside the workplace to become directly involved in handling disciplinary issues. Thus some simply set out a framework for how disciplinary cases are to be handled within the workplace. Others do, however, require senior managers from elsewhere in the organisation either to participate in the latter stages of procedures or to be consulted before dismissal decisions are taken.

Whichever approach is adopted, care must be taken to ensure that the arrangements specified are relevant to all the workplaces covered, since job titles may differ between different locations, as may the depth of the management hierarchy. One way round the first of these problems is to use generic descriptions to indicate the level of management which has authority to take particular types of disciplinary action, i.e. immediate supervisor, first-line manager, second-line manager, etc.

Types of worker

A major objective of disciplinary procedures is to ensure that disciplinary matters are dealt with in a fair and consistent manner. As a general rule, therefore, it is undesirable to operate different procedures for different groups of workers.

The ACAS handbook emphasises that in no circumstances should the application of procedures vary according to an employee's length of service. Not only is such a distinction morally questionable, it can give rise to both legal and practical problems. For example, employers may be vulnerable to claims of indirect sex discrimination if it can be shown that a smaller proportion of women qualify for the superior protection afforded to long-service employees. Such a distinction can also cause confusion and generate feelings of injustice. For similar reasons procedures should apply equally to full and part-time employees.

In some situations the development of separate procedures for different groups of workers may be considered unavoidable. Management structures may vary between one section of a work force and another to such an extent that it is not feasible to have one common procedure. Similarly, variations in procedural arrangements may be required in multi-union situations to deal with differences in union policies and representative arrangements. Where such situations exist every effort should be made to ensure that procedures are as similar as possible and do not afford greater protection to particular categories of staff. Thus attempts by stronger union groups to secure more favourable arrangements should either be resisted, or, if agreed, extended to other groups as well.

According to the 1984 WIRS, the vast majority of organisations operate uniform procedures for all staff.[2] Where this is not the case, the most common situation is for manual and non-manual staff to be covered by separate arrangements. It appears that technical and professional staff in particular are likely to be covered by non-uniform procedures.

Subject matter

Most disciplinary procedures are open-ended in nature. The range of issues to be dealt with under them is not usually limited, and the procedural arrangements laid down are intended to cover the multitude of different types of situation that may give rise to dissatisfaction with an employee's performance. However, in recent years employers have been adopting a more differentiated approach to the handling of disciplinary matters. The result has been that disciplinary procedures are frequently operating in parallel with more specific procedural arrangements dealing with particular topics or else make provision for some issues to be handled in different ways. Absenteeism, race and sexual harassment, alcohol and drug abuse, and work capability, are some of the main issues frequently singled out for special treatment.[3]

The evolution of this differentiated approach reflects a number of influences. One is the emergence of unfair dismissal case law, which has indicated the procedural steps that must be taken by employers if dismissals on grounds of ill health or poor work performance are to be regarded as fair. Similarly, growing awareness of the extent of racial and sexual harassment and the legal liabilities that can flow from it has played a part. Additional factors have been:

- Increased recognition on the part of employers of their wider social responsibilities towards employees.
- Growing awareness of the costs incurred as a result of absenteeism and alcohol and drug abuse.
- The desirability of retaining experienced staff in whom substantial investment has frequently been made.

More generally, the development of these specialised procedural arrangements has frequently been informed by an awareness that there is a need to adopt rather different strategies towards the handling of problems which do not reflect any fault on the part of the employees concerned. Poor work performance, for example, may occur through no deliberate intent on the part of an employee, but may simply reflect inadequate skills or knowledge. For this reason many disciplinary procedures stress that formal disciplinary action should not be initiated in respect of unsatisfactory work performance without steps being taken to try and bring behaviour up to the required standards through counselling, training and other forms of support. The Co-operative Insurance Society's incapability guidelines (opposite) provide a good example of this type of approach.

Disciplinary procedures commonly adopt a similar approach in relation to alcohol and drug abuse. That at Guardian Royal Exchange is a case in point. It states that:

> Where unsatisfactory conduct or performance derives from alcohol or drugs it is more appropriate to deal with the situation as one of ill health or incapability rather than misconduct or incompetence, though much will depend on whether the employee is prepared to accept that such a problem exists and constructively discuss a programme of action.

Where it is decided to develop specific procedural arrangements for dealing with particular issues, and to detail them in a separate document, the question arises as to whether they are to be completely self-contained or whether they are to feed into the general disciplinary procedure at some stage. If it is decided to develop a self-contained procedure, care must be taken to ensure that it operates fairly and consistently, and provides employees with rights equivalent to those provided under the normal disciplinary procedure, for example, the right to be represented and to appeal against decisions. Care must also be taken to ensure that such procedure takes into account the guidance in Chapter 5 on the handling of the relevant issues.

Co-operative insurance society: incapability guidelines

The following guidelines supplement the Society's disciplinary procedure. Where a manager or supervisor is satisfied that an employee has difficulties in performing adequately the duties required because of incapability (by reference to skill, aptitude, health or any other physical or mental quality), and the Society is satisfied that the incapability is genuine, it will be appropriate to follow the following guidelines.

In dealing with such cases, the Society will seek to treat each employee fairly and compassionately, whilst attempting to minimise disruption to the work of the employee's section or department.

Job performance. It is the Society's aim at all times to obtain an improvement in an employee's performance.

The Society will take action which will include:

- Informing the employee as to where there is a shortfall in standards,
- Giving the employee an opportunity to provide an explanation,
- Giving the employee time to achieve the required standard(s) and warning of the likely consequences of failing to improve. Wherever practicable, the employee will be offered assistance in the form of training and/or closer supervision.

If, despite these measures, there is a failure to improve or to maintain the improvement at a level which the Society finds acceptable, the employee will:

- Be informed of the nature of his or her continued unsatisfactory performance and given an opportunity to provide an explanation,
- Be warned of the consequences of a continued failure to improve and the likelihood of dismissal.
- Wherever practicable, be considered for suitable alternative work.

An employee will not normally be dismissed because of unsatisfactory job performance unless warnings and an opportunity to improve have been given.

Ill health. The Society will take action which will include:

- Undertaking a thorough investigation to establish an employee's medical condition and the effect of his or her absence(s) on the section or department, including seeking to obtain a medical report on the employee's condition in accordance with the Access to Medical Reports Act 1988,
- Consulting the employee and discussing the matter with him or her, in order to ascertain the true medical position and the likelihood of the employee's ability to undertake his or her duties to a level which the Society finds acceptable.
- Where a full and prolonged return to work is not anticipated, consideration will be given to other appropriate options, for example, an application for early retirement on the grounds of ill health, suitable alternative work, or return on a part-time basis.

The contract of employment will not be terminated on the grounds of ill health until this procedure has been exhausted.

If it is decided that a specialist procedure will at some stage refer to the general one, thought must be given to the nature of the linkage. For example, if a policy on absence already incorporates a series of warning stages there seems little point in offering further warnings under the formal disciplinary procedure. Clearly, if the purpose of the linkage is to consider the dismissal of an employee it should be spelt out in both procedures. More generally, the nature of the interrelationships between special and general disciplinary arrangements should always be made clear. The extract from the harassment and discrimination procedure at Leicester City Council (below) provides a good illustration of a specialist procedure which does this.

Leicester City Council: extract from harassment and discrimination procedure

THE FORMAL PROCEDURE

Stage 1. Raising a complaint

8   If any person or persons feel that they have been the victim of harassment or discrimination, they should raise the matter with any of the following:

   (a) The Personnel Officer in their department.
   (b) The relevant shop steward or staff representative.
   (c) An officer of Personnel and Management Services Department, Employee Relations Section.
   (d) An officer of the Race Relations Unit and/or Women's Equality Unit.

9   The purpose of this initial stage is to ensure that the employee, or employees, concerned fully understand the procedure and are given assistance in deciding whether or not this procedure is the appropriate one for pursuing the alleged complaint.

10 If the employee, or employees, concerned decides to make a formal complaint, that complaint should be put in writing to the Chief Officer of the department concerned as soon as possible, stating the grounds for the complaint. A complaint against a Chief Officer should be made to the Chief Executive. A complaint against the Chief Executive should be made to the Leader and the Deputy Leader of the Council.

11 The employee or employees concerned will have the right to be represented by their trade union or other representative, who may be a friend or colleague, throughout the procedure. All complainants are strongly advised to seek such representation in making a formal complaint, including assistance with the written complaint as in 12(a) below.

Designing disciplinary procedures

Stage 2. Management investigation

12 (a) The matter will have been referred, in writing, to the departmental Chief Officer. The letter of complaint will state the nature of the complaint and refer to specific occurrence(s).

(b) A senior officer (the 'investigating officer') of at least third-tier level in the department where the person against whom the complaint is made is employed (unless, exceptionally, and by agreement with the Director of Personnel and Management Services, another senior officer is nominated) will normally be delegated to investigate the matter. The Investigation Officer will be conversant with and be briefed on, the procedure.

In the case of a complaint against a Chief Officer, the Chief Executive shall act as 'Investigating Officer' and, in the case of a complaint against the Chief Executive, three elected members shall act in that capacity (subject to any changes which may be made under the model Standing Orders as introduced under the Local Government and Housing Act, 1989).

(c) The Investigating Officer will provide a copy of the complaint to the person against whom the complaint is made, as soon as possible.

(d) The Chief Officer (or the Investigating Officer) may decide, immediately, that the complaint is sufficiently serious to invoke the disciplinary procedure.

13 The Investigating Officer will complete the necessary enquiries into the complaint within ten working days, which should include interviewing all those concerned, separately. The parties involved in the case may be represented at this stage and full notes will be kept by the Investigating Officer. The DPMS or a Personnel Officer from another department* and the Chief Executive through the Race Relations Unit and/or Women's Equality Unit and the representatives of all parties concerned will be present at all interviews. In exceptional cases, the Chief Officer may obtain specialist advice and guidance which may be from outside the Authority.

14 Following investigation, the Investigating Officer with the advice of the DPMS or a personnel officer from another department* and the appropriate units(s), which should be in writing, will decide upon one of the following courses of action, notifying the complainant and the person against whom the complaint is made and confirming in writing within five working days of the decision being taken:

(a) Not to uphold the complaint, with the reasons for that decision.
(b) To take non-disciplinary action.
(c) To take formal disciplinary action. This will be in accordance with paragraphs 7(a) onwards of the Council's Disciplinary Procedure, subject to sub-paragraph 14(f) of this procedure. (Applying to A.P.T.&C. and manual/craft employees only).

* A department other than that in which the person complained against is employed.

During the disciplinary procedure the manager concerned will call upon the advice of the Director of Personnel and Management Services and the Chief Executive through either the Race Relations Unit and/or the Women's Equality Unit. DPMS and the appropriate Unit(s), will be present at all interviews.

At the disciplinary interview, the parties may be interviewed separately, if requested by the complainant or by the person against whom the complaint is made. Where this occurs the representatives of both parties will be present throughout all proceedings.

The Investigating Officer will normally conduct the formal disciplinary interview and the information gathered during the investigation should form the basis of any disciplinary action that may follow, thus avoiding the need to repeat detailed interviews, but subject to the discretion of the officer conducting the disciplinary interview to carry out such further investigations as are considered necessary.

(d) To identify to DPMS changes to the Council's policies and practices as suggested by the case.

15 The outcome of the disciplinary hearing will be communicated, in writing, to the complainant within five working days of a decision being taken.

Stage 3. Seeking a review

16 The complainant will have the right, once the disciplinary procedure has been exhausted, to seek a review by the Council's Harassment and Discrimination Panel against all decisions under paragraph 14(a), (b) and (c) or if the proposed changes to policies and practices under 14(d) were considered insufficient.
17 A panel of five Council members, drawn from the Local Appeals Committee and advised by the Director of Personnel and Management Services or representative and the Chief Executive through either the Race Relations Unit and/or Women's Equality Unit, will hear the case.
18 To request a review the complainant should write to the Director of Personnel and Management Services, stating the grounds, within ten working days of receipt of the written decision.

Disciplinary penalties and offences

The ACAS Code of Practice notes that often supervisors will give informal oral warnings for the purpose of improving conduct when employees commit minor infringements of the established standards of conduct. Where formal disciplinary action, other than summary dismissal, is considered necessary paragraph 12 of the code recommends that the following procedure should normally be observed:

Designing disciplinary procedures

(a) In the case of minor offences the individual should be given a formal oral warning or if the issue is more serious, there should be a written warning setting out the nature of the offence and the likely consequences of further offences. In either case the individual should be advised that the warning constitutes the first formal stage of the procedure.

(b) Further misconduct might warrant a final written warning which should contain a statement that any recurrence would lead to suspension or dismissal or some other penalty, as the case may be.

(c) The final step might be disciplinary transfer, or disciplinary suspension without pay (but only if these are allowed for by an express or implied condition of the contract of employment), or dismissal, according to the nature of the misconduct. Special consideration should be given before imposing disciplinary suspension without pay and it should not normally be for a prolonged period.

The ACAS handbook *Discipline at Work* details a model disciplinary procedure which provides an illustrative example of a procedure incorporating these principles. This is detailed in the box below. As can be seen, it provides for the informal handling of minor offences, the giving of oral, written and final written warnings, and allows for employees to be suspended without pay for up to five days as an alternative to dismissal. An example of a shorter procedure for use in small firms is also given in the handbook. However, it still contains the same number of disciplinary stages as the longer version, although no provision is made for suspension without pay. Both also, as recommended in the ACAS code, provide for warnings to become spent after a certain length of time.

ACAS model disciplinary procedure

1 *Purpose and scope*

This procedure is designed to help and encourage all employees to achieve and maintain standards of conduct, attendance and job performance. The company rules (a copy of which is displayed in the office) and this procedure apply to all employees. The aim is to ensure consistent and fair treatment for all.

2 *Principles*

(a) No disciplinary action will be taken against an employee until the case has been fully investigated.
(b) At every stage in the procedure the employee will be advised of the nature of the complaint against him or her and will be given the opportunity to state his or her case before any decision is made.
(c) At all stages the employee will have the right to be accompanied by a shop steward, employee representative or work colleague during the disciplinary interview.

(d) No employee will be dismissed for a first breach of discipline except in the case of gross misconduct when the penalty will be dismissal without notice or payment in lieu of notice.

(e) An employee will have the right to appeal against any disciplinary penalty imposed.

(f) The procedure may be implemented at any stage if the employee's alleged misconduct warrants such action.

3 *The procedure*

Minor faults will be dealt with informally but where the matter is more serious the following procedure will be used:

Stage 1. Oral warning. If conduct or performance does not meet acceptable standards the employee will normally be given a formal **oral warning**. He or she will be advised of the reason for the warning, that it is the first stage of the disciplinary procedure and of his or her right of appeal. A brief note of the oral warning will be kept but it will be spent after .... months, subject to satisfactory conduct and performance.

Stage 2. Written warning. If the offence is a serious one, or if a further offence occurs a written warning will be given to the employee by the supervisor. This will give details of the complaint, the improvement required and the time scale. It will warn that action under Stage 3 will be considered if there is no satisfactory improvement and will advise of the right of appeal. A copy of this written warning will be kept by the supervisor but it will be disregarded for disciplinary purposes after .... months subject to satisfactory conduct and performance.

Stage 3. Final written warning or disciplinary suspension. If there is still a failure to improve and conduct or performance is still unsatisfactory, or if the misconduct is sufficiently serious to warrant only one written warning but insufficiently serious to justify dismissal (in effect both first and final written warning), a **final written warning** will normally be given to the employee. This will give details of the complaint, will warn that dismissal will result if there is no satisfactory improvement and will advise of the right of appeal. A copy of this final written warning will be kept by the supervisor but it will be spent after .... months (in exceptional cases the period may be longer) subject to satisfactory conduct and performance.

Alternatively, consideration will be given to imposing a penalty of a disciplinary suspension without pay for up to a maximum of five working days.

Stage 4. Dismissal. If conduct or performance is still unsatisfactory, and the employee still fails to reach the prescribed standards, **dismissal** will normally result. Only the appropriate Senior Manager can take the decision to dismiss. The employee will be provided, as soon as reasonably practicable, with written reasons for dismissal, the date on which employment will terminate and the right of appeal.

4 Gross misconduct

The following list provides examples of offences which are normally regarded as gross misconduct:

(a) Theft, fraud, deliberate falsification of records.
(b) Fighting, assault on another person.
(c) Deliberate damage to company property.
(d) Serious incapability through alcohol or being under the influence of illegal drugs.
(e) Serious negligence which causes unacceptable loss, damage or injury.
(f) Serious act of insubordination.

If you are accused of an act of gross misconduct, you may be suspended from work on full pay, normally for no more than five working days, while the company investigates the alleged offence. If, on completion of the investigation and the full disciplinary procedure, the company is satisfied that gross misconduct has occurred, the result will normally be summary dismissal without notice or payment in lieu of notice.

5 Appeals

An employee who wishes to appeal against a disciplinary decision should inform .... within two working days. The Senior Manager will hear all appeals and his/her decision is final. At the appeal any disciplinary penalty imposed will be reviewed but it cannot be increased.

The 1980 WIRS found that disciplinary procedures followed ACAS advice in providing for systems of oral and written warnings prior to the ultimate sanction of dismissal. A more recent survey of disciplinary procedures in seventy organisations carried out by Industrial Relations Services (IRS) confirms this practice.[4] Thus all but one of the procedures examined followed the ACAS recommendations in providing that employees should normally receive an oral and two written warnings before dismissal is countenanced.

Warnings should be used to encourage employees to bring their conduct or performance up to the required standard rather than as a means of supplementing the normal day-to-day process of managing work. For this reason they should, as the ACAS code notes, be disregarded after a specified period of satisfactory conduct. Organisations, as the procedures reproduced in Appendix 2 illustrate, adopt rather different policies as to the period of time that must elapse before a warning becomes spent. The most common period for oral warnings, according to the IRS survey, is six months. In contrast, first and final written warnings were frequently found to remain in force for twelve months, and sometimes even longer. Indeed, some organisations keep final warnings in force for periods of up to two years (see Appendix 2).

The staged approach to handling disciplinary cases recommended by ACAS is not intended to be applied mechanistically. This is confirmed by the ACAS handbook, which observes that it is not always necessary to give three warnings before dismissal is contemplated. It is therefore important that procedures should make it clear that one or more stages can be omitted if appropriate. Behaviour constituting gross misconduct is the most obvious situation where the staged approach to handling discipline is discarded. However, procedures should also draw attention to the fact that one or more stages can be omitted in the case of serious offences falling short of gross misconduct.

Acts of gross misconduct should be spelt out in disciplinary procedures as well as in rules. Some organisations also prefer to detail the types of 'serious offences' which may lead to the full procedure being short-circuited. This is designed to avoid subsequent ill feeling over the way in which management exercises its discretion. Where this is done every effort should be made to specify the offences in as comprehensive a fashion as possible (the types of behaviour listed should not be unreasonable) and it should be made clear that those mentioned are illustrative examples and do not constitute an exhaustive list. An extract from the procedure covering Cadbury's Bournville site (see below) provides a good example of an organisation using such an approach to give employees some indication of the types of behaviour which will be treated as serious or gross misconduct.

Cadbury Bournville: extract from disciplinary procedure

Discipline procedure

The objective of this procedure is to maintain a good standard of conduct and performance at work. It has been developed in line with the ACAS Code of Practice on such matters. The full procedure, 'Bournville Code of Practice – Non-management', which is held by your manager and in your Personnel Department, contains three categories of offence. Details of these and the methods for dealing with disciplinary offences are set out below.

1 *Misconduct* – examples

- Poor timekeeping/attendance.
- Poor work performance.
- Refusal to work.

Designing disciplinary procedures

- Breach of site safety rule.
- Prolonged absence from place of work, e.g. unauthorised visits to other departments.
- Hygiene offences, e.g. untidy or dirty appearance, wearing prohibited jewellery.
- Damage to property, e.g. writing on walls, intentional damage to overalls.
- Horseplay.
- Gambling.

2 *Serious misconduct* – examples. There may be occasions when misconduct is considered to be insufficiently serious to justify dismissal but sufficiently serious to warrant only one written warning, which in effect will be both first and final.

- Hygiene, e.g. failure to notify contact with a notifiable disease.
- Fighting, e.g. intentionally causing minor physical injury.
- Clocking offence.
- Smoking.
- Serious breach of site safety rule or breach of statutory regulations.
- Prolonged absence from place of work, e.g. unauthorised absence from site or whilst in a position of responsibility.
- Drunkenness – incapable of work.
- Falsification of information for fringe benefit purposes.

3 *Gross misconduct* – examples:

- Theft.
- Drunkenness whilst in a position of responsibility.
- Fighting, e.g. attack on an employee, one which causes serious injury.
- Fraud, e.g. serious clocking offence or falsification of work record.
- Damage, e.g. sabotage.
- Use of an offensive weapon.
- Serious breach of safety rule or statutory regulations, which may result in injury or gross damage.
- Hygiene, e.g. continuing to attend work whilst knowingly having a notifiable disease.

Some organisations additionally make it clear that the full procedure does not apply to new employees who are still on trial or on a probationary period and/or those who have been employed for only a relatively short period of time. For example, the procedure at Weidmuller (Kipton Products) Ltd states that:

> New employees working within a recognised trial period who fail to meet the required standards of work or conduct within that period will have their employment terminated with notice. Wherever possible the employee

should be given the opportunity to improve following the receipt of a written warning prior to dismissal.

In similar vein the Co-operative Insurance Society's procedure states that:

> The Society reserves the right not to follow the full warning procedure for an employee with less than 52 weeks' service whose employment is considered unsatisfactory. Except in cases of gross misconduct, the Society would normally issue an oral warning where appropriate and at least one written warning prior to dismissal.

It is also appropriate here to mention that some procedures lay down special arrangements in respect of apprentices or young workers in recognition of their inexperience and possible lack of maturity. The disciplinary procedure of IBC Vehicles, for example, contains the following clause in respect of young trainees:

> Young trainees must observe the Standards of Conduct in Appendix 6 in the same way as other employees. They are also subject, should the necessity arise, to the same corrective and disciplinary measures, but with the inclusion of the following provisions that take account of the training relationship that exists with them:
> (i) While departmental supervision and fellow employees will exercise day-to-day responsibility for the conduct and performance of trainees undergoing training in their areas, the application of formal corrective or disciplinary measures will be the responsibility of the Personnel Department.
> (ii) Trainees have the same right to representation as other employees.
> (iii) At the discretion of a senior member of the Personnel Department, there may be discussion or correspondence with the parents or guardian of a trainee involved in a disciplinary matter.
> (iv) Disciplinary offences on college premises will be considered in the same way as if they had been committed on Company premises.

Where penalties other than warnings or dismissal are to be imposed, they should be identified, together with the stages at which they are to be considered. In particular, it should be made clear whether they are intended to supplement formal warnings or to be used as an alternative to dismissal. If the former is the case, the types of warning which they may be used in conjunction with should be identified. Where penalties such as demotion and suspension are intended to provide a discretionary sanction between a final written warning and dismissal, it goes without saying that procedures should specify what happens if an employee's performance still fails to meet the required standards.

Designing disciplinary procedures

Even if it is decided that suspension without pay should not be used as a sanction, it is advisable for procedures to allow management the right to suspend employees pending the investigation of alleged offences. Such investigatory suspension may be with or – provided there is the necessary contractual authority – without pay. However, as a general rule it is preferable to adopt the paid option. Indeed, this is the option provided for under the ACAS model procedures.

Unpaid investigatory suspension can generate considerable ill will among employees, since it not only penalises employees, but sits rather uncomfortably with the principle that an alleged offender is to be treated as innocent until proved guilty. Consequently, if unpaid suspension is to be used, procedures should make it clear that lost pay will be reimbursed when an employee is cleared of the alleged offence. They should additionally stress that the suspension will be for as short a period as possible and set some maximum limit on its length. A maximum of between three and five days is perhaps the most frequently used. Such limits should incidently also be laid down in respect of paid suspension.

A further issue that needs to be considered with regard to investigatory suspension is whether the right to suspend applies to all types of offences or only to those of a given level of gravity. The most common approach, and arguably the fairest, is to limit its use to more serious categories of alleged offence. For example, County Nat West's procedure states that 'Behaviour constituting gross misconduct will render an employee liable for immediate suspension on full pay, normally for no more than five working days.' In similar vein the procedure at Peradin Ltd limits the right to suspend without pay to circumstances where the conduct of employees has constituted a hazard to themselves or other employees. The following types of behaviour are then listed as examples of misconduct which may be held to constitute such a hazard:

(i) Tampering with safety devices with the deliberate intent to render them inoperable.
(ii) Drunkenness.
(iii) Smoking in a prohibited area.
(iv) Fighting or attacks on personnel.
(v) Wilful damage.
(vi) Arson.
(vii) Other mutually agreed serious offences which may occur from time to time.

The provision of informal counselling

As noted earlier, in practice many minor disciplinary issues will be dealt with informally by line managers and will not become the subject of formal disciplinary hearings. Ideally all issues would be dealt with in this way. It is therefore sensible to make some reference to the role and importance of such informal processes within the disciplinary procedure in order to emphasise the desirability of handling matters in a flexible and non-formalistic manner wherever possible. Some organisations do this by including an informal stage within their disciplinary procedure as the first step in attempting to resolve disciplinary problems. The disciplinary procedure at Komatsu, for example, incorporates the following informal stage:

> By normal day to day and by individual counselling and advice, the supervisor will make employees aware of the improvements in standards required.
>
> Minor offences will be reprimanded by the supervisor informally but formal written records will not be kept at this stage.
>
> It is hoped that most matters can be speedily and effectively resolved at this level. However, in the event of a failure to improve standards to the required level, the following procedure will be invoked.

Counselling should be a two-way process which focuses on the ways in which an employee can deal with identified shortcomings. Having listened to the employee, it may be concluded that the problem has been sorted out or will resolve itself. However, if improvement is still required the counsellor must ensure that the employee understands what is necessary, and how and when performance will be reviewed.

Where employees are offered counselling on the basis that if they do not improve they may face dismissal, counselling can be regarded as constituting the initial stage of the disciplinary procedure. However, counselling sessions should not be transformed into disciplinary hearings, since that could undermine certain fundamental principles, for example the right to be represented. If necessary, a counselling interview should therefore be adjourned on the basis that the issues raised will be dealt with under the formal disciplinary procedure. Advice to this effect is in fact included in some procedures. For example, that at Wiggins Teape gives the following guidance:

> Occasions in which informal warnings are given must not be allowed to escalate into disciplinary interviews as this may mean the employee is denied certain rights such as the right to be accompanied by a trade union representative. If the informal oral warning fails to resolve the matter, the discussion should be adjourned and the issue pursued under the formal disciplinary procedure ...

The informal resolution of disciplinary issues has several obvious advantages:

- It helps to avoid disciplinary matters being handled in a formalistic and more conflictual way, and saves a significant amount of management time being tied up in formal hearings.
- It underlines the fact that it is first-line managers who have primary responsibility for maintaining discipline.
- It provides employees with an opportunity to improve their behaviour 'voluntarily' rather than as a result of managerial enforcement.

This last consideration has led some employers in the United States to adopt so called 'non-punitive' approaches to discipline. The procedure adopted at Tampa Electric provides a typical example of this approach.[5] At Tampa a manager is initially required to meet an employee privately to discuss the disciplinary problem with a view to gaining his or her commitment to improve performance. No formal warning is given at this meeting, although a record of the discussion is kept by the manager. If the necessary improvement does not occur, a further meeting is held. At this stage the manager endeavours to draw up an action plan in conjunction with the employee to resolve the problem. After the meeting the manager writes a memo (a 'written reminder') to the employee, summarising their conversation, and a copy is placed on the employee's personnel file. If an improvement is still not forthcoming, the employee is given a day's paid leave (known as 'decision-making leave'). On the employee's return a further meeting is held at which the individual must express a willingness either to change or to quit. If the employee is willing to give a 'total performance commitment', then a further action plan is drawn up and the employee informed that failure to comply with it will lead to the termination of his or her employment. This option is confirmed in a subsequent memo, a copy of which is also placed on the employee's file.

Proponents of this type of procedure argue that it has a number of distinct advantages over the more traditional methods of dealing with poor performance and misconduct. The most important is that it is seen to reinforce the principles of self-discipline and individual choice. Moreover, a number of organisations report significant improvements in work performance as a result of adopting such procedures. Although unfair dismissal provisions make it impossible to fully adopt such procedures in Britain, it is feasible to incorporate elements of them if this is thought desirable.

The location of managerial responsibility

We have already observed that the ACAS code suggests that procedures should specify the levels of management which have the authority to take various forms of disciplinary action. No official guidance is given as to how organisations should allocate such authority. However, as a general rule responsibility should rest with line managers, since it is they who are charged with supervising the conduct of employees and ensuring that it meets the required standards. To provide otherwise runs the risk of undermining the authority of supervisors and managers, and of encouraging them to see disciplinary issues as somebody else's responsibility.

At the same time it is crucial that disciplinary issues are handled in a sensitive, fair, consistent and flexible manner. This in turn implies that the overall management of disciplinary matters should be monitored centrally to ensure that individual managers are in fact handling issues in accordance with organisational procedures and norms. Where there is a personnel function, that is where the task of monitoring should be located.

Striking a balance between the need for line management responsibility, on the one hand, and the need for consistency and procedural correctness on the other, is difficult. Not surprisingly, the solutions differ considerably between organisations. The IRS survey's findings on the levels of management authorised to take different types of disciplinary action illustrate this clearly (see Table 3, overleaf). As can be seen, wide variations were discovered in the approaches adopted by the responding organisations. For example, in some cases immediate supervision is only given authority for the first and second stages of formal procedures, while in others supervisors are authorised to take decisions up to and including a final written warning. None of the surveyed organisations, however, went against the advice of the ACAS code by giving immediate superiors the right to dismiss.

The disciplinary role of personnel specialists varies greatly between organisations, as is shown by the results of the IRS survey and the procedures reproduced in Appendix 2. Some procedures make no formal provision for their involvement at all, or simply require them to be consulted before certain types of action, such as written warnings and dismissals, are taken. Others give them sole or joint decision-making authority at one or more stages, including that of dismissal. The most common arrangement is for personnel specialists to become involved at some stage, but in an advisory and support capacity only. This is perhaps the preferable approach, given the desirability of providing line managers with the 'ownership' of disciplinary matters.

Whatever approach is adopted to the allocation of management responsibilities, the disciplinary procedure should leave no doubt as to who is to be involved in carrying out disciplinary hearings at different stages. A useful way of doing this in an accessible manner is to present the information in tabular form. An example of how this is done in one organisation, County Nat West, is shown in the box opposite.

Designing disciplinary procedures

Disciplinary stage	Nature	Type	Conducted by
Stage 1 Oral warning	Unsatisfactory job performance or conduct	Investigation and verbal	Line manager
Stage 2 First written warning	Significantly short of required standard or failure to improve	Investigation and written	Line manager and personnel manager
Stage 3 Second written warning (final)	Serious misconduct or sustained poor performance	Investigation and written	Line manager and personnel manager
Stage 4 Dismissal	Sustained poor performance and/or misconduct	Investigation and written	Line manager and personnel manager
	Gross misconduct	Investigation	Line manager and senior member of Personnel Department
		Written	Head of business/cost area and Head of Personnel

County Nat West: extract from disciplinary procedure

It is also important for procedures to indicate what should happen if the manager responsible for dealing with a particular disciplinary case is not available for any reason. This is particularly necessary where employees regularly work without anybody with disciplinary responsibility being present. The need for arrangements to be developed to deal with such situations is stressed in the ACAS code. Thus paragraph 15 of the code states that special consideration should be given to the way in which disciplinary procedures are to operate in respect of 'employees to whom the full procedure is not available'. It goes on to draw particular attention to the fact that:

> special provisions may have to be made for the handling of disciplinary matters among nightshift workers, workers in isolated locations or depots

Table 3 The allocation of disciplinary authority

Organisation	First stage/oral warning	Second stage/first written warning	Final written warning	Sanctions
ASCoMIT Company	Immediate supervisor	Personnel and IR manager	Personnel and IR manager	Personnel and IR manager
Associated Tyre Specialists	Not specified	Not specified	Not specified	Not specified
BT	First level of supervision with formal disciplinary responsibility	Employee's second-line manager	Employee's second-line manager	Employee's second-line manager
Co-operative Insurance Society	Official/supervisor	Official	Manager of department/office	Personnel manager or authorised deputy
Cussons UK	Departmental superintendent/manager	Departmental superintendent/manager	Departmental superintendent/manager	Executive management
European Thread Mills	Immediate supervisor	Departmental manager and personnel manager	Assistant general manager and personnel manager	Assistant general manager and personnel manager
Geest Foods	Immediate supervisor	Immediate supervisor	Next level of divisional management	Senior management/divisional personnel manager

Designing disciplinary procedures

Organisation	First stage/oral warning	Second stage/first written warning	Final written warning	Sanctions
Gulf Oil	Immediate supervisor	Not specified	Not specified	Divisional heads in consultation with local HR representative
Legal and General monthly paid staff	Immediate supervisor in consultation with personnel manager	Immediate supervisor in consultation with personnel manager	Immediate supervisor in consultation with personnel manager	Varies with severity of sanction
Lothian Regional Council (excluding teaching staff and senior management)	Varies with the circumstances	Varies with the circumstances	Varies with the circumstances	Head of department, in consultation with personnel manager
Northcliffe Newspaper Group	Immediate manager	Immediate manager	Immediate manager	Immediate manager
NSPCC	Does not include this stage	Immediate superior (1st level of management)	Second level of management	Third level of management
Polytechnic of East London	At least principal lecturer level (immediate supervisor)	Head of department	Head of school	Member of the management board
Royal Ordnance	Immediate line manager plus member of personnel department	Immediate line manager plus member of personnel department	Appropriate more senior level of management plus member of personnel department	Appropriate more senior level of management, ratified by personnel manager
William Hill Organisation	Employee's manager	District manager	Area manager	Area manager

Source. Adapted from 'Discipline at work 2, Procedures', *Industrial Relations Review and Report*, 16 August 1991.

or others who may pose particular problems for example because no one is present with the necessary authority to take disciplinary action or no trade union representative is immediately available.

The procedure at Weidmuller (Kipton Products) Ltd provides a good example of the types of clause that can be used to deal with situations of this sort. Thus paragraph 3 provides that:

> Where the offence cannot be dealt with owing to the absence of a Supervisor (i.e. outside normal work hours) the Chargehand should attempt to contact the employee's Supervisor or Manager. The Chargehand will then instruct the employee to report to the Supervisor at the earliest convenient time. In the case of alleged Gross Misconduct the employee will also be instructed to clock off and leave the Company premises. Should the final decision be in the employee's favour, he or she will be recompensed for the earnings lost.

More generally, the procedure states that 'When a Department Manager or Director is not available to conduct a disciplinary hearing or appeal the Personnel Executive may nominate a replacement from the same or a higher level'.

The right of appeal

Employees who are dissatisfied with any disciplinary decision should be given the opportunity to have it reviewed (see the ACAS Code of Practice, paragraph 10). At the very least, appeals should be permitted against the most serious penalties, for example final written warnings, demotion or dismissal. Indeed, a dismissal may be unfair if a right of appeal is not provided.[6]

In practice appeals are lodged on two main grounds: that the finding of guilt was wrong; and/or that the penalty imposed was out of proportion to the offence. To avoid subsequent misunderstandings it is therefore advisable to make it clear in procedures that both types of appeal are allowed. It is also sensible to indicate that appeals can be resolved, where appropriate, by the substitution of a lesser penalty. The disciplinary procedure at British Telecom provides a good example of a procedure which does both these things. Thus it states that:

> At the appeal stage an employee or a recognised union on behalf of the employee is entitled to challenge a disciplinary or dismissal decision and the imposition of particular penalty points, and to produce new or additional evidence in the employee's defence. The manager adjudicating an appeal should carefully and objectively consider any points made.
>
> After carrying out any further investigations that are necessary, the

appeal authority may reverse decisions and vary penalty points; points of substance made on appeal must be responded to and an explanation given of the reasons for the decision.

Where an appeal against the severity of a dismissal decision is successful, organisations can find themselves in a quandary if they have decided not generally to make use of such sanctions as unpaid suspensions, transfer or demotion. One way round this, as the Royal Ordnance's procedure illustrates (see Appendix 2), is to allow sanctions of this type to be used exceptionally as a substitute for dismissal at the appeal stage.

So far as possible, procedures should provide for an appeal to be heard by a more senior person than the manager who made the original decision. However, the EAT has accepted that an appeal procedure does not infringe the rules of natural justice simply because the person hearing the appeal had been informed of the original decision before it was given and the person who took the decision was also present throughout the appeal hearing.[7] Indeed, it is suggested that the disciplining manager should attend at some point in order to answer questions and respond to criticisms of the original decision.

Procedures should make clear who in the management hierarchy is to hear appeals. Where employees are given a right of appeal against disciplinary warnings as well as against dismissal and other penalties, it will be necessary to develop different arrangements for appeal, to cope with different types of case. In some organisations it is done simply by stating that appeals will be heard by the next level of management above that involved in the decision which is the subject of appeal. In others rather more complex arrangements have been developed. These too can be usefully detailed in tabular form (see box overleaf).

Procedures should, as the County Nat West example illustrates, state the time period within which an appeal must be lodged and the period within which it will be heard. It is also advisable to require appeals to be lodged in writing and to indicate the grounds on which the appeal is being made. Given that the designated manager will occasionally be unavailable, it would seem sensible to stipulate that a comparable person can deputise in specified circumstances. More detailed guidance on the handling of appeals is given on p. 75.

Third-party intervention

Many procedures provide for the involvement of individuals not directly employed at the establishment where a disciplinary offence is alleged to have taken place. In most cases this involvement remains 'domestic' in the sense that the individuals concerned, who may be managers and/or union officials from elsewhere in the organisation, full-time union

| County Nat West: extract from disciplinary procedure ||||
Disciplinary stage	Line of appeal	Time to appeal	Result of appeal within
Stage 1 Oral warning	Personnel manager	Three working days	Three working days
Stage 2 First written warning	Senior member of business/cost area and independent personnel manager	Three working days	Three working days
Stage 3 Second written warning (Final)	Senior member of business/cost area and independent personnel manager	Three working days	Five working days
Stage 4 Dismissal	Head of Personnel and head of business/cost area	Three working days	Five working days
Dismissal for gross misconduct	Chief executive and head of independent business/cost area	Three working days	Five working days

officials or representatives of an employer's organisation, are directly associated with the collective bargaining arrangements covering the establishment. However, a significant minority of procedures provide for the introduction of an independent element into the appeal process.

This independent element can take one of three main forms: conciliation, mediation or arbitration. Conciliation and mediation are closely related. Both involve the use of a third party to provide assistance where internal discussions have reached an *impasse*. Equally, both leave the internal parties with ultimate responsibility for resolving the issue themselves. The essential difference between them is that a mediator is able to put forward recommendations which are designed to resolve the matter – although the parties remain free to reject, accept or amend the recommendations. By way of contrast, arbitration usually involves the third party making a morally binding award to resolve the issue.

Any form of third-party intervention, by definition, brings an outsider into the internal affairs of an organisation. For this reason many employers are cautious about placing too much reliance on it. This is particularly true

Designing disciplinary procedures

in the case of arbitration, where managerial decision-making is essentially usurped by the third party appointed. Against this has to be set the potential benefits of being able to draw on an outside source of advice and expertise which can view an issue in a more dispassionate manner. Each of the three forms of intervention has the additional benefit of providing a means of resolving disagreements without recourse to damaging management–union disputes. This is of course particularly true of arbitration.

If it is considered desirable to make some formal provision for third-party intervention, thought needs to be given to the type of involvement and the circumstances in which it is to be triggered. The pros and cons of the three possible forms of intervention must be carefully weighed. Some organisations opt for a staged approach to such intervention – conciliation first, followed by mediation and/or arbitration.

A further issue which arises in relation to arbitration is the question of whether it is to be of the 'conventional' or the pendulum type. Under the former, arbitrators are given the freedom to come up with compromise awards, whereas under the latter they must find for either the management or the worker's side. A good deal of debate has taken place recently about the merits of pendulum arbitration. Advocates emphasise its value in concentrating the minds of the domestic parties on finding their own solution and of avoiding the so-called 'chilling effect' – the process whereby the parties conceal their final negotiating position so that they have something to 'give' if the issue goes to arbitration. However, critics draw attention to the rather crude nature of the process if a dispute involves a number of distinct topics and the fact that it precludes arbitrators from formulating awards which take long-term considerations into account.

A crucial factor that will influence thinking on these issues is the more general question of how appeals are to be handled. In most organisations the appeal process is detailed in the disciplinary procedure and as a result retains a fundamentally individualistic orientation. Consequently, arbitration may be considered the most appropriate form of intervention, since it can be viewed as a form of quasi-judicial decision-making. As many appeals will be about whether an offence has been proved or not, this would also seem to make pendulum arbitration attractive. However, it needs to be borne in mind that the use of this option will limit the scope for compromise decisions in the case of appeals which concern the fairness of the penalty imposed in a particular case.

The ACAS code recommends that grievance machinery and disciplinary machinery should normally be kept separate. Nevertheless, some organisations do provide for appeals against disciplinary decisions to be handled through the general grievance/disputes procedure. Where this is the case, disciplinary issues are more likely to take on a collective dimension, and conciliation, mediation and 'conventional' arbitration may become more attractive.

If appeals are handled through the disciplinary procedure, the question of whether the issue is referred to a third party will essentially rest with the appellant and his or her representative. If they are dealt with through grievance procedures, third-party intervention may be triggered in several ways: unilaterally by one side or the other, jointly by both parties, or automatically if an issue remains unresolved at the final internal stage. Clearly the procedure should stipulate which of these methods applies.

Similarly, arguments can be avoided if the procedure identifies the third party to be used. ACAS provides conciliation, mediation and arbitration services, and is the party most commonly referred to in procedures. According to the 1990 annual report of ACAS, issues relating to dismissal and discipline accounted for 13 per cent of completed collective conciliations and 26 per cent of references to arbitration and mediation.

Conciliation and mediation are carried out by ACAS officials, but arbitrators are drawn from a panel of suitably qualified people appointed by the service. In most cases all three of the processes are carried out by individual officers or arbitrators. However, ACAS will set up mediation boards on request and will also assist in the creation of specially appointed boards of arbitration, consisting of an ACAS arbitrator and equal numbers of representatives from employers and employees. If such arrangements are preferred then once again the fact should be stated in the procedure.

Employers can, of course, arrange for third-party assistance to be provided by sources other than ACAS. For example, they may establish their own independent arbitration body, incorporating management and worker representatives, with or without an independent chair. Machinery of this type is in fact employed in certain parts of the public sector, for example in the civil service and electricity supply industry.[8] Nevertheless, most organisations are unlikely to consider the establishment of such machinery as either necessary or desirable, given the alternatives available and the frequency with which third-party intervention is likely to be needed.

Employee representation

The ACAS code states that disciplinary procedures should give individuals the right to be accompanied by a trade union representative or by a fellow employee of their choice (paragraph 10). Thus procedures should stipulate that employees have a right to be represented at all formal disciplinary hearings.

The issue of employee representation is more problematic where informal disciplinary action and counselling are provided for. The presence of a representative at this stage runs the risk of introducing a greater degree of formality into the proceedings and hence undermining what is intended to be an informal process. On the other hand, what may be seen as an informal counselling session from a management perspective may be viewed rather differently by an employee. The presence of a friend or union representative may help provide reassurance and enable counselling to be conducted in a more relaxed and open manner. The involvement of union representatives in any informal stage has the further advantage of enabling them to be well briefed if the matter reaches the formal procedure. Nevertheless, most procedures limit employee representation to the formal stages of disciplinary procedures.

Surprisingly, most procedures are silent as to the precise role that employee representatives are to play at disciplinary hearings – that is whether they are to attend as observer or participant. Thus many procedures simply refer to the right of employees to be 'accompanied' by a fellow employee or a trade union representative. Such phrasing obviously leaves scope for disagreement, and it is therefore advisable, if the representative is to have only observer status, to make this clear in the written procedures. Such an approach, however, is arguably at odds with the spirit if not the letter of the ACAS code.

When disciplinary action is being considered against union representatives, they too have a right to be represented. In addition, the ACAS code (paragraph 15) suggests that no disciplinary action beyond an oral warning should be taken until the circumstances of the case have been discussed with a senior trade union representative or a full-time official. The need to hold such discussions should be made clear in the procedure, together with the persons who should be involved. In the case of ordinary shop stewards, it may be decided that the issue should be discussed with the senior union representative on site or in the organisation as a whole. If, on the other hand, it is a senior representative who is the subject of the action, then the relevant full-time official of the union is the most appropriate person.

Another form of employee representation, albeit of a different kind, also needs to be mentioned. This is the practice, adopted in a small number of organisations, of using joint tribunals consisting of management and worker/trade union representatives to adjudicate on disciplinary issues. In his book *Private Justice* Henry reports on the operation of a number of tribunals of this type and found considerable commitment from both sides to their operation.[9] Union representatives saw them as a valuable additional means of influencing management decision-making, while management considered that they bolstered the legitimacy and acceptability of the rulings that emerged. Managers additionally considered them a useful means of making dismissal decisions less vulnerable to successful challenge before an industrial tribunal.

The use of joint bodies of this type to handle disciplinary cases is far from common. Such limited use reflects both management and union reservations about their role. By definition, their introduction involves some loss of managerial authority over disciplinary decisions. It also has the danger that decisions will become the subject of acrimonious, destructive and long-winded arguments between management and union representatives. From the union perspective, formal involvement in the making of disciplinary decisions raises potential conflicts of interest with their representative role.

If it is considered desirable to introduce some form of joint forum for resolving disciplinary cases, the precise role it is to play needs careful consideration. In particular, thought must be given to whether it is to function as an appeal body or whether it is to partially replace managerial decision-making. Where a joint decision-making body is established it must be determined whether the body's jurisdiction is to extend to all disciplinary matters or is to be restricted to particular types of issue. For example, one of the bodies investigated by Henry operated a dual system for handling disciplinary matters. Under this arrangement management or the joint tribunal itself could choose whether a matter was to be handled through the tribunal or dealt with by management alone. In general the tribunal's activities were found to be concerned largely with such issues as pilferage, smoking and horseplay. Similarly, in other organisations the jurisdiction of a joint forum was limited to making decisions in cases of theft or sick pay eligibility.

Drafting procedures

As with disciplinary rules, the ACAS Code of Practice suggests that, to be effective, procedures must be viewed as reasonable by those they cover and those reponsible for their operation (paragraph 5). Thus it is recommended that management should aim to secure the involvement of employees and all levels of management when formulating or revising procedures. In particular, ACAS emphasises that unions should participate fully with management in agreeing to procedures and ensuring that they are used consistently and fairly.

Widespread consultation over the formulation of procedures should be viewed in a positive light rather than as an unnecessary bureaucratic requirement. Such consultation will help ensure that procedures take sufficient account of internal organisational structures and traditions, and the views and wishes of staff. There is little point in preparing and issuing a procedure which is seen as unpractical, unfair or both.

Designing disciplinary procedures 55

In unionised environments the ordinary negotiating arrangements can, and often are, utilised as the forum for discussing and agreeing disciplinary procedures. Some organisations, however, prefer to consult rather than negotiate over the structure and content of procedures, on the grounds that the process involves less infringement of the principle that it is management's responsibility to devise the disciplinary arrangements that apply in their organisations. Where existing consultative machinery is already in place, it may be viewed as the most appropriate channel through which such consultation can take place.

Alternatively a joint working party can be set up to consider the formulation of procedures. This option may be particularly attractive when there are a number of unions present in an organisation who generally do not bargain jointly, since such bodies can provide a means of bringing the unions together and hence help overcome the duplication of discussions with different union groups. They can therefore also avoid the risk of separate procedural arrangements having to be developed in respect of different groups of workers.

Advice on the formulation of disciplinary procedures can be obtained from ACAS if this is thought desirable. Such advice can take a number of forms. At the most basic level use can be made of the public enquiry points located in each of the ACAS regional offices. Alternatively ACAS officials can be invited along to meet members of management and representatives of workers to discuss problems or to carry out advisory exercises in greater depth. In recent years an increasing proportion of this more in-depth work has involved ACAS advisers acting as independent chairs of joint working parties.[10]

In the light of this shift of emphasis ACAS has produced a video, in conjunction with the former Manpower Services Commission, providing guidance on the role, composition and establishment of joint working parties.[11] A booklet which accompanies the video usefully summarises some of the key issues that must be borne in mind when considering the use of such bodies. In particular it recommends that;

- Membership should be kept as small as possible and in general should not exceed 12 people.
- Care should be taken to ensure that members are representative of all staff likely to be affected by the joint working party's recommendations.
- An agreed constitution should be drawn up which, among other things, makes it clear that discussions are confidential, who the joint working party reports back to and how this is to be done.
- Terms of reference should be clearly defined and agreed.
- Meetings should be held regularly.
- No negotiating should be allowed. However, this does not mean that

joint working parties effectively replace negotiations. Rather they contribute recommendations that can be considered by the negotiators.
- Voting should be prohibited, since the intention is to encourage consensual decision-making.

Whatever approach is adopted towards the formulation of disciplinary procedures, it is important that the process is not viewed as a one-off exercise. Changes in legislation and case law, problems arising in the application of procedures, and the development of new human resource policies and work arrangements, may all lead to procedures being amended. Indeed, paragraph 20 of the ACAS code emphasises the importance of periodically reviewing procedures in the light of such factors.

The importance of keeping the structure and operation of procedures under review is highlighted by the IRS survey. It found that no fewer than forty-nine of the seventy organisations surveyed had revised their disciplinary procedures during the previous four years. The House of Lords' decision in the *Polkey* case, which made clear that if a fair procedure is not followed any resultant dismissal is likely to be unfair, was one of the main factors encouraging this process of reform.[12] New rules on racial and sexual harassment, and the introduction of appraisal schemes and no-smoking policies, were among the other factors which had prompted organisations to revise their procedures.

Implementing procedures

Once the procedure has been finalised, its content and any subsequent amendments should be widely communicated throughout the organisation. As a result all levels of staff (including employee representatives) should be aware of how disciplinary matters will be handled, and their rights and responsibilities in relation to them. Failure to communicate a procedure effectively will not only mean that disciplinary issues will not be handled in the desired way. It will also increase the likelihood of dismissals being held unfair.

A whole range of different methods of communication can be used to bring procedures to the attention of staff, including induction programmes and staff handbooks. However, it should be remembered that the written statement of particulars issued under section 1 of the EPCA 1978 must specify, by description or otherwise, a person to whom employees can apply if they are dissatisfied with any disciplinary decision. As in the case of disciplinary rules, this requirement does not apply to organisations with fewer than twenty employees or disciplinary decisions relating to health and safety.

Designing disciplinary procedures

The mere preparation of a procedure is unlikely in itself to be sufficient to ensure that it is properly implemented by managers. Some managers may lack the skills necessary to handle disciplinary matters effectively. Others may see the procedures as introducing an unnecessary degree of formality and inflexibility into the handling of discipline and as a threat to established ways of resolving issues. A study of disciplinary practice in predominantly small and medium-size workplaces illustrates this point. Very few of the firms studied were found to record instances of corrective discipline systematically. Even more strikingly, 18 per cent of the firms reported that they had never used the formal procedure when dismissing, and another 27 per cent said that they did so only occasionally.[13]

To ensure that procedures are implemented correctly it is important to provide line managers with guidance on their content and operation. This can be done through the preparation of written material and the provision of training. Frequently organisations choose to use both these strategies. For example, the IRS survey found that nine out of ten organisations had drafted some form of written guidance for supervisors and line managers, and sixty-two of the seventy supplied some form of training. Only two organisations, both with small work forces, offered neither guidance nor training.

In some cases organisations simply supply supervisors and managers with the ACAS handbook and/or a copy of their own procedure. Others prepare in-house guidance as a supplement to these documents. Typically such guidance will explain the content of the disciplinary procedure and provide advice on the following types of issue:

- The type of disciplinary action to take in relation to particular issues.
- Who has authority to take different types of disciplinary action.
- The role played by the personnel department.
- Employee rights to representation.
- The processes of investigating disciplinary offences, preparing for disciplinary interviews and conducting such interviews.
- The factors to be taken into account when deciding what kind of disciplinary action to take.

The first four of these issues have already been discussed in this chapter and, as indicated, should be covered within disciplinary procedures themselves. The last two subjects are covered in the next chapter. It is appropriate here, however, to reiterate that guidance on these subjects should be made available to all managers who have responsibilities for disciplinary matters. As can be seen from the examples given in Appendix 2, organisations also frequently choose to include such guidance in their disciplinary procedures.

58   Discipline

The ACAS handbook states that those responsible for applying disciplinary procedures (as well as rules) should be trained for the task (p. 13). The handbook further advises senior management to ensure that, wherever practicable, managers and supervisors have a thorough knowledge of their disciplinary rules and procedures and that they understand how to prepare for and conduct a disciplinary interview. Where unions are recognised, it is suggested that consideration be given to the joint training of managers and trade union representatives.

No hard-and-fast rules can be laid down about how to provide training. Some employers prefer to include disciplinary training as one element in broader-based training programmes, or to deal with discipline and grievance handling together. Others prefer to devise a distinct training course dealing only with discipline. Whichever approach is adopted, training programmes should endeavour to give participants the opportunity to practise interview techniques through role-playing exercises. Any training provided should cover all supervisors and managers likely to be involved in handling disciplinary issues. It should also be compulsory. There is little point in designing a training programme to underline the importance of good disciplinary practice and then allowing individuals to decide whether or not they wish to attend.

Joint management–union training can provide a useful means of ensuring that union representatives have a sound understanding of the structure and purpose of procedures and their importance to the effective operation of the organisation. It can also help avoid subsequent misunderstandings about how disciplinary issues are handled. However, the design and carrying out of such training must be handled sensitively. Supervisors and managers will often be worried about exposing their weaknesses to union representatives. Equally, trade unions may be suspicious that joint training is being used as a propaganda vehicle for pushing the management line and downgrading the independent, representational role of union representatives. It may be possible to overcome such suspicion by making it clear that the training is supplementary to any provided by the unions themselves and/or by giving unions the opportunity to contribute some input to the course. Indeed, the possibility of a union input should be viewed positively, since it could provide managers with a better understanding of union objectives and concerns in relation to discipline.[14]

Key points

- The ACAS Code of Practice on disciplinary practice and procedures provides the fundamental starting point for the preparation, review and implementation of disciplinary procedures. Failure to build the principles

Designing disciplinary procedures 59

detailed in this code into procedures considerably increases the likelihood that dismissals will be ruled as unfair.
- In multi-site enterprises careful consideration must be given to whether procedures are to apply to individual workplaces or more widely across the organisation. Both approaches have advantages and disadvantages. However, if the latter course is adopted care must be taken to ensure that the procedural arrangements are relevant to all the workplaces covered.
- Procedures should as far as possible apply to all workers. Under no circumstances should the application of procedures vary according to employees' length of service or whether they work full or part time. Not only is this morally questionable, but it can give rise to both legal and practical problems.
- Increasingly organisations are developing distinct procedural arrangements for dealing with such issues as absenteeism, racial or sexual harassment, alcohol or drug abuse and poor work performance. Where these arrangements are contained in separate, self-contained procedures care must be taken to ensure that they provide employees with rights equivalent to those provided under the normal disciplinary procedure. If issues handled under specialist procedures may at some stage be referred to the general disciplinary one, then the interrelationships between the two types of procedure should be made clear.
- The ACAS code recommends that, except in cases of gross misconduct, a staged approach to the taking of disciplinary action should be used which incorporates both oral and written warnings. However, this approach does not have to be applied mechanistically and it is therefore sensible to indicate in the procedures the circumstances in which one or more stages may be omitted.
- Acts of gross misconduct should be defined as comprehensively as possible. It should, however, be made clear that the types of behaviour listed are intended as illustrative examples only.
- Many minor disciplinary issues are invariably dealt with informally, and procedures should stress the value of such informal resolution. Some organisations actually incorporate an informal stage into their procedures. If this is done, it must be stressed to managers that informal counselling sessions should not be transformed into formal disciplinary hearings.
- Procedures should clearly outline who has the authority to take particular types of disciplinary action. As a general rule, responsibility for taking such action should rest with line managers.
- The role played by personnel specialists under disciplinary procedures varies considerably. Some procedures make no formal provision for their involvement at all, or simply require them to be consulted before certain types of action are taken. Others give them

sole or joint decision-making responsibility at one or more stages.
- Procedures should give employees a right of appeal against disciplinary decisions. Ideally this right should be provided under disciplinary rather than grievance procedures. Procedures should additionally specify the time periods within which appeals have to be lodged and heard. As far as possible appeals should be heard by a more senior manager than the one involved in the original decision.
- Employees should be granted the right to be accompanied by a colleague or union representative at all formal disciplinary hearings. If it is intended that the person accompanying them is attending only as an observer, this should be made clear.
- No disciplinary action beyond an oral warning should be taken against a union representative without first contacting their senior representative or a full-time official of the union.
- Management should aim to secure the involvement of employees and all levels of management when formulating or revising procedures. In particular, ACAS emphasises that unions should participate fully in agreeing them. Existing negotiating or consultative machinery can be used for this purpose. Alternatively a joint working party could be set up to consider the structure and content of procedures.
- Once procedures have been finalised they should be widely communicated throughout the organisation. In addition managers with disciplinary responsibilities should be given guidance on the structure and operation of the procedures. They should also receive training on how to carry out their responsibilities.

References

1. W. W. DANIEL and N. MILLWARD. *Workplace Industrial Relations in Britain*, Heinemann, 1983.
2. N. MILLWARD and M. STEVENS. *British Workplace Industrial Relations, 1980-84*, Gower, 1986.
3. Detailed guidance on each of these issues is given in Chapter 5.
4. *Industrial Relations Review and Report*. 'Discipline at work' 2, August 1991, 7-14; 'Discipline at work: procedures', 16 August 1991, 7-14.
5. D. N. CAMPBELL, R. L. FLEMING and R. C. GROTE. 'Discipline without punishment at last'. *Harvard Business Review*, July–August 1985, 162-78.
6. *West Midlands Co-operative Society* v. *Tipton* [1986] IRLR 112.
7. *Rowe* v. *Radio Rentals* [1982] IRLR 187.
8. R. UPTON, 'What makes disciplinary procedures appealing?', *Personnel Management*, December 1987, 46-9.

9. S. HENRY. *Private Justice*, Routledge, 1982.
10. Details of ACAS advisory work are provided in that body's annual reports.
11. *A Problem Shared: a case study on joint problem solving*, video, ACAS/MSC.
12. *Polkey* v. *Dayton Services* [1987] IRLR 503.
13. S. EVANS, J. F. B. GOODMAN and L. HARGREAVES. *Unfair Dismissal Law and Employment Practice in the 1980s*, Department of Employment Research Paper 53, HMSO, 1985.
14. Guidance on the carrying out of joint union–management training is given in C. BREWSTER and S. CONNOCK. *Industrial Relations Training for Managers*, Kogan Page, 1980.

Chapter 4
Putting the rules and procedures into operation

Having examined the role of disciplinary rules and procedures, we now turn to the practice of discipline handling. As indicated earlier, one obvious method of trying to ensure that disciplinary matters are handled fairly is to train the supervisors and managers involved. Another useful strategy is to provide them with written guidance on how to apply the rules and procedures. In this chapter we discuss how investigations and hearings should be conducted; the selection of appropriate penalties; the appeal process; the communication of decisions and the keeping of records. In the next chapter we suggest how particular disciplinary issues might be dealt with.

Conducting preliminary investigations

In order to hold a fair hearing (see below) employers must be in a position to put allegations to the employee clearly, together with supporting evidence. This means that it will frequently be necessary to conduct a preliminary investigation into the complaint before the disciplinary hearing commences. Unfair dismissal law demands that the investigation must be reasonable in the circumstances.[1]

Proper investigations lead to better decisions, which in turn minimise the number of appeals and reduce the possibility of industrial conflict. Thus it is essential that investigations are completed before a disciplinary hearing is held. Not only is the employee spared distress if the allegations are unsubstantiated but management time can be saved. Additionally there is less chance of being caught out by a surprise defence.

Although it is the employer's responsibility to check documents, interview witnesses and take statements, where criminal offences are alleged employers may choose to rely on police investigations instead of launching their own. Employers should bear in mind that, unless the contract of employment provides otherwise, they have no power to search employees. The mere fact that an employee has been charged with a criminal offence is not normally sufficient evidence of guilt.[2] However, the evidence collected by the police may be used by employers in disciplinary proceedings even if it would be inadmissible at a trial. It is also important to remember that in a criminal court guilt must be established 'beyond reasonable doubt'. By way of contrast, employers may dismiss fairly if they have reasonable grounds for their belief. Thus the fact that no prosecution takes place or the employee is acquitted by a criminal court does not necessarily mean that dismissal for the same conduct is unjustified. Conversely, a criminal conviction generally entitles employers to regard the employee's guilt as established. For example, the following paragraph in Walsall Metropolitan Council's procedure deals with cases which may have a criminal content:

> When it is considered that an alleged criminal offence at work has serious implications for future employment, then in the course of any disciplinary action there is not a requirement to establish whether the employee committed the offence beyond all reasonable doubt but rather whether the employee committed the offence on the balance of probability. Disciplinary action need not be deferred until the outcome of the case is known. Where the police are called in they should not be asked to conduct the disciplinary investigation, nor to be present at any disciplinary interview.

In some circumstances it may be thought desirable to suspend the employee while an investigation takes place. As mentioned earlier, this could be either with or without pay. However, because of the legal and practical problems involved in suspending without pay, it is good practice to pay wages during an investigatory suspension. Disciplinary procedures should indicate not only that such suspension may sometimes be imposed but should also make it clear that suspension is not intended as a penalty in itself. For example, the Polytechnic of East London procedure states:

> Such suspension in itself is not regarded as a disciplinary sanction, rather it enables investigations to be made where the possibility of dismissal may arise or there are grounds for doubt as to the suitability of the employee to continue to work pending the hearing, or conclusion of the investigation.

An investigatory suspension should last for as short a period as possible. Employees should be told the reason for it, and that an investigation and formal hearing will be conducted, and the terms of suspension should be explained. Ideally this information should be confirmed in writing. The following letter provides a useful model:

> Dear .... Date ....
> I am writing to confirm that you have been suspended from duty until .... This has occurred so that an investigation can be conducted into the following serious allegations:

64   Discipline

It is expected that the investigation will take about ....
days, and you may be called for an interview during this time. As a result of the investigation you may be required to attend a disciplinary hearing. This will be conducted in accordance with the normal disciplinary procedure.

During the period of suspension you will receive full pay, although you are only required to attend work if instructed to do so.

Yours sincerely,

Manager.

Preparing for a disciplinary hearing

Like counselling, the aim of a disciplinary interview should be to improve the employee's conduct or performance. Before an interview is arranged the manager must be clear about what is alleged, what evidence is already available and the purpose of the interview. For example, if there is a complaint about timekeeping it would be useful to draw up a schedule of the days on which the employee was late and by how much. The timekeeping records of others should be available for comparative purposes and the manager will need to know if there are any special circumstances to be taken into account.

Where relevant, written statements should be sought from the person making the complaint and any witnesses. This should be done well before the interview so that the documents can be shown to the employee in advance. If possible, witnesses should attend the interview. However, where allegations are made by an informant, a balance must be struck between the desirability of protecting people who are genuinely in fear and providing a fair hearing of the issues for employees accused of misconduct.[3]

Once all the available information has been collected and an interview is thought to be appropriate, the employee should be notified in writing as soon as possible that a disciplinary interview will be held to discuss the matter. The following example letter appears in the ACAS advisory handbook:

Dear ....   Date ....
I am writing to tell you that you are required to attend a disciplinary hearing on .... at .... a.m./p.m. which is to be held in ....

At this interview the question of disciplinary action against you, in accordance with the Company's disciplinary procedure, will be considered with regard to:

You are entitled, if you wish, to be accompanied by another work colleague or your trade union representative.

Signed ....
Manager

If the letter cannot be delivered in person by the line manager, hand or recorded delivery to the last known address is advisable. A delay could be unfair because it might deprive the employee of the chance to refute allegations while the events are still fresh in everyone's mind. Thus when a shop assistant was suspected of breaching her employer's till procedure it was held unfair to have allowed seven days to elapse before the allegations were put to her (*Marley Homecare* v. *Dutton* [1981][4]). Nevertheless, sufficient time should be allowed to enable the employee to prepare a defence and to arrange for representation (see below). Where the procedure specifies that a particular manager should conduct the hearing, and this would cause unreasonable delay in the circumstances, a comparable or more senior person should be substituted.

Not only must employees be told where and when the interview will be held but full details of the nature of the complaint should be supplied. If dismissal is contemplated as a possible outcome this should also be made clear. According to the EAT, it is a fundamental part of a fair disciplinary procedure that employees should know the case against them. Thus when an employer deliberately decided not to give a sales representative details of the nature and seriousness of the allegations against him (falsifying reports of visits made) before starting disciplinary proceedings, his dismissal was found to be unfair (*Spink* v. *Express Foods* [1990][5]).

It is important that employees are reminded of any right to be accompanied at the interview by a union representative or colleague. Additionally, refusing to allow an employee to exercise a contractual right to be represented could give rise to a claim of constructive dismissal[6]. So far as possible managers should try to accommodate the commitments of representatives. For example, there may be no representative immediately available to deal with problems arising on a night shift.

Employees have no general right to legal representation at an internal disciplinary stage, so unless the procedure expressly provides for it such a request can be refused. However, legal representation may be appropriate if criminal proceedings are pending or if the employer has a lawyer in attendance. Where young people are involved it may be advisable to allow parents to attend. Indeed, they may well be parties to an apprenticeship contract.

If the procedure allows a representative to be present, then that person should also be given full details prior to the interview. In theory, so long as the employee's representative is present there is no need for the employee to attend at all. Nevertheless, if it emerges at the hearing that further information is needed from the employee the proceedings will have to be adjourned until the employee is available. Where possible a second manager should attend to witness the proceedings and take notes.

Careful attention should be paid to the timing of interviews and the physical environment in which they are to be held. The interview should be held in a quiet place at a convenient time – perhaps in the afternoon, to save the employee having to go back to work immediately afterwards. Where employees are in an isolated location, the ACAS advisory handbook points out, it may be sensible to allow time off with pay to attend a hearing on the main site during working hours. Alternatively, if a number of witnesses are required it may be advisable to have the hearing at the particular location out of normal hours.[7] Comfortable seating should be provided and the furniture suitably arranged. For example, putting a manager behind a desk suggests greater formality than may be intended. Efforts should also be made to ensure that the proceedings are uninterrupted. For example, there should be no phone calls unless an emergency arises. Obviously if there is a possibility of language difficulties arising, arrangements should be made for an interpreter to be present.

Conducting a disciplinary hearing

So long as the rules of natural justice are adhered to, employers have some flexibility in deciding how to conduct a disciplinary hearing. Nevertheless, in *Clark* v. *Civil Aviation Authority* [1991][8] the EAT gave a broad indication of what is required:

- The purpose of the meeting should be explained.
- The people present should be identified.
- If appropriate, representation should be arranged.
- The employee should be informed of the allegations being made.
- The evidence should be presented, whether in the form of statements or the calling of witnesses.
- The employee and representative should be allowed to ask questions.
- The employee should be invited to call witnesses.
- The employee or representative should be allowed to explain and argue the case, including mitigating circumstances.
- The employee should be asked whether there is any further evidence which could help his or her case.
- After suitable deliberation the decision should be put in writing, whether or not an oral indication has already been given.

Normally the manager will start by making a detailed statement about the nature of the problem or complaint and the evidence that has been obtained. This statement should not express disapproval, since the blameworthiness of the employee has not been determined at this stage. If the employee challenges a witness's statement, ideally he or she should be permitted to question the person concerned. Although employees can be instructed to attend as witnesses in some cases, this could be impracticable, for example because a witness is unwilling to be confronted (see above on informants). In these circumstances it may be sufficient to show the employee the witness's statement or to provide a detailed summary so that the employee knows what has been said about him or her.[9]

The employee should be given the opportunity to reply by presenting his or her case, asking questions and producing evidence. Certainly a dismissal without giving the opportunity to explain is likely to be deemed unfair.[10] Additionally, the imposition of a lesser penalty, for example a warning, could give rise to a complaint of constructive dismissal on the ground that trust and confidence had been undermined. Where misconduct is admitted the employee must still be given the chance to raise any mitigating circumstances. These may suggest that the matter is not as serious as it may appear.

However conclusive the evidence may appear at first sight, employees are entitled to a fair hearing and should be listened to patiently and courteously. Indeed, it is a basic principle of natural justice that the person conducting the proceedings should not be biased. Thus if a letter imposing a sanction has already been drafted, either the employee has not been given a proper opportunity to state his or her case before the decision was taken or the person conducting the hearing was biased because he or she had already determined what the outcome would be.

Nevertheless, by the very nature of the process of investigation it is inevitable that in many cases the manager will have reached a preliminary view before the hearing. In order to avoid the appearance of bias neither the person bringing the complaint nor the person who undertook the initial investigations should conduct the hearing. Equally, it is undesirable that the person conducting the hearing should also have been a witness to the complaint. Even if people who have taken part in the prior investigation do not actually adjudicate at the hearing, an appearance of bias may be created if it looks as though they have influenced the eventual decision. Nevertheless, the EAT has observed that there will 'inevitably be cases in industrial relations where a witness to an incident will be the person who has to make the decision to dismiss' *(Moyes* v. *Hylton Castle Working Men's Club* [1986][11]. Thus it is acknowledged that there is a limit to the extent to which employers can ensure a complete lack of bias. For example, a small business may have no option but to have the same person conducting the disciplinary proceedings as investigated the initial complaint simply because there are insufficient managers to split these functions.

After the employee has responded, further discussion may be required to ensure that the necessary information has been obtained to enable a decision to be made. If it is clear that there is insufficient evidence to uphold the complaint, or the employee has provided an adequate explanation, the interview should cease. If the manager cannot decide between conflicting versions of events, or if additional investigation is necessary, the proceedings should be adjourned. If further investigation does not resolve the matter the interview may have to be reconvened. Ultimately the manager will have to decide which version to believe on the balance of probabilities. It is not unfair to prefer the employer's evidence so long as the manager has listened to all that has been said on the employee's behalf. What the law requires is that there are reasonable grounds to sustain the employer's belief.[12]

Where the employee refuses to give his or her version of events the reasons for not doing so should be explored. To this end he or she should be invited to discuss the matter with someone from the personnel department. If such an invitation is declined it should be made clear that the organisation can take account of the employee's explanation of events only if such an explanation is forthcoming.

Where criminal proceedings are being brought, managers must act cautiously, since the employee may have been advised to remain silent. If the organisation is willing to await the outcome of these proceedings the employee should be informed that a disciplinary hearing will be held when the result of the criminal trial is known. However, on the basis of the information already available, the manager may be able to judge whether the employee's behaviour merits disciplinary action. In these circumstances the employee's refusal to defend himself or herself can be taken into account. Certainly there is no rule of law to say that once an employee has declined to give evidence the employer's hands are tied.[13]

It is obviously important that neither manager nor employee should lose their temper. If employees become unduly distressed or aggressive a short adjournment will allow them time to regain their composure. Given the stressful nature of the situation, some 'letting off of steam' is to be expected. Thus the following advice is offered at William Hill:

> A disciplinary interview can be a very traumatic occasion for many employees and their presentation should be listened to sensitively. At the end the manager may wish to ask further questions or a brief discussion may take place. This should be encouraged but arguments and unpleasantness should be avoided at all costs. If the meeting is getting out of control it is advisable for the manager to call an adjournment for a few minutes to allow the situation to calm down.

The rules and procedures in operation

Nevertheless the ACAS advisory handbook suggests that if misconduct occurs during the interview – for example, abusive language or threatening behaviour – it should be treated as such. This will require the interview to be adjourned and reconvened at a later date, when the subsequent misconduct can also be considered.[14]

Employees have no general duty to report their own misdeeds or those of others[15] but they can be required to attend disciplinary hearings. If an employee fails to turn up it is advisable to arrange another hearing in order to give the employee the opportunity to put his or her case. Where the employee has already failed to attend a hearing it may be acceptable to continue in his or her absence as long as the employee has been informed in writing that if he or she fails to turn up a second time without good reason the hearing will still take place.

Selecting an appropriate penalty

Some employers regard the use of one or more stages of the disciplinary procedure as a sanction in itself, but we turn now to more directly punitive measures. As regards the range of sanctions available, at the two extremes we have oral warning and dismissal. In between most employers impose penalties which hit employees in the pocket, for example withholding service increments, bonuses or merit pay, suspending without pay or demoting. Occasionally an employee may be punished by the removal of privileges. For example, the option of flexible working hours may be denied to a poor timekeeper. According to the IRS survey, employers dismiss an average of just under 1 per cent of their work force each year because of disciplinary offences. However, an average of 3·5 per cent of the work force were disciplined each year.

Rules and procedures must be applied consistently if their moral authority is to be preserved and legal problems are to be avoided. However, this does not necessarily mean that all similar cases must be dealt with in an identical fashion. Individuals must be treated on their merits, with all relevant circumstances taken into account,[16] for example:

- The employee's disciplinary record. A good record may lead to the imposition of a less severe sanction and vice versa.
- The employee's position within the organisation. Higher standards may be expected from senior employees.
- The employee's length of service. Generally employers may be expected to deal more leniently with long standing employees.
- The employee's age. Is the employee young and inexperienced or old enough to know better?

- Are there any mitigating circumstances, for example provocation, health or domestic difficulties?

Because of the danger of unfairness if one employee is treated differently from others in respect of their involvement in the same incident, it is advisable for employers to complete their investigations in relation to all employees before deciding what sanction to impose.

Warnings

The least severe formal penalty is an oral warning (on informal warnings see p. 34). Nevertheless the manager should keep a note on the employee's personnel file in case further disciplinary action proves necessary. In more serious cases, or where there is an accumulation of minor offences, a formal written warning is appropriate. Where the employee has received a previous warning, further complaints may warrant a final written warning or a sanction short of dismissal (if this is provided for in the contract of employment).

Occasionally a complaint will be serious enough to justify only one written (in effect final) warning. Warnings should always tell the employee the consequences if further complaints are upheld. This is especially important in the case of final warnings, when the penalty is likely to be dismissal. The ACAS advisory handbook provides the following example letter:

Dear .... Date ....
   You attended a disciplinary interview on .... I am writing to confirm the decision taken that you should be given a written/final warning* under the second/third stage* of the Company Disciplinary Procedure.
   This warning will be placed in your personal file but will be disregarded for disciplinary purposes after a period of .... months, provided your conduct** improves/ performance reaches a satisfactory level.
   (a) The nature of the unsatisfactory conduct or performance was:

   (b) The conduct or performance improvement is:

   (c) The time scale within which improvement is required is:

   (d) The likely consequence of further misconduct or insufficient improvement is:
Final written warning/dismissal.*
You have the right to appeal against this decision (in writing**) to

.... within .... days of receiving this disciplinary warning.

Yours sincerely,

Manager.

*The wording should be amended as appropriate.
**Delete if inappropriate.

Issuing more than one final written warning should be avoided, since it may make eventual dismissal more difficult to justify and will generally undermine the value of such warnings.

Confusion may arise where warnings relate to different types of behaviour. However, employers are entitled to take account of the fact that an employee has received a previous warning even if that warning related to behaviour of a different kind from that which forms the potential ground for dismissal. Thus in deciding to dismiss Mr Curtis for mishandling company property it was not improper for his employer to take into account two previous final written warnings. The first concerned his relationships with other employees and the second referred to unsatisfactory documentation and absenteeism (*Auguste Noel* v. *Curtis* [1990] IRLR[17]).

Paragraph 19 of the ACAS Code of Practice specifies that 'except in agreed special circumstances breaches of disciplinary rules should be disregarded after a specified period of satisfactory conduct' (see also example letter above). Ideally this period should be stipulated when the rules are drafted. It is normal for different periods to operate in relation to different types of warnings. For example, warnings for minor offences may stand for up to six months, while final warnings may be valid for a year or longer.[18] If there is evidence of abuse – for example, the employee's behaviour is acceptable only when a warning is in force – this can be considered when determining how long another warning should endure. Where a complaint is so grave that it merits a final written warning which the employer will be unwilling to disregard in the future, it should be made clear that the slate will never be wiped clean.

Many employers provide employees with a right of appeal against warnings (see ACAS example letter, p. 70). Where this is the case care must be taken if it is decided to dismiss an employee for a further offence before the right has been exercised. Indeed, the Court of Appeal has commented that where a disciplinary procedure provides for a warning as a prerequisite of dismissal, a reasonable employer should bear in mind the fact that a warning is subject to an appeal which has yet to be determined. Thus if the appeal against the warning was scheduled to be heard the day after the dismissal occurred, the employer might be held to have acted unreasonably. However, where the time scale is in weeks or months:

the fact of the warning, providing it is given on adequate evidence and not for any oblique or improper motive, and the fact that it is still subject to appeal, remain throughout at least two of the circumstances in a case which a reasonable employer and industrial tribunal should take into account. [*Tower Hamlets Health Authority* v. *Anthony* [1989][19]

Withholding a pay rise

Unless the employee has a contractual right to an annual increase in pay, it may be lawful for an employer to withhold a rise. Where a contract of employment makes no reference at all to pay increases, it would seem that there is no implied contractual term which guarantees a rise.[20] However, it should be borne in mind that there is an implied term to the effect that employers will not treat employees arbitrarily, capriciously or inequitably in matters of remuneration.[21] As with all penalties, it is important for managers to assess the effect of a particular sanction on the individual concerned. Clearly, a refusal to pay a wage increase could be demoralising and counter-productive.

Deductions and fines

Employers wishing to impose either of these penalties must ensure that they comply with the Wages Act 1986. The Act provides that a deduction from wages (or payment to the employer from a worker) is unlawful unless it is required by statute or the worker has agreed to it. The worker must give oral or written consent to the deduction before it is made and, where the agreement constitutes a term of the contract of employment, it must be in writing and drawn to the employee's attention. In retail employment, deductions (or payments made to an employer) in relation to stock or cash shortages are subject to a limit of one-tenth of gross pay, except for the final payment of wages.

Suspension

Suspension can reinforce the employer's commitment to using dismissal as a sanction of last resort. However, suspension with pay can be an expensive penalty and one that may not be perceived as imposing any great disadvantage on the employee. On the other hand, suspension without pay may result in the employee becoming even less committed to the organisation. Both options carry the further risk of lowering the morale of those who have the task of covering the work of the person suspended. More generally, there is little point in providing for periods of suspension, with or without pay, unless it is intended to invoke them. Otherwise their presence in the procedure may simply serve to raise expectations and, if they are not met, engender further disgruntlement on the part of an employee or his or her colleagues. The IRS survey found that 40 per cent of respondents used suspension without pay as a sanction.

Demotion and transfer

According to the IRS survey, these were the most common sanctions, short of dismissal, used for disciplinary purposes. As mentioned earlier, employers have no general right to demote or transfer. The employer must either have contractual authority or obtain the employee's consent to the proposed change. Of course, this consent may be easier to achieve where it is made clear that the only alternative is dismissal. Demotion is particularly useful in relation to incapability, since employees who are genuinely incompetent are unlikely to improve in response to warnings. Transfers may be appropriate, for example, where there is a clash of personalities. A distinguishing feature of both these sanctions is that they are likely to involve the removal of one employee and his or her replacement by another. The implications of this should be discussed with union representatives.

Dismissal with notice

When all the alternatives have been considered the ultimate step will be dismissal. Save where gross misconduct has been committed the employee should be given the appropriate period of notice or payment in lieu. A contract of employment can lawfully be terminated by payment in lieu if the contract provides for such payment or the parties agree that the employee will accept it. However, the payment must relate to a period no shorter than that of the notice to which the employee would be entitled either under the contract of employment or under section 49 of the EPCA 1978. This section states that after a month's service an employee is entitled to a week's notice, and this applies until the employment has lasted for two years. At that point two weeks' notice is owed, and from then on the employee is entitled to receive an extra week's notice for each year of service up to a maximum of twelve weeks. It is sometimes forgotten that payment in lieu should compensate for the loss of any fringe benefits – for example, a company car and medical insurance – and any bonus or commission which would have been earned.

The ACAS advisory handbook includes the following letter confirming a dismissal after previous warnings:

Dear .... Date ....
On .... you were informed in writing that you would be given a final written warning in accordance with Stage .... of the

Company Disciplinary Procedure. In that letter you were warned that if your conduct/performance* did not improve, you were likely to be dismissed.

At the disciplinary hearing held on .... it was decided that your conduct/performance* was still unsatisfactory and that you should be dismissed.

I am therefore writing to you to confirm the decision that you should be dismissed in accordance with Stage .... of the Company Disciplinary Procedure and that your last day of service with the Company will be .... The reasons for your dismissal are:

You have the right of appeal against this decision (in writing**) to .... within .... days of receiving this notice of dismissal.

Your sincerely,

Manager.

*The wording should be amended as appropriate.
**Delete if inappropriate.

Dismissal without notice

In order to justify dismissal without notice (known as summary dismissal) the employee must be guilty of gross misconduct. Summary dismissal must be distinguished from instant dismissal. The latter expression has no legal meaning but normally refers to dismissal 'on the spot', i.e. without investigation. Whereas summary dismissal may be lawful under both statute and common law, instant dismissal is likely to be unfair. In all situations employees should be told the nature of the complaint and be given the opportunity to state their case. For example, it may emerge that a person caught fighting was subject to extreme provocation.

The ACAS advisory handbook provides the following example of a letter confirming dismissal without notice:

Dear ....   Date ....
I am writing to confirm the decision taken at the disciplinary hearing held on .... that you be summarily dismissed without notice or payment in lieu of notice, in accordance with the Company Disciplinary Procedure. Your last day of service was ....
The reasons for your dismissal are:

You have the right of appeal against this decision (in writing*) to .... within .... days of receiving this notice of dismissal.

Yours sincerely,

Manager.

*The wording should be amended as appropriate.

Group dismissal

According to the EAT, where a group of employees could have committed a particular offence, provided that the employer's beliefs are based on solid and sensible grounds, the employer is entitled to dismiss each member of the group if the following conditions are satisfied:

- An act has been committed which if committed by an individual would justify dismissal.
- The employer has made a sufficiently thorough investigation into the matter, using appropriate procedures.
- As a result of that investigation the employer reasonably believes that more than one person could have committed the act.
- The employer acted reasonably in identifying the group of employees who could have committed the act and each member of the group was individually capable of doing so.
- As between the members of the group, the employer could not reasonably identify the perpetrator.[22]

Needless to say, only very rarely will all of these conditions be met.

Appeals

An appeal may be lodged on various grounds. For example, it may be alleged that:

- The employee was not given a fair hearing.
- The sanction imposed was not appropriate to the employee's circumstances.
- New evidence has emerged which could have affected the outcome of the original hearing.

Except where a disciplinary procedure states otherwise – for example, in parts of the public sector – an appeal is intended to be a review rather than a rehearing. However, whether a procedural defect can be rectified on appeal will depend on the degree of unfairness at the initial hearing. If there is to be a correction by the appellate body, then the appeal must be of a comprehensive nature, in essence a rehearing.[23] In this situation it is advisable to provide a further appeal, since the appellate body has in effect stepped into the shoes of the original decision-maker.

As with the initial hearing, the manager should indicate how the meeting will be conducted, who is to be present and why. Ideally the employee should be accompanied by a union official or colleague, and another manager should attend to take notes of the proceedings. The ACAS advisory handbook gives the following example of a notice of appeal hearing letter:

> Dear .... Date ....
> You have appealed against the oral warning/written warning/final written warning/ notice of dismissal* confirmed to you in writing on .... Your appeal will be heard by .... in .... on .... at ....
> The decision of this appeal hearing is final and there is no further right of review.
> You have the right to appear alone or to be accompanied by your Trade Union/Staff Organisation representative or a fellow employee.
>
> Your sincerely,
>
> Manager.
>
> *The wording should be amended as appropriate.

Particular attention should be paid to any new evidence which is offered. It is a vital part of the appeal process to assess whether the disciplinary decision should be confirmed in the light of any new information as well as the information which was available when the original decision was made. However, employers cannot use information which comes to their knowledge during the appeal to establish a new reason for dismissal instead of the original one. For example, a Mr Monie was dismissed for suspected dishonesty when cash went missing from a safe. In rejecting his appeal the employer substituted failure to follow cash procedures as the reason for dismissal. The Court of Appeal held that this was unfair, since the employee had been denied the right to appeal against the new reason (*Monie* v. *Coral Racing* [1980][24]. Thus, if the original reason cannot stand, the appeal should be allowed. Of course, where the different reason would justify dismissal the disciplinary procedure could be reinvoked.

When all the relevant issues have been examined they should be summarised and the hearing should be adjourned for a decision to be taken. The employee should be informed of the reasons for the decision and these should be confirmed by letter. If appropriate it should be made clear that the decision is final. The ACAS Advisory Handbook gives the following example of a letter notifying the result of an appeal hearing:

Dear .... Date ....
You appealed against the decision of the disciplinary hearing that you be given a .... warning/be dismissed* in accordance with Stage .... of the Company Disciplinary Procedure. The appeal hearing was held on ....
I am now writing to confirm the decision taken by the Manager who conducted the appeal hearing, namely that the decision to .... stands**/the decision to .... be revoked** [specify if no disciplinary action is to be taken or what the new disciplinary action is].
You have now exercised your right of appeal under the Company Disciplinary Procedure and this decision is final.

Your sincerely,

Manager.

*The wording should be amended as appropriate.
**Delete if inappropriate.

Although there may be reluctance to undermine managerial authority by overturning the original decision, it is better to correct mistakes internally than risk external opprobrium. In theory there is nothing to stop a harsher penalty being substituted on appeal, although in practice this is likely to be regarded as unfair.

Appeals assume a particular importance in the context of unfair dismissal. In *West Midlands Co-operative Society* v. *Tipton* [1986][25] the House of Lords confirmed that dismissal will be unfair if the employer unreasonably treats the reason for dismissal as sufficient, either when the original decision was made or when that decision was maintained after an internal appeal. Where two employees are dismissed for the same incident and one is successful on appeal but the other is not, the fairness of the latter's dismissal will depend on whether the appeal panel's decision was so irrational that no employer could reasonably have accepted it.[26]

When there has been an appeal against dismissal the effective date of termination (see p. 113) will be the date of the original dismissal. It will not be the date on which the employee was informed that the appeal had failed, unless there is a contractual provision to this effect.[27] The effective date of termination should be clearly stated in a dismissal letter, and many employers feel that it is in their interest to point out that unfair dismissal complaints must normally be presented within three months of that date. Indeed, employees who delay making a claim because they are awaiting the outcome of an internal appeal will normally not get a tribunal hearing. As a matter of principle, the fact that a tribunal claim has been lodged before an internal appeal has been heard should not have any effect on the way the appeal is handled.[28]

Communicating decisions and keeping records

In all cases employees should be verbally told what disciplinary decision has been taken. This should be followed by a letter which confirms the details of any sanction that has been imposed (see the example letters above). Some employers find it useful to get employees to sign a statement that they have both received and understood such a communication. A copy of the letter should be sent to the employee's representative and another copy should be retained by the employer.

Sacked employees who have two years' continuous service have the right to be supplied with a written statement giving particulars of the reasons for dismissal. The employer must provide this statement within fourteen days of a specific request, unless it is not reasonably practicable to do so.[29] Perhaps the main significance of the written statement is that it is admissible as evidence in any proceedings. It is therefore vital to ensure that there is no inconsistency between the particulars supplied and the reasons offered as a defence against an unfair dismissal claim.

The need for consistency in discipline handling has already been emphasised (see p. 69). This will be difficult to achieve unless proper records are maintained. Paragraph 18 of the ACAS Code of Practice recommends that such records should be confidential and should indicate 'the nature of any breach of disciplinary rules, the action taken and any reasons for it, whether an appeal was lodged, its outcome and any subsequent developments'.

Key points

- It will often be necessary to conduct a preliminary investigation into a complaint before a disciplinary hearing is held. In some cases it may be desirable to suspend an employee on full pay while an investigation takes place.
- In preparing for a disciplinary hearing, written statements should be sought from witnesses. If possible, witnesses should attend the hearing.
- Employees should be notified in writing that a hearing will take place and be given sufficient time to prepare for it. Full details of the com-

plaint should be given and employees reminded of their right to be represented.
- Disciplinary hearings should be conducted in accordance with the principles of natural justice.
- Although employers must act consistently in applying disciplinary penalties, individuals must be treated on their merits, with all the relevant circumstances taken into account.
- Penalties should not be imposed which are disproportionate to the offence.
- Oral and written warnings should be issued formally but may be disregarded after a specified period of satisfactory behaviour.
- Payments can be withheld and demotions and transfers effected only if the employer has contractual authority to do so.
- Unless there is gross misconduct, dismissals should be implemented only after notice has been given.
- Employees should normally be given the right to appeal against a disciplinary decision. At this stage any new information should be assessed as well as the information that was available when the original decision was made.
- All disciplinary decisions should be confirmed in writing and proper records need to be maintained to ensure consistent treatment.

References

1 *British Home Stores* v. *Burchell* [1978] IRLR 379.
2 *Scottish Special Housing* v. *Cooke* [1979] IRLR 264.
3 *Linfood Cash and Carry* v. *Thomson* [1989] IRLR 235.
4 IRLR 380.
5 IRLR 320.
6 *Lucas Services* v. *Cary* (EAT 917/83).
7 ACAS, *Discipline at Work*, 37.
8 IRLR 412.
9 See *Ulsterbus* v. *Henderson* [1989] IRLR 251.
10 *Weddell* v. *Tepper* [1980] IRLR 96.
11 IRLR 482.
12 *British Home Stores* v. *Burchell* [1978] IRLR 379.
13 *Harris* v. *Courage* [1982] IRLR 509.
14 ACAS, *Discipline at Work*, 24
15 *Walton* v. *TAC* [1981] IRLR 357.
16 *Proctor* v. *British Gypsum* [1992] IRLR 7.
17 IRLR 326.
18 ACAS, *Discipline at Work*, 30.
19 IRLR 394.

20 *Murco Petroleum* v. *Forge* [1987] IRLR 50.
21 *Gardener* v. *Beresford* [1978] IRLR 63.
22 *Parr* v. *Whitbread* [1990] IRLR 34.
23 *Whitbread* v. *Mills* [1988] IRLR 501.
24 IRLR 464.
25 IRLR 112.
26 *Securicor* v. *Smith* [1989] IRLR 356.
27 *Savage* v. *Sainsbury* [1980] IRLR 119.
28 See ACAS, *Discipline at Work*, 34.
29 Section 53, EPCA 1978.

Chapter 5
Putting discipline into practice

Earlier chapters have examined the nature and purpose of disciplinary rules and procedures and have outlined the general principles of discipline handling. In this chapter we discuss the main situations in which discipline may be imposed and suggest how operational principles can be put into practice in order to ensure fairness.

Absenteeism

The IRS survey found that this issue was the most common cause of disciplinary action. However, the word 'absenteeism' covers a variety of situations which demand different approaches from employers. We have therefore distinguished between long-term absence through ill health, persistent short-term absences, problems associated with HIV/AIDS, unauthorised absence and overstaying leave.

Long-term absence through ill health

Strictly speaking, long-term absence through ill health is not a disciplinary issue. We have included it here because the procedure that should be followed to deal with such absence closely resembles that used for disciplinary action.

In order to monitor absenteeism, records must be kept. These should indicate the duration of, and reasons for, all periods of absence. The employer will then have to assess how much harm is being caused by an individual's absence.[1] Is there a crisis or could the organisation continue for a while without a permanent replacement? In exceptional situations a job may demand that employees need to be in particularly robust health and have impeccable levels of attendance. For example, a steel fixer working to a deadline on an oil platform in severe conditions had a term in his contract stipulating that if he was absent for two shifts in a fourteen-day period he would be regarded as unfit for employment.[2] As regards the feasibility of providing temporary cover, it would seem that those who work in smaller organisations and those doing the most important jobs may be more vulnerable because they can be less easily replaced.

The employer should obviously be in regular contact with the employee, who must be consulted and kept fully informed if his or her employment is at risk. The importance of consultation and medical investigation has been emphasised by the EAT:

> if in every case employers take such steps as are sensible according to the circumstances to consult the employee and to discuss the matter with him, and to inform themselves upon the true medical position, it will be found in practice that all that is necessary has been done. [*East Lindsey District Council* v. *Daubney* [1977][3]].

The employee's GP should be asked whether a return to work will be possible and, if so, what type of work that employee will be capable of. For example, a resumption of work might be possible if the job was redesigned. In order to comply with the Access to Medical Reports Act 1988, the employee should be notified that an application for a medical report is proposed and the employee's consent must be obtained. In addition, the employer must inform both the individual and the doctor, in writing, of certain matters.[4]

Where there is doubt about the nature of the illness or injury it may be advisable to seek an examination by a doctor appointed by the employer. However, unless medical examinations are provided for in the contract of employment, an attempt to compel an employee to undergo one may constitute constructive dismissal (see p. 115).[5] If employees refuse to provide medical evidence or submit to independent medical examination they should be told in writing that a decision will be taken on the basis of the information available to the employer and that this may result in the termination of their employment. In cases where there are conflicting medical reports, failure to obtain another opinion will not necessarily be unfair. Yet if the employer relies on one report rather than another there should be a valid reason for doing so. For example, a company doctor's view might be preferred because such a person has specific knowledge of the work environment in which the tasks were performed.

In the end the decision to take action is not a medical one but a matter to be determined by the employer in the light of the medical evidence. Indeed, since for unfair dismissal purposes an employee's incapability need only 'relate to' the performance of contractual duties, there is no legal requirement to show that the performance of all those duties has been affected. According to the EAT, the basic question is whether in all the circumstances the employer should be expected to wait any longer for the employee to recover.[6] In this context the existence of sick pay arrangements is simply one factor to be weighed. Dismissal during a period of occupational or statutory sick pay entitlement is not necessarily unfair. Equally it is not necessarily fair to dismiss when such an entitlement has been exhausted.[7]

If an individual's job cannot be kept open the employer should enquire whether alternative work is available, perhaps of a lighter or less stressful nature. The psychological value of knowing that there is some job to return to cannot be underestimated. Although many employers accept that they have a greater moral obligation where the illness or injury is job-related, an employer is not legally required to create a special job for the employee. Where no suitable alternative work is available, and the possibility of early retirement has been considered but rejected, the employee may be dismissed with notice. One difficulty with this is that the fairness of a dismissal is to be judged at the effective date of termination (see p. 113). Thus if a suitable vacancy arises during the period of notice it may be unfair not to offer it. To avoid the problem, many employers make a payment in lieu. The effect is to make the date of termination the date on which the payment is accepted.

Where there is little likelihood of the employee returning to work it may be argued that the contract of employment has automatically terminated through frustration, i.e. there is no dismissal at law and therefore no notice is due. A contract is deemed to be frustrated when, without the fault of either party, some event makes future performance either physically impossible or radically different from what was contemplated. Although this doctrine can be applied to contracts which are determinable by short notice, it is good practice not to rely on it and to give full notice where employees are entirely blameless. By definition the employee will be unable to work during this period.

It is generally accepted that disabled persons are entitled to special consideration.[8] However, the mere fact that people are disabled does not prevent them from being dismissed. Of course, if an employer was aware of an employee's disability at the time of hiring, an increased level of absence might reasonably have been anticipated.

Persistent short-term absence

Simple scrutiny of personnel records will reveal which individuals are constantly absent.[9] In such cases employers should undertake prompt investigations and invite the employee to explain the situation. Where there is no apparent medical justification for frequent absences the individual should be asked to consult a doctor to determine whether treatment is necessary and whether the underlying cause is work-related.[10] If the absences stem from domestic problems the employer should assess the likelihood of an improvement in attendance being achieved.

The normal disciplinary procedure should be applied when there appear to be no good reasons for the absences. In particular, the individual should be informed specifically about what improvement is required and warned of the possible consequences if it does not materialise. If no improvement occurs, the employer will have to decide what action to take.

In *Lynock* v. *Cereal Packaging* [1988][11] the EAT offered detailed guidance to employers in cases where an individual has an unsatisfactory record of intermittent sickness absence. Here dismissal following a final written warning was held to be fair, even though the company had failed to submit medical evidence. According to the Appeal Tribunal, where there are unconnected periods of intermittent illness it is impossible to give a reasonable projection of what will happen in the future. Whilst the employer may make enquiries there is no obligation to do so because of the transient nature of the employee's symptoms and complaints. In this situation the employer's approach should be based on sympathy, understanding and compassion. However 'there is no principle that the mere fact that the employee is fit at the time of dismissal makes his dismissal unfair; one has to look at the whole history and the whole picture'. The factors which may prove important in reaching a decision include:

- The nature of the illness.
- The likelihood of it recurring or some other illness arising.
- The lengths of the various absences and the spaces of good health between them.
- The employer's need to have the work done by the particular individual.
- The impact of the absences on other employees.
- The extent to which the difficulty of the situation and of the employer's position was made clear to the employee.

Other relevant factors not mentioned in this case are the employee's age and length of service and the availability of suitable alternative employment.

Problems associated with HIV/AIDS

As regards individuals who are believed to be suffering from a medical condition which has rendered them unacceptable to colleagues, employers may be under pressure to dismiss. To avoid unfairness, employers will have to consider not only the nature of the medical condition but also its impact on working relationships and the possibility of alternative employment. For example, since in most jobs there is no risk of the HIV virus being transmitted, there are normally no grounds for discriminating against employees simply because of suspected or actual HIV infection. Indeed, employers have a duty to provide reasonable support for an employee who is being harassed by colleagues. Thus good practice suggests that the employer's response to pressure to dismiss should be education and persuasion. If they prove unsuccessful the disciplinary procedure may have to be invoked against those who refuse to work normally.

Employees cannot be forced to take a blood test unless it is stipulated in the contract of employment. Even if employees are obliged to have regular check-ups it is arguable that an HIV test cannot be included without consent. Indeed, ACAS suggests that testing for HIV infection is 'expensive, inconclusive and unjustified' and may amount to indirect sex discrimination.[12] Where there is an express contractual term relating to HIV tests, refusal to submit to such a test does not necessarily mean that dismissal will be fair. An employer would need to have a valid reason for requiring the test and should explain to the employee what the consequences of refusing to take the test would be. In the absence of an express term governing HIV screening, an employer's insistence on such a test will probably be a fundamental breach of the implied term of trust and confidence, which will entitle the employee to resign and claim constructive dismissal (see p. 115).

ACAS advises all organisations to develop a policy on AIDS/HIV 'so that if and when problems arise they can be handled in a considered way'. An IRS survey found that 70 per cent of respondents had policies on HIV/AIDS and that the vast majority had consulted trade unions and employees over them.[13] Such policies are found more frequently among larger organisations and to some extent reflect the importance attached to equal opportunities and anti-discrimination measures in the public sector. Although the scope of HIV/AIDS policies varies considerably it is nevertheless possible to identify a number of common principles:

- The provision of basic information on HIV/AIDS, including reassurance that the chances of transmission in most workplace situations are minimal.
- The need for confidentiality.
- An assurance that there will be no HIV testing either before or during employment.
- An assurance to employees that their antibody status will have no effect on their continued employment with the organisation, including promotion and training opportunities.
- A commitment that an asymptomatic seropositive employee will be treated as in full health and that people with AIDS will be treated in the same way as any other person with a non-contagious debilitating condition.

According to the IRS, a broad consensus emerged among the survey respondents as to how to approach the situation where an employee becomes HIV positive or develops AIDS:

- Such an employee would not be obliged to inform the employer of the condition.

- If the employee chose to disclose the information it would be treated in strict confidence. The employee might be advised to consult the organisation's medical department.
- If the employee consented, his or her immediate supervisor would be informed.
- The employee would be offered advice on any steps that could minimise the risk of transmitting HIV to other employees.
- Advice on counselling would be offered.
- Unauthorised disclosure of a person's antibody status would be treated as an offence within the usual disciplinary structures.
- If the employee developed AIDS, resultant sickness would be treated as any other long-term disabling non-contagious illness.
- Eventually the employee might have to be retired early on ill-health grounds and would be entitled to any sickness pension or benefit the organisation provided.

Unauthorised absence

Unauthorised absences constitute a serious breach of contract. Yet, as in other instances of misconduct, it is important for the employer to investigate the situation and give the employee the opportunity to explain. For example, even if the employer does not believe that there is genuine illness, time must be allowed for a medical certificate to be submitted. Where medical evidence is received an employer may still be entitled to take disciplinary action on the grounds that the employee has an unsatisfactory record of intermittent absence (see above). Unauthorised leave would normally be regarded as a matter justifying warnings rather than dismissal for a first offence. However, if it is suspected that a sick note is being abused – for example, an employee has been seen participating in a demonstration while on sick leave – dismissal may be justified.[14]

It is now well established that employees who take leave after having been refused permission, and warned of the potential consequences of doing so, can be fairly dismissed. In these circumstances the Court of Appeal has indicated that employers do not have to wait for the employee to return in order to hear a possible explanation.[15] Nevertheless, whenever it is practical to do so a decision should be postponed until a investigation has been carried out.

Overstaying leave

Many employers grant extended leave without pay to enable employees to visit relatives or care for dependants. Where such a policy exists, the ACAS advisory handbook suggests that the following matters should be considered:

- The policy should apply to all employees, irrespective of sex, marital status or racial group.
- Any conditions attached to the granting of extended leave should be carefully explained to the employee and the employee's signature should be obtained as an acknowledgement that he or she understands and accepts them.
- If an employee fails to return on the agreed date this should be treated as any other failure to abide by the rules and the circumstances should be investigated in the normal way as fully as possible.
- Care should be taken to ensure that foreign medical certificates are not treated in a discriminatory way: employees can fall ill while abroad just as they can fall ill in this country.
- Before deciding to dismiss an employee who overstays leave, the employee's age, length of service, reliability record and any explanation given should all be taken into account.

Agreement that the employee will return at a specified time will not prevent the individual complaining of unfair dismissal if he or she is sacked for not returning as agreed. The agreement will be treated as an attempt to exclude or limit the operation of the EPCA 1978 and therefore cannot be enforced.[16] In this situation all the matters listed above and the general duty to behave reasonably should be borne in mind before any disciplinary action is taken.

Poor performance

According the IRS survey, poor standards and performance are the second most common cause of disciplinary action. Clearly poor performance is an expression which covers a multitude of sins. In certain circumstances employees may be blameless – for example, if they were wrongly selected for promotion. By way of contrast, an employee may be at fault by not working to the best of his or her ability. Unfair dismissal law suggests that whereas the latter situation can be treated as misconduct, in the former situation the reason for taking disciplinary action relates to capability. According to section 57(4) of the EPCA 1978, capability is to be assessed by reference to 'skill, aptitude, health or any other physical or mental quality'. From a practical point of view it is important to consider poor performance separately from absenteeism caused by ill health.

Setting standards and monitoring performance

It is the employer's duty to ensure that employees can achieve satisfactory levels of performance. This involves proper instruction and support, although, generally speaking, the more senior and experienced the employee the less supervision is required. Having commented that careful recruitment, selection and training can minimise the risk of poor performance, the ACAS advisory handbook suggests that the following principles should be observed when employment commences:

- The standard of work required should be explained and employees left in no doubt about what is expected of them. Special attention should be paid to ensuring that standards are understood by employees whose English is limited and by young persons with little experience of working life.
- Where job descriptions are prepared they should accurately convey the main purpose and scope of each job and the tasks involved.
- Employees should be made aware of the conditions which attach to any probation period.
- The consequences of any failure to meet the required standards should be explained.
- Where an employee is promoted, the consequences of failing 'to make the grade' in the new job should be explained.

As regards work standards, it is clear that these must be realistic and measurable. For example, it may be demonstrated that a salesperson failed to reach a target but that would not justify dismissal if the target was virtually impossible to meet.

The absence of a job description does not preclude disciplinary action so long as it can be demonstrated that employees knew what was required of them. However, it is important to remember that employees can be fairly dismissed only if they are incapable of performing the job that they were contractually obliged to do. Given the current two-year qualifying period, it is highly unlikely that employees will be entitled to complain of unfair dismissal while they are on probation. Nevertheless the way in which a probationary period is handled may be relevant to a claim of unfairness. To this end it is worth noting that there is an implied obligation on employers 'to take reasonable steps to maintain an appraisal of a probationer during a trial period; giving guidance by advice or warning where necessary' (*White* v. *London Transport Executive* [1981][17]).

In order to encourage improvement and to identify problems as early as possible, performance should be discussed regularly with employees – for example, by using an appraisal system to monitor an employee's performance, potential and development needs.[18] One complication here is that employers who operate appraisal systems will have to decide in what circumstances poor performance should become a disciplinary issue rather than one that is dealt with at an appraisal interview. Problems can arise if appraisal and disciplinary procedures are not properly distinguished. On the one hand, criticism at an appraisal interview may be perceived as a warning by the employee. On the other hand, if it is not clear that a disciplinary warning is being given, individuals may regard the criticism as relating solely to the appraisal exercise and not realise that they are being disciplined. It follows that warnings should be recorded as part of the disciplinary procedure and not on the appraisal form.

Dealing with poor performance

All instances of poor performance should be investigated. However, it is not necessary to prove that the employee is in fact incompetent. As Lord Denning put it, 'Whenever a man is dismissed for incapacity or incompetence it is sufficient that the employer honestly believes on reasonable grounds that the man is incapable or incompetent' (*Alidair* v. *Taylor* [1978][19]). This means that the employer must produce some evidence of poor performance (see chapter 5 on investigations and hearings).

Where poor performance is identified, the individual should be invited to provide an explanation – for example, pressure of work, health or domestic difficulties. If it appears that the employee lacks the requisite skills he or she should be offered training and given time to improve, especially if new technology has rendered certain skills obsolete. The training which is carried out must be adequate and systematically recorded. Factors to be considered in determining the period allowed for improvement might include:

- Length of service.
- Previous performance.
- The extent to which the employee is functioning below standard.

The targets set during the period allowed for improvement must again be realistic, and in some instances it may be useful to lower expectations in order to help restore confidence. Obviously the employee's progress should be monitored during this period.

Warnings can be particularly valuable in distinguishing cases of genuine incapability from those where there is a failure to exercise to the full such talent as is possessed. Employees who are genuinely incapable will not improve simply because a warning has been issued. According to the EAT, cases where people have not come up to standard through their own carelessness, negligence or idleness are much more appropriately dealt with as cases of misconduct than of incapability.[20]

In certain cases, where the consequences of a single error are very grave, a warning may not be necessary. For example, when a pilot damaged a plane during a faulty landing, the Court of Appeal endorsed the following view:

> in our judgment there are activities in which the degree of professional skill which must be required is so high, and the potential consequences of the smallest departure from that high standard are so serious, that one failure to perform in accordance with those standards is enough to justify dismissal. [*Alidair* v. *Taylor* [1978][21]]

Of course the disciplinary rules should have indicated that dismissal might result in these circumstances.

If despite help and encouragement the employee cannot achieve an acceptable level of performance attempts should be made to find suitable alternative work. In this context 'suitable' means anything which the employee is capable of doing, and may include demotion or transfer if it is contractually provided for. However, the law does not oblige employers to create artificial posts for employees. The ACAS advisory handbook suggests that where performance problems stem from changes in the nature of the job the situation may be treated as one of redundancy.[22] Even if the statutory definition of redundancy is technically not satisfied[23] there can be no impropriety in making a payment, since employers are no longer eligible for rebates from State funds. Undoubtedly the availability of redundancy payments can be an important sweetener when changes in job content are being negotiated with trade unions.

It almost goes without saying that when someone is sacked for poor performance consistency requires employers to ensure that others are not performing at a lower standard. If lower standards have been accepted in the past without dismissal it is vital that employees understand the reasons.

Timekeeping

According to the IRS survey, this issue was the third most common cause of disciplinary action. In cases of poor timekeeping the employee should be invited to give an explanation and, if none is forthcoming, a warning should be issued. Where a warning has already been given but the problem continues the employee should again be invited to explain before a more severe sanction is imposed.

Disobedience

All those engaged under contracts of employment have a duty to obey lawful and reasonable orders. There are two distinct aspects to this obligation. First, it means that employees are not required to obey an order if to do so would break the law, for example falsifying accounts or flouting health and safety legislation. Second, it also suggests that employees are not obliged to follow instructions which fall outside the scope of the contract. This is consistent with the legal principle that contractual terms cannot be unilaterally varied. However, case law shows that employees have been fairly dismissed for refusing to obey instructions which are outside their contractual obligations (see below).

Where disobedience is alleged, employers should undertake the usual investigations (see Chapter 3). In particular it will be important to check that the order issued was both lawful and reasonable and to ascertain the reasons for the employee's disobedience. To establish whether there is contractual authority for an instruction the employer may need to consider all the possible sources of contractual terms – express and implied terms in individual contracts of employment, statements issued under section 1 of the EPCA 1978, collective agreements, works rules and custom and practice.

One potential problem is that employees may have a contractual duty to perform tasks beyond the type of work they normally carry out. For example, a Ms Glitz was employed as a copy typist/general clerical duties clerk. At the time of hiring, the operation of a duplicating machine was not discussed and for three years she was not required to use such a machine. Nevertheless the EAT ruled that, since she worked for a small business, the operation of such a machine was within the scope of her duties (*Glitz* v. *Watford Electrical Company*).[24] It should also be noted that even when employees are absent from work on grounds of ill health, their obligations are modified only to the extent that they are incapable of carrying them out. For example, when a sales representative is ill it may be physically possible to obey an instruction to secure the employer's property by having it removed from a company car.[25]

The law of unfair dismissal has had a major impact on the notion of reasonable orders. In particular the statutory concept of reasonableness has been used to impose obligations on employees in situations where no contractual right to demand obedience exists. For example, although they had no contractual right to insist on mobility, the EAT thought John Menzies Ltd were justified in dismissing a manager who was underperforming when he refused to move from Letchworth to Swansea on a temporary basis for the purposes of retraining (*Coward* v. *John Menzies* [1977]).[26] Indeed, in *Millbrook Furnishing* v. *McIntosh* [1981][27] the EAT accepted that

> if an employer, under the stresses of the requirements of his business, directs an employee to transfer to other suitable work on a purely temporary basis and at a diminution in wages that may, in the ordinary case, not constitute a breach of contract.

In relation to the employee's reasons for refusing to obey orders, the Court of Appeal has indicated that

> the primary factor that falls to be considered by the reasonable employer deciding whether or not to dismiss his recalcitrant employee is the question 'Is the employee acting reasonably or could he be acting reasonably in refusing to obey my instruction?' [*UCATT* v. *Brain* [1980][28]]

It follows from what has been said above that the reasonableness of disciplinary action is not to be determined solely by job descriptions or contractual obligations. For example, employees may be disciplined for refusing to accept changes in job content or working hours if it can be demonstrated that the employer had a sound business reason for reorganising (see p. 000).[29] However, before taking disciplinary action an employer should consult both the individual and his or her union, consider any representations and allow exceptions to be made where appropriate.

Equally, it is not automatically fair to dismiss a person for a clear breach of the employer's rules. All discipline must be a reasonable reaction to the circumstances. For example, a Ms Oliphant was sacked for failing to record a sale on her till. Although the disciplinary rules indicated that till irregularities amounted to gross misconduct, it was held that the dismissal was unfair. According to the EAT, it was unreasonable to sack her on the grounds of one unexplained failure to comply with the till procedure, especially as no allegation of dishonesty had been made (*Laws Stores* v. *Oliphant* [1978][30]).

Employers have a duty to act reasonably in dealing with health and safety matters but the reasonableness of disciplinary action is not to be determined solely by statutory and contractual obligations. Where employees disobey orders on safety grounds the matter should be investigated promptly and the results disseminated before any decision on disciplinary action is taken. The crucial question is whether the employers could reasonably be expected to take more action than they did, for example, by offering a transfer to alternative work.[31]

Dishonesty

It is an implied term of the contract they have entered into that neither employer nor employee will destroy the mutual trust and confidence upon which their relationship is based. Clearly employees can jeopardise this relationship if they act dishonestly, for example by stealing, fiddling expenses, falsifying timekeeping records or failing to disclose relevant information. Nevertheless, dismissal in such circumstances will not always be fair. Apart from possible procedural errors (see Chapter 4), it may be argued that in the light of the individual's circumstances a warning would be more appropriate for a relatively minor offence.

In the case of stealing or fraudulent behaviour employers are not obliged to demonstrate 'beyond reasonable doubt' that the employee was dishonest. In order to act fairly the employer merely has to show:

- A genuine belief in the employee's guilt based on reasonable grounds.
- That having conducted an investigation into the matter as thoroughly as was appropriate, it was reasonable to dismiss in the circumstances.

However, it will not always be wrong to dismiss before a belief in guilt has been established. Quite apart from guilt, involvement in an alleged criminal offence often means that a serious breach of discipline has been committed. For example, a cashier charged with a till offence may well have ignored the proper till procedure.

Ordinarily, employees have no duty to volunteer information about themselves otherwise than in response to a direct question.[32] Indeed, section 4 of the Rehabilitation of Offenders Act 1974 relieves certain persons of the obligation to disclose 'spent' convictions. It also states that a 'conviction which has become spent . . . shall not be a proper ground for dismissing'. Sentences of over thirty months never become 'spent', otherwise convictions become 'spent' after periods which are related to the gravity of the sentence imposed. Protection does not extend to certain occupations, for example doctors, nurses, teachers, social workers and probation officers.

Problems can obviously arise if employees conceal convictions which are not 'spent'. Although it might be argued that as a matter of public policy employees should not be dismissed simply because of previous convictions, the EAT has taken a firm line on non-disclosure. Thus, despite the fact that one Mr Torr had worked satisfactorily as a British Rail guard for sixteen months before the concealment of his conviction was discovered, it was held that he had been fairly dismissed. According to the EAT:

> it is of the utmost importance that an employer seeking an employee to hold a position of responsibility and trust should be able to select for employment a candidate in whom he can have confidence. It is fundamental to that confidence that the employee should truthfully disclose the history so far as it is sought by the intending employer. [*Torr* v. *British Rail* [1977][33]]

This kind of reasoning would apply also to the deliberate concealment of other matters, for example a history of mental illness. Even so, every case should be investigated and considered on its merits.

Bad language

The form of disciplinary action which is appropriate for dealing with abusive or foul language will depend not only on the actual words used but also on their context. Clearly it will be necessary to distinguish cases where there is a history of swearing from a single, if significant, outpouring. As many commentators have remarked, bad language is usually the symptom rather than the cause of poor working relationships.

In assessing what response to make, employers should consider the employee's status and the effect on discipline in the organisation as well as the actual words used. For example, language which is acceptable on a building site may not be tolerated in other work contexts. However, disciplinary action for abusing a superior will be justifiable if managerial authority is challenged, and trust and confidence are undermined. Although employers are not expected to condone insubordination, it should be acknowledged that sometimes both parties are at fault. Thus the dismissal of an employee who has been provoked may be unfair.

In order to act reasonably, the events prior to the bad language should be examined as well as the incident which gave rise to the complaint. For example, a heat-of-the-moment outburst may be unlikely to recur and an apology may suffice.

Smoking

Employers have a common law duty to take reasonable care of the health and safety of their employees, and under the Health and Safety at Work Act 1974 they have a general duty to ensure, so far as is reasonably practicable, the health, safety and welfare of employees. Additionally, section 2(2)(e) of this Act requires employers 'to provide and maintain a safe working environment which is, so far as is reasonably practicable, safe, without risks to health and adequate as regards facilities and arrangements for their welfare at work'. This sub-section has attracted increasing attention recently because of its apparent application to the problem of passive smoking.

It may therefore be entirely appropriate for disciplinary action to be taken if an employee deliberately breaks a no-smoking rule which has been widely publicised and imposed for health and safety purposes. Indeed, where there are exceptional risks smoking may be regarded as gross misconduct. Nevertheless disciplinary action should be taken only if it is reasonable to do so in the circumstances. Thus it is necessary to distinguish between the employee who takes a conscious decision to infringe smoking rules and an inexperienced employee who innocently smokes in a prohibited area. In essence, this is another area where it is important to consider whether or not the employee is at fault.

If the employee is not at fault, in the sense that he or she is trying to adhere to the smoking rules but is unable to do so owing to dependence on cigarettes, there is a strong case for providing support and assistance. Indeed, although employers are not legally obliged to have a smoking policy, an increasing number of organisations are seeking to deal with the issue through the development of formal policies. According to research commissioned by the IPM, by 1989 over 20 per cent of companies had such policies and 80 per cent of companies had introduced no-smoking areas. Guidance on the preparation and content of such policies has been published by ACAS and a number of other organisations.[34]

The aim of a smoking policy is to provide workers with a healthy and efficient working environment and to avoid conflict at work. The first step should be to investigate the situation in order to assess the nature of the problem. For example, how many smoke, where are the smokers located, how will employees react to any curtailment of their freedom to smoke? As regards the content of the policy, pp. 17–18 of the ACAS advisory booklet offers a checklist of items to be considered. One crucial decision will be whether to introduce a total ban on smoking in all working and communal areas (with the exception of a 'smoking permitted' area) or a partial ban, for example, with separate working areas for those who wish to smoke. A further choice must be made between implementing the policy in full or phasing it in over a period of time. In making these and other decisions workplace safety representatives should be consulted. Apart from the statutory duty to consult imposed by section 2(6) of the Health and Safety at Work Act 1974, the involvement of safety representatives is likely to result in greater employee co-operation with the implementation of the policy and better industrial relations. Ultimately the new policy and the justification for it should be presented to the work force in a suitable format. It almost goes without saying that the penalties to be invoked in cases of non-compliance should be made clear.

Where smoking rules are introduced and operated in a reasonable fashion, and fair procedures are followed in dealing with any breaches, employers are likely to be found to have behaved reasonably. The IPM advises that employers wishing to introduce smoking policies which involve the creation of new rules should, in addition to carrying out adequate consultation, give plenty of notice of the change. Along with ACAS, the IPM suggests that ninety days would be a suitable period. It is also advisable to include a term in the contract of new employees whereby they agree to abide by the smoking rules.

As regards the enforcement of a smoking policy, the ACAS advisory booklet makes the following observations:

If employees have been properly consulted and their views taken into account most organisations should find little difficulty in introducing and maintaining a smoking policy. Any problems that do arise can usually be dealt with by counselling. Where an employee persistently disregards a smoking policy, employers may wish to consider whether it is appropriate for this to be treated in the same way as other breaches of company rules and dealt with under the disciplinary procedure.

Drinking and drugs

As with smoking, difficulties can arise either because the employee consciously chooses to break the employer's rules or because dependence on these substances leads to a breach of the rules or a failure to achieve acceptable work standards. Unfortunately it is not always easy to distinguish between the two types of situation. In recognition of the fact that employees may find themselves in trouble through no fault of their own, a growing number of employers have developed formal policies to deal with those who have an alcohol and/or drug problem. These lay down procedures for dealing with alcohol and drug abuse which are intended to help employees overcome their problems. Guidance on designing policies of this type has been produced by a variety of bodies, including ACAS and the Health and Safety Executive.[35]

Drinking

ACAS urges all employers to 'develop a policy that will enable them to deal with alcohol-related problems sympathetically, fairly and consistently'. As regards rules and procedures, these will obviously vary according to the nature of the organisation and the job content. What is appropriate should be the subject of careful consideration, including consultation with trade union or employee representatives. Breaches of the rules should be dealt with under the normal disciplinary procedure, which should allow each incident to be fully investigated and give employees the opportunity to state their case. The investigation needs to establish not only whether the employee was drinking but whether there was reasonable explanation for the behaviour or if there were other mitigating factors. It has been suggested that the opportunity to apologise is particularly important where employees lose their temper under the influence of drink.[36]

Since drinking (or being under the influence of drugs) at work often has health and safety implications, it is frequently treated as gross misconduct. If such is the case the disciplinary rules should indicate that dismissal without notice is the normal penalty. For example, a Mr Beverstock was summarily dismissed for drinking in a pub during working hours, although others who had behaved similarly had not been sacked. The dismissal was found to be unfair despite the employer's argument that previous cases had involved drinking on company premises and that Mr Beverstock's offence was more serious. According to the EAT, if an employer wishes to apply a particular penalty to alcohol misuse, or certain types of drinking are to be regarded in an unusual way, it should be dealt with in the contract of employment (*Dairy Products* v. *Beverstock* [1981])[37]. It goes without saying that employees should be fully informed about any change in the rules.

According to ACAS, 'where an employee's absences, deterioration in performance or even misconduct at work are due to consistent heavy drinking then it may be appropriate to treat the problem as one of illness'. It is suggested that the following steps should help:

- Keep accurate, confidential records of instances of poor performance or other problems.
- Interview the employee in private. If the employee is actually drunk, wait until he or she is sober.
- Concentrate on the instances of poor performance and question whether it could be due to a 'health' problem, without specifically mentioning alcohol in the first instance.
- Discuss possible work-related causes, such as excessive workload or too much responsibility.
- If appropriate discuss the organisation's alcohol policy and the help available inside and outside the organisation.
- Agree future action.
- Arrange regular meetings to monitor progress and discuss any further problems if they arise.

Clearly it is important that an alcohol policy should spell out the disciplinary position of employees who agree to undergo treatment. For example, at Legal & General the disciplinary procedure applies only if employees refuse to accept medical help or counselling to deal with their problem of alcohol abuse.

Drugs

The problems of drug and alcohol abuse are sometimes associated but they are not truly analogous, for one fundamental reason. Whereas the consumption of alcohol is normally legal, the possession of certain non-prescribed drugs is an offence under the Misuse of Drugs Act 1971. Indeed it is also an offence for an individual knowingly to allow such drugs to be offered for supply and, in some cases, used on premises for which he or she is responsible. Since drug users are likely to be less willing to discuss their habit for fear of prosecution, confidentiality becomes imperative. This may mean that no formal records can be kept.

ACAS suggests that, as with alcohol misuse, it is best to focus on performance problems and to follow the steps recommended for dealing with a suspected alcohol problem (see p. 97). Of course, if employees refuse help, or it does not prove successful, disciplinary action may have to be taken. Whether drug misuse gives rise to conduct or capability problems, it is important to follow a fair disciplinary procedure, conduct a full investigation and allow employees to put their case.

Even though it may be assumed that drug-taking at work is prohibited (because it is illegal), employers are advised to make specific mention of the subject in their disciplinary rules. As regards the use of drugs outside working hours, it should be dealt with in the same way as other conduct committed outside employment (see p. 105). According to the EAT, dismissal for such conduct will be justified only if it adversely affects relationships at work or otherwise harms the employer's business.[38]

Fighting

Although fighting at work may be treated as gross misconduct, not all fighting is equally serious, and in some cases a warning will be appropriate. The EAT has commented that 'in these days it ought not to be necessary for anybody to have a rule in black and white that a fight is going to be regarded very gravely by management' (*C. A. Parsons* v. *McLaughlin* [1978][39]). Nevertheless, employers should be able to demonstrate that they have rules on violence (and the threat of it) which have been fully explained to all concerned.

Given the general requirement to behave reasonably in all the circumstances, and the specific need to show that the employer held a genuine belief on reasonable grounds that the employee had been guilty of misconduct, it follows that it cannot be automatically fair to dismiss someone even where there is an obvious breach of an express rule. For example, it was held unfair to sack a long-serving employee (with a good previous record) for hitting a colleague solely on the basis that the employer's rules stated that such violence would lead to dismissal. According to the EAT, 'the proper test is not what the policy of the employer was but what the reaction of a reasonable employer would have been in the circumstances' (*Taylor* v. *Parsons Peebles* [1981][40]).

What matters ought to be considered in assessing a reasonable response to fighting? Attention should be paid to:

- The employee's length of service.
- The employee's general work record.
- The extent of any provocation and the proportionality of the employee's response to it.

Where violence has been threatened but not carried out, an important factor will be the atmosphere generated by the threat. Similarly, as regards violence outside the workplace, or outside working hours, the crucial factor is whether there is a sufficient link with the employment relationship. For example, has the incident put employees in fear?

Although it is readily assumed that attacks on managers amount to gross misconduct, it should not be forgotten that attacks by managers on their staff are equally serious. Indeed, it may be argued that an act of managerial aggression will have undermined trust and confidence to such a degree that the victim was constructively dismissed (see p. 115).

As indicated in Chapter 4, in all cases proper procedures should be followed, and employers must be consistent in imposing penalties for violence. This means not only behaving consistently as between employees accused of the same misconduct but also not acting out of line with the response in previous cases without giving employees proper warning that a different attitude has been adopted.

Sexual or racial harassment

Employees who suffer sexual or racial harassment may claim that they have been both unfairly dismissed and discriminated against under the Sex Discrimination Act 1975 and the Race Relations Act 1976 respectively. Thus harassers are not only guilty of misconduct but they also infringe the anti-discrimination legislation. Under this legislation employers are also liable for the acts of their employees committed in the course of employment, irrespective of whether they were done with the employer's knowledge or approval, unless it can be proved that the employer 'took such steps as were reasonably practicable to prevent the employee from doing that act'.[41]

It follows that an employer should have an equal opportunities policy and disciplinary rules which make it clear that discrimination amounts to misconduct and will attract appropriate penalties. Allegations of harassment must always be taken seriously. Indeed, failure to do so might entitle a victim to resign and claim constructive dismissal.[42] Investigations should obviously be carried out sensitively, and ideally the person investigating should be of the same sex and race as the complainant.

Some employers have chosen to develop special policies and procedures for dealing with allegations of harassment. These lay down both formal and informal mechanisms for resolving complaints, including how formal disciplinary action is to be carried out.[43] The Department of Employment guidance on sexual harassment, which can be applied equally to racial harassment, suggests that suitable policies will:

- Set out what kind of conduct is unacceptable.
- State that harassment may be treated as a disciplinary offence and that it may be unlawful.
- Make clear to employees their responsibility to treat colleagues of both sexes (and all races) with dignity and respect.
- Describe how to complain about harassment.
- Assure staff that allegations of harassment will be dealt with seriously.
- Make it the duty of managers and supervisors to implement the policies.

The guide warns that managers and supervisors may need training in order to implement the policy and recommends that, wherever possible, employees who have complained of harassment should be given access to advice and, if necessary, counselling.

The breakdown of working relationships

Disruptive relationships are obviously detrimental to a work environment and disciplinary action may need to be taken. However, employers should endeavour to take such measures as are reasonable to alleviate the situation, for example transferring one or more of those involved. Dismissal will be reasonable only if:

- The breakdown in relationships is irremediable.
- Efforts have been made to improve the situation, for example by counselling.
- All the alternatives to dismissal have been considered.[44]

Disloyalty

The common law implies a duty of fidelity in all contracts of employment. This is intended to prevent employees putting themselves in a position whereby their own interests conflict with those of their employer. Nevertheless, questions of loyalty should ideally be dealt with by express terms covering disclosure of information (see also p. 105 on media activity), the receipt of gifts or hospitality and working for others without prior permission. Obviously, if such terms are to be relied on for disciplinary purposes they must be reasonable. For example, a general clause preventing employment elsewhere may be too broad to justify disciplinary action for engaging in a totally different job outside working hours.

Carefully worded restraint clauses (restrictive covenants) can be used to limit the activities of *former* employees. By definition ex-employees are immune from disciplinary action, and restraint clauses will only be enforced by the courts if they:

- Provide protection against something more than competition.
- Are reasonable in the circumstances and are not contrary to the public interest.

Such clauses are of interest to us because disciplinary action may be contemplated against those who refuse to sign them during the course of their employment. What have to be considered are:

- The extent of the limitation which the employer wants to impose. (Was it too extensive in terms of time, geography or the range of activities covered?)
- The importance of the restriction to the employer's business.
- The reaction of other employees. (Did they comply with the employer's request?)

For example, a manufacturer of electrical components discovered that ex-employees were working in competition and soliciting former customers. Since profits were being reduced, the manufacturer thought it necessary to impose a new contractual term on his sales team, prohibiting them from soliciting customers for up to a year after leaving the company. In these circumstances it was decided that a Mr Irwin, who was one of four out of the ninety-two sales team who refused to accept the new terms, was fairly dismissed. (*RS Components* v. *Irwin* [1973]).[45]

Although an actual breach of the duty of fidelity must be demonstrated before an employer can bring a claim at common law, the law of unfair dismissal suggests that disciplinary action can be taken when the employer merely has reasonable grounds for believing that there was a breach of trust. As in other cases, proper procedures must have been applied, i.e. investigation must provide sufficient evidence to give rise to a reasonable belief in the employee's guilt, and it must be reasonable to discipline in the circumstances, for example because of the threat posed to the business. We will now consider the two main aspects of the duty of fidelity.

The obligation not to compete with the employer

Unless there is an express contractual term prohibiting it, spare-time working can be the subject of disciplinary action only if it causes serious harm to the employer. (Indeed, in certain circumstances an injunction may be granted to prevent an employee working for a competitor.) In assessing whether the harm suffered is such as to breach the employee's duty of fidelity, attention has to be paid to all the circumstances, including the nature of the job and the number of hours of employment. For example, where an odd-job man did work for a competitor in his own time which hardly affected his employer it was held that there had been no breach of trust.[46]

Where employees establish a rival business in competition with their current employer, trust and confidence are so obviously undermined that it is not necessary to show that serious losses have actually been suffered. However, the mere intention to set up in competition does not in itself justify dismissal. According to the EAT, it has to be shown that the employee misused confidential information (*Laughton* v. *Bapp* [1986]).[47] In such circumstances the opportunity to explain will prove crucial, and in many cases employees will respond positively to warnings about the consequences of their actions.

The obligation not to disclose confidential information

The extent of this duty varies according to the nature of the contract but in principle the leaking or misuse of confidential information may warrant disciplinary action – for example, if an employee copied or deliberately memorised a list of the employer's customers for use after the employment had ceased. Nevertheless regard must be had to:

- The importance of the information.
- The employee's position in the organisation.
- Whether or not the employee was motivated by gain.

Thus the inadvertent disclosure of insignificant material may not justify dismissal.

Disciplinary action may be thought appropriate either because a breach of confidence has taken place or it is suspected that it might happen in the future. Whether such action is fair or not will depend on the circumstances, perhaps the most crucial factor being the existence or absence of a genuine threat to the business. As in other cases, a proper investigation should be conducted, and it should not be assumed that consultation or warnings will necessarily be futile in these circumstances. For example, when an employer's concern is made clear the employee may voluntarily decide to look for work elsewhere. Where employers have a policy of not employing people whose partners or relatives work for rival organisations, this should be made clear from the outset.

Reorganisation of the business

If the employer has a sound business reason for reorganising, it may be fair to take disciplinary action against employees who refuse to accept changes in their terms and conditions of employment.[48] It is not necessary for employers to show that in the absence of a reorganisation there would be a total collapse of the enterprise. All that has to be demonstrated is that there were reasonable grounds for believing that their business reasons were sound and that they reacted sensibly to the employee's refusal to comply with the new terms. For example, could dismissal have been avoided by a transfer?

Where changes are proposed, employers should engage in the fullest possible consultation with both unions and individuals. If general agreement to accept the changes has been secured, it is clearly easier to take disciplinary action against isolated individuals who resist the new terms – for example, if an employee's refusal to co-operate undermines a new payment or shift system. Although employees may have perfectly valid reasons for opposing change, perhaps because of a sizeable drop in income, ultimately the matter is one of managerial prerogative. Thus the test to be applied is whether the terms offered are ones which a reasonable employer could offer in the circumstances. Weighing the advantages to the employer against the disadvantages to the employee is merely one factor.[49]

It should be noted that some reorganisations may involve redundancies. If in essence the employee's work remains the same but a different mode of performance is required there may be a substantial reason for taking disciplinary action. However, if there is a reallocation of functions such as to alter the particular kind of work which the employee is required to perform the procedure for handling redundancies should be invoked.[50] Indeed, when a redundancy payment is claimed, dismissal is presumed to be on the grounds of redundancy unless the contrary is proved.[51]

Contravention of statute law

If there is a statutory prohibition making it illegal to allow the employee to continue to do the same work it may be fair to take disciplinary action. Perhaps the most obvious example is that of a driver who loses his or her licence. Additionally, it would seem that, if there is a genuine belief, based on reasonable grounds, that continued employment would be illegal, then that may amount to 'some other substantial reason' for dismissal even if the belief turns out to be erroneous (see p. 116): for example, a genuine belief that the employee needed a work permit to remain legally employed.[52]

In deciding what is a reasonable response an employer's attention will focus on whether the ban is permanent or temporary. If the former, an employer might be expected to consider the feasibility of redeployment; if the latter, short-term alternative work might be offered. Whether such measures need to be taken will depend on the type of business and the employee's work record. Indeed, after consultation it may emerge that it is possible for the employee to continue in his or her normal job by making special arrangements. For example, a sales representative who has been disqualified from driving may be prepared to hire a driver in order to remain in employment.

Where the illegality comes about because the employee lacks vocational qualifications, it will be relevant to know the extent to which the employer assisted the individual to obtain the necessary qualifications. If it is possible for further time to be given to enable the employee to obtain the necessary qualification – for example, by a professional body – it may be unreasonable to take disciplinary action before it is learned whether an extension will be granted.[53]

Third-party pressure

Where a third party – for example, an important client – puts pressure on an employer it may be reasonable to remove an employee even though no misconduct has been established. The employer must show that the third party has threatened not to continue normal business contact unless the employee concerned has been replaced. It is obviously desirable that employers who may be required to take action in these circumstances make this clear in the contracts of employment they issue.

In considering the range of reasonable responses an employer will have to assess the seriousness of whatever the employee is alleged to have done as well as the opportunities for redeployment. However, it has been accepted that, subject to the usual procedural safeguards, termination can be fair even if the employer is reluctant to dismiss and believes that the third party is acting unreasonably.[54]

The refusal of colleagues to work with an employee may justify disciplinary action, although management must take reasonable steps to dispel fears and assimilate employees. Giving in to pressure to dismiss may not only reinforce prejudices and create problems for the future, it may also lead to a finding of unfair dismissal. Section 63 of the EPCA 1978 provides that, in determining the reason for dismissal or whether it was sufficient to dismiss, a tribunal cannot take into account any pressure, in the form of industrial action or the threat of it, which was exercised on the employer to secure an employee's dismissal.

Conduct outside employment

Employees may be disciplined for behaviour outside the work context so long as it reflects in some way on the employment relationship. Since we have already discussed 'moonlighting' as an aspect of disloyalty (p. 101), we will now consider bringing the employer into disrepute through media activity or criminal offences outside employment.

Media activity

Many people would think it unfair if employees were disciplined for media activities privately engaged in on subjects unconnected with their employment. However, in certain circumstances express or implied criticism of an employer in the media may be the subject of disciplinary action. Indeed, some employers – for example, in the National Health Service – have introduced so-called 'gagging clauses' to make it easier to discipline individuals who reveal information to the media. Some would argue that such clauses are against the public interest and therefore should not be relied upon. Whatever moral view is adopted, in deciding whether to take disciplinary action against a 'whistle-blower' employers will need to consider the following matters:

- Whether the employee has abused his or her position.
- The degree of harm inflicted.
- Whether trust and confidence have been undermined.

As in other cases, an investigation will be essential, especially given the ability of the media to put people under pressure and to misrepresent their views.

Criminal offences outside employment

Paragraph 15 of the ACAS Code of Practice suggests that the main considerations should be:

> whether the offence is one which makes the individual unsuitable for his or her type of work or unacceptable to other employees. Employees should not be dismissed solely because a charge is pending or because they are absent through having been remanded in custody.

(On imprisonment see p. 106.)

Whether disciplinary action should be taken will depend on a number of factors, for example:

- The nature of the crime.
- The employee's job. (Does the work involve contact with the public?)
- The potential harm to the employer's business.
- The employee's length of service.

Thus in *Moore* v. *C & A Modes* [1981][55] the dismissal of a retail supervisor for shoplifting from another store was held to be fair despite her twenty years' service.

Imprisonment

People who are remanded in custody or sentenced to imprisonment often do not resign because they would like to retain their employment if possible. However, if it is impracticable to keep a person's job open it may be argued that the contract has been frustrated or that the loss of trust and confidence makes it fair to dismiss for 'some other substantial reason' (see p. 116).

We have discussed the doctrine of frustration in the context of ill health (see p. 83). A lengthy term of imprisonment may be treated as frustrating the contract of employment. However, a shorter custodial sentence may not, unless the employer can demonstrate that the business could not function without an immediate permanent replacement. In deciding whether it is reasonable to keep the job open, employers should take into account the employee's:

- Work record.
- Length of service.
- Expected period of absence.

For example, could it be argued that the employer regularly tolerated such periods of absence on the grounds of ill health?

Before reaching a decision it is advisable to make enquiries of the employee's family or lawyers about the likelihood of an appeal being lodged. If there is doubt as to whether dismissal would be a reasonable response, the safest course would be to inform the employee that the job is being kept open and that a disciplinary hearing will be held when the sentence has been served. This will give the employee the chance to make representations and the employer will have the opportunity to explore the alternatives to dismissal, for example demotion or transfer.[56]

Personal appearance and hygiene

Employers have a discretion in regulating the physical appearance of their employees if health and safety factors are involved or their work necessitates contact with the public. Ideally, there should be clear rules about what can or cannot be worn, and before any new rules are introduced there should be proper consultation. Even if there are no written rules, it is generally implied that employees will wear suitable clothes at work and that jewellery which could be offensive or a source of danger will not be displayed.[57]

In striking a balance between individual freedom and the interests of the business, the employer will have to weigh the reasons for imposing the dress requirements against the reasons why the employee objects. It goes without saying that the rules on appearance should not be capricious or fanciful and that employers must behave reasonably in enforcing the standards they desire. For example, if an employer decides that uniforms should be worn, an exception may be appropriate when there is an objection on the grounds of genuine religious belief.

Where a breach of appearance rules is alleged it needs to be investigated and management should check that the rules have been interpreted reasonably. Only rarely will it be fair to treat a breach of such rules as amounting to gross misconduct. In many cases employees will respond positively to warnings that their job is in jeopardy unless they can provide a good excuse for disobeying a reasonable rule.

The standard of personal hygiene required of employees will be influenced by a number of factors, for example:

- The nature of the product.
- The production process.
- The reaction of workmates.

References

1. See ACAS, Advisory Booklet 5, *Absence*.
2. See *Leonard* v. *Fergus & Haynes* [1979] IRLR 235.
3. ICR 566.
4. See sections 3-5, Access to Medical Reports Act 1988.
5. See *Bliss* v. *South East Thames Regional Health Authority* [1985] IRLR 308.
6. See *Spencer* v. *Paragon* [1976] IRLR 373.
7. See *Hardwick* v. *Leeds Area Health Authority* [1975] IRLR 319.
8. See *Hobson* v. *GEC* [1985] ICR 777.
9. On personnel records generally see ACAS Advisory Booklet 3, *Personnel Records*.

10 See ACAS, *Discipline at Work*, p. 41.
11 IRLR 510.
12 ACAS Advisory Booklet 15, *Health and Employment*. See also 'Aids and the workplace: a guide for employers', Employment Department/Health and Safety Executive. 1990.
13 *Health and Safety Information Bulletin* 186, June 1991 (IRS).
14 See *Hutchinson* v. *Enfield Rolling Mills* [1981] IRLR 318.
15 *London Transport Executive* v. *Clarke* [1981] IRLR 355.
16 See section 140, EPCA 1978, and *Igbo* v. *Johnson Matthey* [1986] IRLR 215.
17 IRLR 261.
18 See ACAS Advisory Booklet 11, *Employee Appraisal*.
19 IRLR 445.
20 See *Sutton & Gates* v. *Boxall* [1978] IRLR 486.
21 IRLR 445.
22 See ACAS Advisory Handbook page 49.
23 See section 81(2), EPCA 1978.
24 [1979] IRLR 89.
25 See *Marshall* v. *Sloan & Co.* [1981] IRLR 264.
26 *Coward* v. *John Menzies* [1977] IRLR 428.
27 IRLR 309.
28 IRLR 357.
29 See *Hollister* v. *National Farmers Union* [1979] 238.
30 *Laws Stores* v. *Oliphant* [1978] IRLR 251.
31 See *Piggott* v. *Jackson* [1991] IRLR 309.
32 *Walton* v. *TAC* [1981] IRLR 357.
33 IRLR 185.
34 See ACAS, *Health and Employment*, Advisory Booklet 15, 1990; IPM, *Smoking Policies at Work*. 1990.
35 See, for example, ACAS, *Health and Employment*; Health and Safety Executive, *The Problem Drinker at Work*, 1981; *Drug Abuse at Work*, 1990; Department of Employment, *Alcohol in the Workplace: a guide for employers* and *Drug Misuse and the Workplace: a guide for employers* (both published by the Employment Department in 1989).
36 See *Charles Letts & Co.* v. *Howard* [1976] IRLR 248.
37 [1981] IRLR 265.
38 See *Norfolk County Council* v. *Bernard* [1979] IRLR 220.
39 IRLR 65.
40 IRLR 119.
41 Section 41, Sex Discrimination Act 1975; section 32, Race Relations Act 1976.
42 See *Bracebridge Engineering* v. *Darby* [1990] IRLR 3.
43 See M. Rubenstein, *Preventing and Remedying Sexual Harassment*,

Industrial Relations Services, 1990; Department of Employment; *Sexual Harassment in the Workplace – a guide for employers.* 1992, IPM. *Sexual Harassment in the Workplace – a review of the literature and current developments.* 1992.

44 See *Turner* v. *Vestric* [1981] IRLR 23.
45 IRLR 239.
46 *Nova Plastics* v. *Froggatt* [1982] IRLR 146.
47 IRLR 245.
48 See *Hollister* v. *National Farmers Union* [1979] IRLR 238.
49 *Richmond Precision* v. *Pearce* [1985] IRLR 179.
50 See *Murphy* v. *Epsom College* [1984] IRLR 271.
51 Section 91(a), EPCA 1978.
52 See *Bouchaala* v. *Trust Houses Forte* [1980] IRLR 382.
53 See *Sutcliffe* v. *Pinney* [1977] IRLR 349.
54 See *Dobie* v. *Burns* [1984] IRLR 329.
55 IRLR 71.
56 See generally *Releasing the Potential: a guide to good practice for the employment of people with criminal records.* Apex Trust.
57 See *Boychuk* v. *Symons* Ltd [1977] IRLR 395.

Chapter 6
The consequences of getting it wrong

This chapter examines the legal consequences that can follow from the mishandling of disciplinary issues. However, it must be reiterated that the avoidance of such consequences should be viewed as only one of a number of considerations which need to be taken into account when developing and operating disciplinary rules and procedures. Arguably they are not even the most important consideration.

The poor handling of discipline at work can have important implications for all aspects of human resource management. Organisations which develop a reputation for arbitrary and harsh disciplinary practices can harm the recruitment process by reducing their attractiveness to potential recruits. More important, poor disciplinary practices can adversely affect workforce attitudes and motivation, with potentially harmful consequences for effort levels, staff retention and management–worker relations. For example, official statistics indicate that in the year ending April 1991 dismissal or other disciplinary measures were the third most common cause of strike action. Similarly, research has shown that over-strict disciplinary regimes can have dysfunctional consequences for absence levels.[1] More positively, advocates of non-punitive approaches to discipline used by some employers in the United States claim that organisations utilising them have frequently achieved reductions in disciplinary incidents, labour turnover and discipline-related grievances.

While the development of disciplinary policies should not be viewed as essentially about compliance with legal rules and norms, the legal framework within which discipline must be handled cannot be ignored. The remainder of this chapter deals with the most common sources of legal action that arise in relation to disciplinary matters: complaints about breach of contract and unfair dismissal. However, it should not be forgotten that those who feel they have been subjected to unfair discipline on the grounds of their sex or race can bring claims under the anti-discrimination legislation.

Injunctions and damages for breach of contract

Although it will be possible to make a statutory complaint about action short of dismissal only if the behaviour challenged amounts to discrimination on the grounds of sex, race or union membership or activities, the common law offers greater scope for redress where no dismissal has taken place. Once it is established that the employer has committed a breach of contract – for example, by making unauthorised deductions from wages or failing to abide by a disciplinary procedure which forms part of the individual's contract of employment – an employee may seek damages, an injunction to prevent disciplinary action being imposed or a declaration of his or her rights.

Injunctions

Traditionally, great emphasis was placed on the personal nature of the contract of employment, and the courts were extremely reluctant to order a party to continue to perform such a contract. However, in recent years the courts have been more willing to grant injunctions against employers who act in breach of contract. Nevertheless an injunction is a discretionary remedy, and the circumstances in which one will be granted are likely to be exceptional. Before an injunction is issued a court will need to be satisfied that the following conditions have been met:

- The employer's breach has not been accepted by the employee as bringing the contract to an end, i.e. there is still a contract in existence to enforce. In practice, almost any act which indicates that the employee has accepted that the employment has ceased is treated as terminating the contract. For example, in *Dietman* v. *London Borough of Brent* [1988][2] it was held that Ms Dietman had accepted that her contract had ended by taking employment elsewhere and lodging a complaint of unfair dismissal.
- Damages would not be an adequate remedy in the particular circumstances.
- The employer still has sufficient confidence in the employee to make the contract workable. The mere fact that the employer and employee are in dispute does not mean that mutual confidence has evaporated. For example, in *Robb* v. *London Borough of Hammersmith and Fulham* [1991],[3] although the local authority had lost confidence in the Director of Finance's ability to perform his job, the effect of the injunction was that he was suspended on full pay until the employer's disciplinary procedure had been complied with.

The consequence of an injunction being granted is not that the employee must be retained until retirement. It is simply that disciplinary action cannot continue in breach of the employer's contractual obligations, i.e. the rules and procedures must be followed.

Damages

Those who seek damages at common law can be compensated for the direct and likely consequences of the breach of contract, although nothing can be recovered for the mental stress, frustration and annoyance involved.[4] Thus an employee who has been dismissed in breach of contract will normally recover only the amount of wages lost between the actual date of dismissal and the date when the contract could lawfully have been terminated. For example, Ms Dietman's contract was breached when she was denied the disciplinary hearing that was provided for in the rules. She was awarded damages to reflect the pay she would have received during the period the employer should have carried out the proper procedure. Additionally she obtained a sum as compensation for loss of her notice entitlement.[5]

Employees have a duty to mitigate their loss, which means, in effect, that they are obliged to look for another job. At the time of writing, industrial tribunals still have no jurisdiction to hear ordinary breach of contract cases. These have to be brought before the County Court if the claim is worth up to £25,000 or the High Court.[6]

The right to claim unfair dismissal

Section 54 of the EPCA 1978 gives employees the right not to be unfairly dismissed, and it is worth noting that more than half the respondents to the IRS survey had faced an unfair dismissal claim in the previous five years. In the remainder of this chapter we outline:

- The exclusions and qualifications that apply to the exercise of this right.
- The meaning of dismissal.
- The potentially fair reasons for dismissal.
- The concept of reasonableness.
- The remedies available to successful complainants.
- The role of ACAS conciliation officers.

Exclusions and qualifications

There are a number of exclusions from and qualifications for unfair dismissal which seriously restrict the number of individuals who can bring such claims.

Unless sex or race discrimination is alleged, or the reason for dismissal is related to trade union membership or activities, those who complain of unfair dismissal need to have two years' continuous service.[7] Those who are employed for between eight and sixteen hours a week

The consequences of getting it wrong 113

need five years' continuous service, and those who are employed for less than eight hours are totally excluded. Given the nature of female involvement in the labour market, it goes without saying that such provisions have a disproportionate impact on women. At the time of writing the continuity rules are being challenged in the courts by the Equal Opportunities Commission as being inconsistent with EC discrimination law.[8]

No complaint can be made if on or before the effective date of termination the individual had attained the normal retiring age for an employee in his or her position or, where there is no normal retiring age, was sixty-five years old.[9]

There is no right to complain if 'under his contract of employment the employee ordinarily works outside Great Britain'. However, employees who work on oil rigs or offshore installations in British territorial waters or areas designated under the Continental Shelf Act 1964 are not excluded.[10]

Where at the date of dismissal the employee was locked out, or taking part in industrial action, a tribunal cannot determine whether the dismissal is fair or unfair unless it is shown that one or more 'relevant employees' of the same employer have not been dismissed or that, within three months of the complainant's dismissal, any such employee has been offered re-engagement and the complainant has not. In no circumstances can employees complain of unfair dismissal if at the time of dismissal they were taking part in unofficial industrial action.[11]

Only employed persons can complain (including Crown employees). Thus self-employed persons are excluded, as are certain share fishers and members of the armed forces and of the police service. Additionally, an industrial tribunal must dismiss a complaint if a Minister of the Crown certifies that the action was taken for the purpose of safeguarding national security.[12]

Complaints of unfair dismissal must normally arrive at an industrial tribunal within three months of the effective date of termination. If it is not reasonably practicable for a complaint to be presented within this period it must be submitted within such further period as the tribunal considers reasonable.[13]

The employer and employee can contract out of the unfair dismissal provisions. This may occur in one of three ways:

- An employee will be excluded if a dismissal procedures agreement has been designated by the Secretary of State as exempting those covered by it. An application must be made by all the parties to the agreement and the Secretary of State must be satisfied about all the matters listed in section 65(2) of the EPCA 1978. Only one such exempt agreement exists to date, in the electrical contracting industry.
- There is no right to complain of unfairness where the dismissal con-

sists only of the expiry of a fixed-term contract for a year or more without it being renewed, if before the term expires the employee has agreed in writing to waive his or her right to claim.[14]
- An agreement to refrain from presenting a complaint will be binding if it has been reached after the involvement of an ACAS conciliation officer (see p. 121).

Is there a dismissal at law?

If an employee can establish the right to complain, the next hurdle is to show that there has been a dismissal at law. For this purpose an employee is to be treated as dismissed if:

- The contract under which he or she is employed is terminated by the employer with or without notice, or
- A fixed-term contract expires without being renewed under the same contract, or
- The employee terminates the contract with or without notice in circumstances such that he or she is entitled to terminate it without notice by reason of the employer's conduct.[15]

For the giving of notice to constitute a dismissal at law the actual date of termination must be ascertainable. Where an employer has given notice to terminate, an employee who gives counter-notice indicating that he or she wishes to leave before the employer's notice has expired is still to be regarded as dismissed.[16]

We have already indicated that there is no dismissal if the contract terminated owing to frustration (see p. 83). Equally, there is no dismissal if there is a mutually agreed termination. However, as a matter of policy, tribunals will not hold that there is an agreement to terminate unless it is proved that the employee really did agree with full knowledge of the implications. Thus in *Igbo* v. *Johnson Matthey* [1986][17] it was held that an employer could not rely on a provision for automatic termination upon the employee's failure to report for work on a specified date following a period of extended leave.

Obviously, if people resign of their own volition there is no dismissal at law, but if pressure has been applied the situation will be different – for example, where the employee has been given the choice of resigning or being dismissed. There may also be no dismissal where an employee resigns on the terms offered by an employer's disciplinary sub-committee. According to the EAT:

> it would be most unfortunate if, in a situation where the parties are seeking to negotiate in the course of disciplinary proceedings and an agreed

form of resignation is worked out by the parties, one of the parties should be able to say subsequently that the fact that the agreement was reached in the course of disciplinary proceedings entitled the employee thereafter to say that there was a dismissal.[18]

Problems can arise in determining whether the words used by an employee can properly be regarded as amounting to resignation. Normally, when the words are unequivocal and are understood by the employer as a resignation, it cannot be argued that a reasonable employer would not have so understood the words. However, exceptions will be made in the case of immature employees, or where a decision was taken in the heat of the moment or under pressure exerted by an employer.[19] An objective test of whether there was an intention to resign will be applied by a tribunal only where the language used by the employee was ambiguous or where it is not plain how the employer understood the words. In deciding whether words used by an employer constitute a dismissal in law tribunals must consider all the circumstances to determine whether the words were intended to bring the contract to an end.

Employees are entitled to treat themselves as constructively dismissed only if the employer is guilty of conduct which is a significant breach going to the root of the contract or which shows that the employer no longer intends to be bound by one or more of its essential terms. However, if employees continue at work for any length of time without leaving they will be regarded as having elected to affirm the contract and will lose the right to treat themselves as discharged.

It is not necessary to show that the employer intended to repudiate the contract. In determining whether there has been a constructive dismissal tribunals will look at the employer's conduct as a whole and determine whether its cumulative effect is such that the employee cannot reasonably be expected to tolerate it. Many cases have been decided on the basis that the employer failed to display sufficient trust and confidence in the employee. Thus, as indicated in Chapter 4, unjustified accusations of theft, harassment or a refusal to act reasonably in health and safety matters have all given rise to successful claims of constructive dismissal.

Finally, it should be noted that the courts have refused to accept the notion of constructive resignation. Thus if an employee acts in a manner which demonstrates that he or she no longer intends to be bound by the contract of employment, for example through lengthy unauthorised absence, the contract will be regarded as terminated only if the employer has accepted the repudiation.[20]

Giving a reason for dismissal

Once employees have proved that they were dismissed the employer will have to show a reason or, if there was more than one, the principal reason for the dismissal.[21] As indicated in Chapter 5 disciplinary dismissal could fall within any of the following categories:

- It related to the capability or qualifications of the employee for performing work of the kind which he or she was employed to do.
- It related to the conduct of the employee.
- The employee could not continue to work in the position held without contravention, either on the employee's part or on that of the employer, of a duty or restriction imposed by statute.
- Some other substantial reason of a kind such as to justify the dismissal of an employee holding the position which the employee held.

The fact that an employer has used a wrong label is not fatal to his or her case, for it is the tribunal's task to discover what reason actually motivated the employer at the time of dismissal.[22]

According to section 152 of TULR(C)A 1992, a dismissal is automatically unfair if the reason for it (or, if there was more than one, the principal reason) was that the employee:

- Was or proposed to become a member of an independent trade union, or
- Had taken, or proposed to take, part in the activities of an independent trade union at any appropriate time, or
- Was not a member of any trade union or of a particular trade union, or had refused or proposed to refuse to become or remain a member.

Employers must therefore ensure that disciplinary dismissal cannot be interpreted as discrimination on grounds of union activity. A distinction has to be drawn between the dismissal of an employee for deceit about previous trade union activities and dismissal for involvement in, or a reputation regarding, those activities. According to the Court of Appeal, attention should focus on whether the reason which motivated the employer to dismiss fell within the meaning of the words 'activities that the employees . . . proposed to take part in'. It does not matter that the activities could not be precisely identified as present in the employment from which the person was dismissed. Thus:

> if an employer, having learnt of an employee's previous trade union activities, decides that he wishes to dismiss that employee, that is likely to be a situation where almost inevitably the employer is dismissing the employee because he feels that the employee will indulge in industrial activities of a trade union nature in the current employment.[23]

For the sake of completeness it should be noted that if dismissal occurs in circumstances that amount to direct or indirect discrimination the employer may fall foul of the Sex Discrimination Act 1975, the Race Relations Act 1976 or the Fair Employment Act 1976. For example, it has been suggested that insistence on geographical mobility may have a disproportionate impact on women (see p. 5).

Reasonableness in the circumstances

Where the employer has given a valid reason for dismissal the determination of the question whether the dismissal is fair or unfair will depend on:

> whether in the circumstances (including the size and administrative resources of the employer's undertaking), the employer acted reasonably or unreasonably in treating it as a sufficient reason for dismissing the employee; and that question shall be determined in accordance with equity and the substantial merits of the case.[24]

At this stage tribunals must take account of the wider circumstances, including the ACAS Code of Practice 1977. As noted earlier, the code does not carry the force of law in the sense that failure to comply with it makes dismissal automatically unfair. Nevertheless, failure to follow one of its recommendations can be taken into account in tribunal proceedings.

As indicated in Chapter 4, in assessing reasonableness attention will focus on the personal attributes of the employee as well as on the employer's business needs. The words 'equity and the substantial merits' also allow tribunals to apply their knowledge of good industrial relations practice and to ensure that there has been procedural fairness. It is not normally permissible for an employer to argue that the proper procedural safeguards would have made no difference to the outcome in the particular case. It is what the employer did that has to be judged, not what he or she might have done. However, if the employer could reasonably have concluded in the light of the circumstances known at the time of dismissal that the procedural safeguards would have been 'utterly useless' he or she may well have acted reasonably.[25]

Finally, it is important to appreciate that it is not the function of tribunals to ask themselves whether they would have done what the employer did in the circumstances: it is merely to assess the employer's decision to dismiss, to see whether it falls within a range of responses which a reasonable employer could have taken.[26]

Remedies

The remedies available to a successful claimant are re-employment or compensation.

Re-employment
Here we are using the word 're-employment' to cover both reinstatement and re-engagement. Technically, people who are reinstated are to be treated in all respects as if they had not been dismissed. By way of contrast, those who are re-engaged may return to work in a different job and on different terms and conditions. Nevertheless, except where a tribunal has taken contributory fault into account, re-engagement must be ordered on terms which are, so far as is reasonably practicable, as favourable as an order for reinstatement.

Where re-employment is sought, a tribunal must first consider whether reinstatement would be appropriate and in so doing must take into account the following matters:

- Whether the complainant wishes to be reinstated.
- Whether it is practicable for the employer to comply with an order for reinstatement.
- Where the complainant caused or contributed to some extent to the dismissal, whether it would be just to make such an order.[27]

If reinstatement is not ordered the tribunal must decide whether to make an order for re-engagement and, if so, on what terms. If neither reinstatement nor re-engagement is ordered the tribunal must turn to the question of compensation.

The fact that the employer has hired a permanent replacement will not be taken into account unless it is shown either:

- That it was not practicable to arrange for the dismissed employee's work to be done without engaging a permanent replacement, or
- That the employer took on a replacement after the lapse of a reasonable period without having heard that the dismissed employee wanted re-employment, and that when the replacement was engaged it was no longer reasonable to arrange for the dismissed employee's work to be done except by a permanent replacement.

Practicability is a question of fact for each tribunal, and in *Boots* v. *Lees* [1986][28] the EAT agreed that it was practicable to reinstate notwithstanding that the employee's ultimate superior remained convinced that he was guilty of theft. On the other hand the following arguments have been used to prevent an order being made:

- The employee was unable to perform the work.
- A redundancy situation arose subsequent to the dismissal.
- Other employees were hostile to the complainant's return to work.

Where a person is re-employed as a result of a tribunal order, but the terms are not fully complied with, a tribunal will award such compensation as it thinks fit, having regard to the loss sustained by the complainant in consequence of the failure to comply.[29] If the complainant is not re-employed after an order has been made compensation will be awarded together with an additional award unless the employer satisfies the tribunal that it was not practicable to comply with the order.[30] However, a re-engagement order does not place a duty on an employer to search for a job for the dismissed employee irrespective of the vacancies that arise.[31]

Compensation
Compensation will usually consist of a basic and a compensatory award.

Basic award. Normally this is calculated in accordance with the following formula, with a maximum of twenty years' service being taken into account. Starting at the end of the employee's period of service and calculating backwards:

- One and a half weeks' pay for each year of employment in which the individual was between the ages of forty-one and sixty-four. Those who are aged sixty-four have their entitlement reduced by one-twelfth in respect of each month they remain in employment.
- A week's pay for each year of employment in which the individual was between the ages of twenty-two and forty-one.
- Half a week's pay for each year of employment under the age of twenty-two.

The basic award can be reduced by such proportion as the tribunal considers just and equitable on two grounds:

- The complainant unreasonably refused an offer of reinstatement.
- Any conduct of the complainant before the dismissal or before notice was given.

The basic award will also be reduced by the amount of any redundancy payment received, and no award will be made if the employee has already received an *ex gratia* sum in excess of the total of the maximum compensatory and basic awards.

Compensatory award. This is the amount which a tribunal 'considers just and equitable in all the circumstances, having regard to the loss sustained by the complainant in consequence of the dismissal in so far as that loss is attributable to action taken by the employer'.[32]

It is the duty of tribunals to enquire into the various heads of damage – for example loss of wages and benefits, loss of statutory rights – but it is the responsibility of the complainant to prove the loss. The legislation aims to reimburse the employee rather than to punish the employer. Thus employees who appear to have lost nothing – for example, where it can be said that irrespective of the procedural unfairness that occurred they would have been dismissed anyway – do not qualify for a compensatory award.

A compensatory award can be reduced if the employee's action caused or contributed to the dismissal, or if the employee failed to mitigate his or her loss. Before holding that a complainant caused or contributed to the dismissal, a tribunal must be satisfied that the employee's conduct was culpable i.e. foolish, perverse or unreasonable in the circumstances.[33] Having found that an employee was to blame, a tribunal must reduce the award to some extent, although the proportion of culpability is a matter for the tribunal.

In relation to dismissals for incapability, the EAT has observed that if an employee is incompetent this cannot be regarded as a contributory factor: 'the whole point about contribution is that it is something by way of conduct on the part of the employee over which he has control'.[34] Although ill-health cases will rarely give rise to a reduction on the grounds of contributory fault, one possible example is where the employee had blatantly and persistently refused to obtain appropriate medical reports or attend for medical examination. However, there may be ill-health cases where an award may be drastically reduced under the overriding 'just and equitable' provisions. For example, a dismissal may be unfair on procedural grounds but it may be apparent from the medical evidence that, at the date of dismissal, the employee was incapable of performing the job.[35]

Where the employee's conduct on which the employer seeks to rely to reduce compensation was not known to the employer at the time of dismissal, it may be just and equitable to reduce compensation if a thorough investigation might have resulted in the employee still being dismissed.[36] However, the mere fact that the employer could have dismissed fairly on another ground arising out of the same factual situation does not render it unjust or inequitable to award compensation. Thus in *Trico-Folberth* v. *Devonshire* [1989][37] a compensatory award was made where the employee was unfairly dismissed on medical grounds even though the employer could have dismissed fairly for poor attendance.

Clearly complainants are obliged to look for work and should not unreasonably refuse an offer of re-employment, but failure to utilise an internal appeal procedure does not amount to failure to mitigate. The onus is on the employer to prove that there was such a failure. While acknowledging that the employee has a duty to act reasonably, the EAT has indicated that this standard is not high in view of the fact that the employer is the wrongdoer.[38]

No account can be taken of any pressure which was exercised on the employer to dismiss the employee, but compensation can be reduced if the employee in some way brought about both the pressure and the subsequent dismissal. For example, a Mr Dutton was a dustcart driver whose workmates refused to ride with him after several incidents of careless driving. Although industrial pressure was found to be the reason for dismissal, the EAT decided that his driving was a factor and that his compensation should be reduced.[39]

At the time of writing the maximum compensatory award is £10,000. This limit applies only after credit has been given for any payments made by the employer – for example, payments in lieu of notice and *ex gratia* payments – and any reductions have been made on the grounds indicated above.[40]

Conciliation

Copies of an unfair dismissal application are sent to an ACAS conciliation officer, who has a duty to try and promote a settlement of the complaint:

- If requested to do so by the complainant and the employer (known as the respondent), or
- If, in the absence of any such request, the conciliation officer considers that he or she could act with a reasonable prospect of success.

Where the complainant has ceased to be employed the conciliation officer must seek to promote that person's re-employment on terms which appear to be equitable. If the complainant does not wish to be re-employed, or it is not practicable, the conciliation officer must seek to promote agreement on compensation. Additionally, conciliation officers are required to make their services available before a complaint is presented if requested to do so either by a potential applicant or by a respondent.

Where appropriate, a conciliation officer is to 'have regard to the desirability of encouraging the use of other procedures available for the settlement of grievances' and nothing communicated to a conciliation officer in connection with the performance of the above functions is admissible in evidence in any proceedings before a tribunal except with the consent of the person who communicated it.[41] Normally a conciliated settlement will be binding, even though it is not in writing, and the employee will be prevented from bringing the case before a tribunal.[42] However, a settlement reached after a tribunal has found the employee to have been unfairly dismissed but before the remedy has been determined will be void unless a conciliation officer was involved.[43]

For an agreement to refrain from proceeding with an unfair dismissal complaint to be valid, a conciliation officer must have 'taken action'. It follows that the conciliation process should not be seen as a method of rubber-stamping private deals by recording them on the appropriate form.[44] Indeed, the ACAS explanatory guide to individual conciliation states that a conciliation officer has no duty to act where a settlement has already been achieved, unless the settlement is provisional and the parties undertake that if a conciliation officer becomes involved the terms of their agreement might be changed 'as a result of that action'.[45] It is also worth noting that a conciliation officer has no duty to advise on the merits of an employer's offer or to explain to the parties what their rights are.

In deciding whether to settle a claim at the conciliation stage employers will bear in mind a number of factors. These will include the fact that tribunal hearings:

- Take time to arrange and are normally held in public.
- May involve complex legal arguments and considerable cost.
- Often result in awards of compensation higher than those which emerge from conciliated settlements.

While many employers act on the merits of each case, some have adopted the view that willingness to compromise is conducive to harmonious industrial relations. On the other hand, some organisations have a policy of not settling claims, in order to discourage applications. So far as employees are concerned, the risk and cost of a tribunal hearing may mean that they are prepared to accept a lower sum at the conciliation stage than a tribunal might be expected to award. Conversely, it may be possible to secure through conciliation something that could not be obtained at a tribunal, for example, a reference.

The ACAS annual report for 1991 reveals that 69 per cent of unfair dismissal complaints were resolved without reference to an industrial tribunal; 40 per cent of these were disposed of as a result of conciliation, the remainder being withdrawn.

Key points

- Employers who do not abide by fair rules and procedures may suffer industrial relations consequences in terms of distrust and possibly unrest.
- Where contractual rights are infringed, an employee may seek an injunction to restrain the unlawful disciplinary action. However, it is more likely that damages will be sought for breach of contract.
- Unfair dismissal law requires the employer to show a fair reason for

The consequences of getting it wrong 123

dismissal and a tribunal to be satisfied that the employer acted reasonably in all the circumstances.
- The remedies for unfair dismissal are re-employment or compensation.
- Employers who wish to avoid an industrial tribunal hearing may involve a conciliation officer in the settlement of a claim.

References

1 See P. Edwards and H. Scullion, *The Social Organisation of Industrial Conflict*. Blackwell. 1982.
2 IRLR 299.
3 IRLR 72.
4 See *Bliss* v. *South East Thames Regional Health Authority* [1985] IRLR 308.
5 *Dietman* v. *London Borough of Brent* [1988] IRLR 299.
6 Courts and Legal Services Act 1990.
7 Section 64(1)a, EPCA 1978.
8 See *R.* v. *Secretary of State* ex parte *Equal Opportunities Commission* [1991] IRLR 493.
9 Section 64(1)b, EPCA 1978.
10 Section 141(2), EPCA 1978.
11 Sections 238, 237 TULR(C)A 1992.
12 Sections 144(2), 138, 146 and Schedule 9, paragraph 2, EPCA 1978, respectively.
13 Section 67(2), EPCA 1978.
14 Section 142(1), EPCA 1978.
15 Section 55(2), EPCA 1978.
16 Section 55(3), EPCA 1978.
17 IRLR 215.
18 *Staffordshire County Council* v. *Donovan* [1981] IRLR 108.
19 See *Sovereign House* v. *Savage* [1989] IRLR 115.
20 See *London Transport Executive* v. *Clarke* [1981] IRLR 166.
21 Section 57(1)(2), EPCA 1978.
22 See *Abernethy* v. *Mott Hay & Anderson* [1974] IRLR 213.
23 *Fitzpatrick* v. *British Rail* [1991] IRLR 376.
24 Section 57(3), EPCA 1978. On the importance of looking for alternative employment, see now *P.* v. *Nottinghamshire County Council* [1992] IRLR 362.
25 See *Polkey* v. *Dayton Services* [1987] IRLR 503.
26 See *British Leyland* v. *Swift* [1981] IRLR 91.
27 Section 69(5), EPCA 1978.
28 IRLR 485.

29 Section 71(1), EPCA 1978.
30 Section 71(2), EPCA 1978.
31 See *Freemans* v. *Flynn* [1984] IRLR 486.
32 Section 74(1), EPCA 1978.
33 See *Nelson* v. *BBC* (No. 2) [1979] IRLR 304.
34 *Kraft Foods* v. *Fox* [1979] IRLR 431.
35 See *Slaughter* v. *Brewer* [1990] IRLR 426.
36 See *Tele-trading* v. *Jenkins* [1990] IRLR 430.
37 IRLR 397.
38 See *Fyfe* v. *Scientific Furnishings* [1989] IRLR 331.
39 *Colwyn Borough Council* v. *Dutton* [1980] IRLR 420.
40 See *Braund* v. *Murray* [1991] IRLR 100.
41 Section 134, EPCA 1978.
42 Section 140(2)d, EPCA 1978.
43 See *Courage* v. *Keys* [1986] IRLR 427.
44 COT3.
45 COT5.

Appendix 1
Sample disciplinary rules

Brush Electrical Systems

1 *Discrimination*

The company policy requires that entry into the company and progression within it, are determined solely by application of objective criteria and personal merit and that no applicant or employee will be treated less favourably than another on grounds of sex, marital status, race, nationality, ethnic or national origin, colour or creed.

Any offence, therefore, which infringes such laws as the Sex Discrimination Act 1975 and the Race Relations Act 1976 will be treated as gross misconduct.

2 *Company/personal property*

Deliberate or calculated misuse of, theft of, or damage to company property or any other person's property on company premises, will be treated as gross misconduct.

Any loss of either company or personal property should be reported immediately to your supervisor/manager, who will then liaise with the site security officer.

The Company will not accept any liability or responsibility for any personal possessions damaged or lost on the premises.

3 *Assault*

The physical assault of any person on the company premises by any employee will be treated as gross misconduct.

The issuing of threats or verbal abuse are not acceptable forms of behaviour.

4 *Fire*

Employees should familiarise themselves with fire regulations and procedures exhibited on notice boards and co-operate in practice and fire drills.

All employees have a responsibility to practise fire prevention and good housekeeping requirements.

There are certain areas on the site which are designated as 'no smoking' areas. Disregard of such regulations may endanger the employee's own life and the lives of other employees.

5 *Health and safety regulations*

The Health and Safety at Work Act 1974 imposes a legal requirement upon both the company and its employees to comply with the content of this Act and any regulations, codes of practice or guidance notes issued pursuant to this Act.

Specifically employees are required to take reasonable care for the health and safety of themselves and others who may be affected by their acts or lack of action at work and are required to co-operate with their employer to enable him to perform or comply with the duties placed upon him. Any failure to do so may involve the company and/or employees in prosecution.

The company has an established health and safety policy designed specifically to assist in safeguarding its employees against hazards which may arise in employment.

Protective clothing and equipment are issued to employees whose work requires their use, and where deemed necessary, protective goggles, etc. *must* be worn. Employees must utilise this clothing/equipment. Further more, employees must not misuse anything provided in the interests of health, safety or welfare.

Employees are required to read, observe and comply with all safety instructions, notices or signs displayed on company premises.

Notices to the effect that toxic material is in use are displayed in areas where lead, cyanide or other potentially harmful materials are utilised. Employees must not eat or drink in these areas.

Where it is considered necessary, employees are expected to co-operate by attending consultations arranged with the works medical officer.

Further guidance on all aspects of health and safety matters can be provided by the company's safety officer on request.

6 *Traffic regulations*

All employees are required to comply with traffic regulations on the site. Employees' cars must not be parked within the site boundaries, except in designated car parks, without special permission.

Similarly, cycles, mopeds, motor cycles, etc., must be placed in the areas provided and not left in any other places on the company premises.

It should be noted that vehicle parks are provided for the convenience of employees and any contractual relationship between the company and employees using them, or liability for any loss or damage thereto, is expressly excluded.

7 *Company vehicles*

Company vehicles (licensed or unlicensed) must only be used by authorised personnel.

8 *Travel on company business*

Employees who travel on company business must ensure they have the agreement of their supervisor/manager.

Reimbursement of authorised expenses will be made in accordance with the company's standard reimbursement arrangements.

Private cars used on company business. When travel by car is authorised, a company car should be used whenever possible. Employees using their privately owned car on company business should familiarise themselves with the rules appertaining to such use. Reimbursement will be in accordance with the current scales stipulated by the company.

9 *Attendance/hours of work*

Every employee is required, as a condition of employment, to devote to the company's service the normal business hours of the company and such additional hours as the exigencies of the company's business require.

Shift working is necessary in certain areas where activities are closely associated with production. It is a condition of employment that operatives will co-operate with shift working as required.

Employees who leave the site during working hours must always have prior permission from their supervisor/manager. Where appropriate a 'pass out' will be issued to employees who normally record their attendance by clock card. This 'pass out' should be handed in to the site security staff.

Habitual lateness or persistent absence will be dealt with within the disciplinary procedure guidelines.

Employees who are prevented from attending work have a duty to notify their supervisor/manager as to the reason for non-attendance at the earliest possible opportunity.

Absence through reasons of sickness in excess of three days must be covered by certification.

Employees must comply with attendance recording/time-booking procedures.

10 *Falsification of records and clocking offences*

The deliberate falsification of records is gross misconduct and will result in dismissal.

Clock cards are provided to maintain a record between the individual and the company. It is gross misconduct for any employee to interfere with the clock card of his own or any other employee for whatever reason.

The deliberate clocking of another employee's clock card will be treated as gross misconduct and will result in dismissal. Any employee accidentally clocking on the wrong card must report the incident to his immediate supervisor at the earliest opportunity. Equally, any employee discovering his card has been clocked in error must report the error to his immediate supervisor at the earliest opportunity.

Note. 'At the earliest opportunity' means before the end of the next normal shift at the latest.

Clock cards must not be removed from the racks adjacent to the employee's usual clocking station except for recording of clock times or by authorised personnel. It is the individual's responsibility to check his card every time he clocks in and out.

The deliberate tampering with, or alteration of, clocking equipment, will also be treated as gross misconduct.

11 *Security*

It is the duty of site security officers to advise and assist management in the overall security of the site.

Employees leaving the premises with company property must first obtain a 'pass out' signed by an authorised member of management. This should be handed in to the site security staff on demand.

Site security staff are required to assist in the controlling of entry and exit to the site, and the company reserves the right, in the interests of all employees, to request any person entering or leaving the site to disclose to a member of site security staff the contents of any parcel, bag or any other container carried by them.

They may also be asked to disclose the contents of any vehicle in their charge on company property.

Refusal of any such inspection will render the employee concerned liable to disciplinary action.

12 Unauthorised persons on company premises

The company has a responsibility for all individuals when they are on company premises and, therefore, no unauthorised persons are to be brought on to company premises.

Children must not be brought on to company's premises without prior authorisation.

All visitors are required to report to the appropriate gate/reception before being admitted to the company premises and report as they leave (so that in the case of fire, for example, account can be taken of their presence). All staff employees should ensure that visitors comply with this procedure.

13 Confidential information

All documents, information, data, specifications relating to the company's business and/or its trading specialities must be treated as confidential and not divulged, used or employed except in the company's services.

Employees should be aware that, regardless of any disciplinary action, the company may take legal proceedings against any individual for any misuse or unauthorised disclosure of such confidential information whether during employment with the company or afterwards.

14 Cameras

Only authorised personnel may use a camera on the company's premises. No one may take photographs on the company's premises without written permission.

15 Legitimate instructions

All employees are required to comply with a reasonable request or a legitimate instruction from their supervisor/manager.

16 Trade union and similar meetings on company premises

Facilities and authorisation for any meetings on company premises must be obtained from Management. Payment for attendance at meetings will only be made when the meeting has been specifically authorised by management.

17 Leaving the section office

Where employees are required to work outside their department they should always ensure that their supervisor/manager knows where they can be contacted. Where employee representatives have to leave their department to carry out trade union activities they must obtain permission from their supervisor/manager and of the supervisor/manager of any department they wish to enter.

18 *Notices and notice boards*

Notice boards are provided throughout the site for displaying approved company notices and general communications.

All employees should read the notices on the notice boards; ignorance of them will not be accepted as an excuse for non-compliance.

Facilities are available on certain designated notice boards for displaying forthcoming social events and advertising of personal items on the understanding that such transactions are carried out outside normal working hours.

19 *Misuse of drugs and alcoholic drink*

The misuse of drugs or alcohol in an industrial environment can cause serious injury. No employee should be on the company's premises under the influence of alcohol or drugs. Employees must advise their supervisor/manager if they are taking medically prescribed drugs which may affect their performance or safety at work. In particular, it is totally unacceptable behaviour for any employee under the influence of alcohol or drugs to operate machinery or to drive a vehicle on company premises. Any employee in this condition will be sent home prior to disciplinary action being taken. They will be advised not to drive themselves.

20 *Gambling*

Gambling on company premises is expressly forbidden.

21 *Collections*

No collections of money for any reason, other than for personal gifts, may be made without the permission of the Personnel Manager.

22 *Sale of goods on company premises*

Individuals should not conduct a private business on company premises, involving the sale of goods or services, without written authorisation from the Personnel Manager.

23 *Inventions and patents*

Any inventions or improvements which an employee makes in the course of, during the period of, or connected with, his employment with the company, whether such inventions or improvements are patentable or not, should be immediately communicated by him to the company.

The obtaining of letters patent or any other adequate protection required will be obtained at the company's cost and will be vested in the company for its exclusive benefit.

Where current patent legislation provides for an emolument to the employee, such arrangements will be honoured.

24 *Private correspondence/telephone calls*

Private letters must not be addressed to employees at the works, neither may an employee make or receive private telephone calls except in extreme emergencies. In the case of an emergency where the employee cannot be contacted direct, the Personnel Director will arrange for a message to be conveyed.

Several telephone booths are located on the company site for employee use during the mid-day break. Visits to the telephone booths during working hours should be limited to definite emergencies.

25 *Standard of work*

All employees are expected to maintain the required standard of work performance.

26 *Code of ethics*

In dealing with suppliers, distributors, consultants, agents and other external entities, all employees must:

- Declare any personal interest which may impinge, or be deemed by others to impinge, on an employee's impartiality in any matter relevant to their duties.
- Respect the confidentiality of information received in the course of duty and not use such information for personal gain.
- Avoid any arrangement with a supplier which might prevent the effective operation of fair competition.
- Not accept business gifts other than items of very small intrinsic value.
- Not accept a level of hospitality which might be deemed by others to have influenced the making of a business decision. The frequency and scale of hospitality accepted must not be greater than the company would provide in return.
- Claim through the normal expense recovery channels authorised expenditure incurred in the furtherance of company business. Payment of travel and accommodation by third parties must not be accepted.

27 *Acts contrary to the law of the land*

Any act contrary to the law of the land, carried out within the establishment, will be subject to disciplinary action in addition to any legal proceedings which may be taken by the company or the police.

Cadbury, Bournville

Introduction

The running of a site of this size would be impossible without some rules to regulate our conduct as members of an industrial and commercial community. Accordingly this booklet has been jointly prepared by management and trade union representatives for the benefit of all non-management employees, regardless of category or whether they work in the offices or factories.

You must read these rules through carefully and fully familiarise yourself with them. The rules are for guidance purposes and are not exhaustive. Disciplinary action will follow the guidelines set out in this booklet and the 'Code of Practice – Non-management' which is held by your manager and your

Personnel Department. The minimum category of offence is stated in the text for each rule.

From time to time existing rules may be amended following consultation with trade union representatives. Details of any such amendments will be included in special notices posted on notice boards and it is your responsibility to read these.

Ignorance of a rule or the ensuing penalties will not be accepted as an excuse for breaking it.

Recording of time

Dependent upon grade/area you will be issued with a clock card/time sheet and payroll number. The clock card/time sheet is used to record the hours which you have worked and is used when calculating wage payments due to you. Working time is recorded and you are required to record time according to departmental requirements. You must clock in when you arrive to start work and clock out at the end of your day or shift, where appropriate. Similarly you should always use your clock card to record absences from your department during working hours, for example, for meals, attendance at meetings, visits to the surgery, etc. If you are absent from your department for any reason, other than for recognised meal breaks, the reason for absence from your workplace must be noted on your clock card by your manager. If you forget to clock in you should tell your manager immediately so that you will not be marked late or absent. Likewise, if you make a mistake of any sort it should be reported to your manager at once.

Your clock card must be kept in the rack provided and you must only use your departmental clock when recording time.

You should not attempt to alter or deface your clock card in any way, or should you alter another employee's clock card. You must not record time for any other person.

Misuse of clock/time sheet is dealt with as *serious misconduct.*

Late arrival

We require a good standard of punctuality to ensure the efficient running of the factories and commerical operations.

If you are late for any reason you must report as soon as possible to your manager. Lateness will be recorded and you will lose payment according to your terms of employment.

Persistent lateness will be treated as *misconduct.*

Unauthorised absence from place of work

Unauthorised absence from place of work, with visits to the dining area, Crush Hall, Men's/Clerk Club, staff sales shop, Bournville Club, etc., or unauthorised absence from place of work whilst in a position of responsibility will be deemed to be *serious misconduct.*

Absence from work

If, for any reason, you are unable to come to work, you must notify the company of your absence through the appropriate procedure as soon as possible on the first day of absence, preferably within the first two hours of the commencement of your shift. Give your name, payroll number, pay point, department, reason for absence and, if possible, your expected date of return to work. If you are away from work for any reason other than personal illness, works accident, infectious disease or agreed holidays/time off, payment for time off will not be made.

Repeated absence without permission or good cause will be taken up through the appropriate discipline procedure.

Repeated failure to notify of absence at the required time will be dealt with as *misconduct*.

Entry at unauthorised times

You are not allowed inside the factory or office departments more than ten minutes before or after your normal working hours without management permission. Entry at unauthorised times will be treated as *misconduct*.

Outside work

You are not permitted to undertake outside work if it interferes with your capability to do your job.

Failure to comply with this regulation is regarded as *serious misconduct*.

Private work

No private work may be done in the factories and offices during working hours.

Contravention of this rule will be dealt with as *misconduct* or *serious misconduct*, depending upon the circumstances.

Private trading

You are not allowed to privately trade or operate clubs or agencies in company time or on company premises and any contravention of this rule will be dealt with as *misconduct*.

Collections

If you wish to hold a collection or sell tickets then permission from management/Personnel Department must be obtained.

Failure to do so will be treated as *misconduct*.

Unauthorised notices

No notices, leaflets or propaganda shall be displayed or distributed on site without permission of management.

Any contravention of this rule will be treated as *misconduct*.

Provision is made for authorised trade unions' notices.

Correspondence

Private correspondence must not be sent to you at the company's address.

Any contravention will be dealt with as *misconduct*.

Private telephone calls

In cases of emergency permission may be given by management for you to make or receive a telephone call. Otherwise private telephone calls may not be made or received on company telephones.

Any contravention will normally be dealt with as *misconduct*.

Personal visitors

You are not allowed to receive private visitors, for example relatives, on the site except in emergencies and with the permission of management. Visitors must report to the lodge.

Any contravention will normally be dealt with as *misconduct*.

Conduct

You are expected at all times to conduct yourself in an orderly and proper manner and to carry out reasonable instructions given by management. Such actions as wasting, damaging or destroying the company's property, horseplay, using bad language, loitering, dropping litter, harassing other employees or preventing them from carrying out their work will render you liable to be dealt with as *misconduct*, *serious misconduct* or *gross misconduct*, dependent upon the circumstances.

Fighting

Threatening behaviour, intimidation or physical violence is forbidden. Any contravention of this rule will be dealt with as *serious* or *gross misconduct*, depending upon the circumstances.

Gambling

You are not allowed at any time to engage in gambling of any nature on company premises.

Failure to observe this rule will be treated as *misconduct*.

Sleeping on duty

Sleeping on duty, depending on the circumstances, will be dealt with as *serious* or *gross misconduct*.

Smoking

With the exception of designated areas, you are not allowed to smoke at any time, anywhere within the factories or offices.

Failure to comply with this regulation will be considered as *serious misconduct*.

Alcohol

Alcoholic drinks for consumption must not be brought into the factories or offices. Drinking which affects your performance or behaviour at work or on site may be a reason for dismissal when it affects your capability or results in intolerable behaviour, unauthorised absence, lateness, etc.

The surgery staff or management will determine whether you are competent to work and if not you will not be allowed to enter the premises and you will be told to leave. Failure to do so will result in you being escorted off the premises. If you are sent home you must report to the Personnel Department before returning to work.

Any contravention of this rule could be dealt with as *serious* or *gross misconduct*, depending upon the circumstances.

Drug taking

If your doctor prescribes drugs for you to be taken during normal working hours you must report this in your own and your colleagues' interest to your manager or to the Surgery so that it can be confirmed with the Surgery that it is safe for you to work at your normal job.

Drug taking that affects your performance or behaviour at work or on site may be a reason for dismissal when it affects your capability or results in intolerable behaviour, unauthorised absence, lateness, etc.

The Surgery staff or management will determine whether you are competent to work and if not you will not be allowed to enter the premises and you will be told to leave. Failure to do so will result in you being escorted off the premises. If you are sent home you must report to the Personnel Department before returning to work.

Such drug taking is treated as *serious* or *gross misconduct*, depending upon the circumstances.

Recording of information

If you are required to record details of your own work or the work of another employee, or prepare records for payment or reimbursement, you should do so ensuring that such information is accurate.

Falsification of such records will normally be dealt with as *serious misconduct*.

Falsification of information for fringe benefit purposes

In order to qualify for sick pay, documentary evidence will need to be furnished of the reason for your absence. Such evidence will take the form of self-certification forms and/or medical certificates. Similarly, attendance at hospitals, dentists, etc., will require appointment cards to be submitted as proof prior to attendance.

Falsification of such information will normally be treated as *serious* or *gross misconduct*, depending upon the circumstances.

Disclosure of information

Any confidential information which you receive or obtain whilst in the company's employment:

(a) Should be used only in the company's interests.
(b) Should not be divulged by any means to any person or persons outside the company or to any unauthorised person within the company.
(c) Should not knowingly be allowed by you to be so divulged or used other than in the interests of the company.

Information of any nature concerning the company which is to be divulged to any person or persons outside the company should first be discussed by you with your immediate superior and the person or persons to whom it is to be divulged shall enter into an appropriate undertaking as to confidentiality prior to the disclosure of such information.

These restrictions shall apply both during your employment and afterwards but shall cease to apply to information which becomes public knowledge otherwise than through unauthorised disclosure.

Any violation of security will be regarded as *serious* or *gross misconduct*, depending upon the circumstances.

Cameras

The taking of unauthorised photographs on the premises is strictly forbidden and cameras must be deposited at the lodges.

The company reserves the right to confiscate and develop any film taken on the premises.

Any contravention of this rule will be treated as *gross misconduct*.

Sabotage

Any deliberate attempt to sabotage the company's goods or property will be dealt with as *gross misconduct*.

Issue of company equipment

In normal circumstances you will be held responsible for all the equipment supplied to you in the course of your work. All such property (for example, protective safety equipment) must be handed in before leaving the company's employ.

The return of such items must be confirmed by your immediate manager before administration details of termination of employment are completed.

Failure to return such items may mean that you will be liable to pay the company for the cost of the items not returned.

Cash

Money, even in cash boxes, whether belonging to the company or to employees, should not be left in any desk or drawer. Personal monies must always be deposited in the safe deposits at No. 2 lodge. The company accepts no liability for loss, however arising.

Consumption of company products on company premises

Saleable finished products from work-in-progress or finishing stocks, either wrapped or unwrapped, must not be consumed unless by specific authority where this is necessary in the course of your job.

Waste or rework products in your own department may be consumed.

Neither waste nor finished products may be taken to other departments on site, without legitimate business reason.

Consumption or removal of products from departments except as defined above will be treated as *misconduct* or *serious misconduct*, dependent upon the circumstances.

Staff shop goods

Both to avoid confusion with manufactured products, and for reasons of good housekeeping, staff shop goods must not be taken to places of work. They must either be left at lodges or taken to authorised dressing rooms. A receipt should be retained as proof of purchase.

Removal of company products from company premises

Company products taken outside controlled company premises, i.e. outside lodges, without authorisation from a senior manager will be regarded as theft and will be treated as *gross misconduct*. The proper documentation for the removal of company products from company premises for outer quantities is a 'miscellaneous despatch note'. For smaller quantities a 'pass out' specifying the name of the person authorised, date of removal, the quantity of goods and the reason for removal. The original authorisation document must be handed in at a manned lodge on leaving and a copy retained in the department.

Theft

All cases of theft of company products or property of other employees (however small the quantity or value) will be treated as *gross misconduct*. The penalty for gross misconduct is summary dismissal. In addition theft may result in prosecution.

Personal belongings and outdoor clothing

You may only bring personal handbags or briefcases to your place of work. These are liable to inspection in the department or at lodges. Personal bags must be kept in places provided in production areas and must not be brought on to the production line. All other bags or parcels, including shopping or staff shop purchases, must be left at the lodge or placed in the lockers provided. Should you take them into departments you will be sent back to the lodge.

Offences of this nature will be treated as *misconduct*.

Outdoor clothing and/or other articles not needed at work must be left in the dressing room unless you have a proper reason for not doing so.

Valuable items may be deposited at No. 2 lodge.

All employees are liable, on leaving the site, to have bags, etc., inspected or to be asked to produce the requisite pass-out and attention is drawn to the rule on theft.

Employees are reminded that they should only bring those items on to the site which are necessary to enable them to do their job.

The company accepts no liability, however arising, in respect of any loss or damage to personal belongings and outdoor clothing brought on to site.

Lost property

If you find any property or money on the company's premises you must hand it in at the reception area of No. 2 lodge outside normal day working.

Retaining lost property is regarded as stealing and will be dealt with as such (see rule on theft).

The company accepts no liability, however arising, in respect of any loss or damage to personal belongings and outdoor clothing brought on to site.

William Grant and Sons

1 *Safety*

(a) Employees must conduct themselves in a safe and orderly fashion at all

times, giving full consideration to their personal safety and to the safety of others.
(b) Employees will remember that bad housekeeping is frequently the cause of accidents. No articles or litter will be left on catwalks, stairs, passageways or any other place where they can create a hazard.
(c) An employee seeing any conduct, machinery or anything which appears unsafe will report the matter immediately to the departmental Safety Committee representative or the head of the department concerned.
(d) Sensible shoes must be worn by all employees. Employees will not be permitted to work while wearing unsafe shoes.

2 *Accidents*

Accidents, no matter how trivial they may appear, must be reported immediately to the appropriate head of department for arranging treatment at the ambulance room and recording in the Accident Register.

3 *Medical examination*

Employees may be required to undergo medical examination from the company's medical officer.

4 *Protective clothing*

(a) Protective clothing is issued by the company to every employee who is required to wear it in the course of their work at no cost to the employee. This will be worn, when appropriate, at all times.
(b) Replacement of protective clothing will be made after a reasonable period, providing reasonable care has been taken of such clothing. In cases where no reasonable care has been taken, employees will be charged for replacement.
(c) On the termination of employment any protective clothing issued by the company must be returned before the payment of wages is made.
(d) All clothes should be worn under overalls.
(e) Any employee not safely dressed will not be permitted to commence work. Refusal to wear protective clothing supplied by the company will lead to disciplinary action.

5 *Fire prevention*

The danger of fire is extreme in this industry and it is most important for employees to ensure that they are aware of the local 'Fire Prevention Rules' and the 'Procedure in Case of Fire' which can be obtained from your supervisor.

6 *Smoking*

There are certain 'no smoking' areas within the bond and distillery. Notices have been posted clearly defining these and any person found smoking in these areas will be instantly dismissed.

7 *Security*

(a) The Security Department will be responsible for security in all its aspects within the company premises and employees should co-operate with this department at all times.

(b) An employee will not be permitted to collect the wages of another employee without written personal authority from the employee concerned.
(c) An employee found in unauthorised possession of any goods or spirits, or who steals or aids and abets another employee to steal, will be instantly dismissed.
(d) Any employee found to have been consuming or be in unauthorised possession of intoxicating liquor within the premises, renders himself liable to instant dismissal.
(e) Employees at all times within the company premises will submit themselves for search in private if so instructed. The employee may request that a witness be present.
(f) In addition to personal search, employees' lockers and cars are liable to be searched in the presence of the employee and a witness if requested.
(g) Employees' cars may be parked in the car park or where otherwise authorised, but the company does not accept responsibility for any loss or damage which may occur to these cars.
(h) The company takes every reasonable precaution to safeguard personal property, but it cannot be held responsible for any loss or damage. You are therefore advised not to leave money or valuables about. If a case of pilfering arises, the matter is usually referred to the police.
(i) Wilful damage to company property will involve instant dismissal.
(j) Employees should leave any valuables, messages or authorised liquor at the gatehouse before entry.

8 *Your supervisor*

Your supervisor, chargehand or foreman is responsible for the well-being of all employees under their control in addition to being responsible for the control of efficient production, the maintenance of quality and ensuring that works rules are maintained.

If you have any problems, require help or advice on any aspect of your work, please discuss it in the first instance with your Supervisor.

9 *Absence from work*

(a) Any employee(s) absent from work must, where possible immediately contact their departmental manager in order that work arrangements can be changed.
(b) In order to maintain efficient production, regular attendance is essential and a disciplinary procedure is agreed to deal with cases of unreliable attendance and timekeeping.
(c) Employees returning from absence must report immediately to their supervisor or, failing that, the manager.

It should be noted, however, that the company may terminate the employment of any employee who incurs prolonged or recurring absences through illness.

10 *Retirement*

The retirement age for male employees will be sixty-five years of age and for female employees sixty years of age.

Oxford City Council

The council has a formal locally agreed disciplinary procedure and to promote good industrial relations it is necessary to demonstrate that individual employees will be treated fairly, reasonably and consistently. Rules are necessary to ensure order and fairness and the council's disciplinary rules are detailed below.

The council realises that in general there is no cause to question the discipline and effectiveness of most of its employees, who can be relied upon to conduct themselves sensibly and with credit to the council. There are, however, certain matters and possible breaches of discipline which need to be brought to all employees' attention, particularly those matters regarded as gross misconduct.

Disciplinary action normally relates to behaviour at work and, exceptionally, where misconduct outside work had a direct relationship with the employee's duties or amounts to a breach of contract on the part of the employee.

(a) Gross misconduct is behaviour of such a nature that the council would be justified in dismissing the employee without notice of circumstance.

Disciplinary appeals are heard and determined by Personnel (Appeals) Sub-committee. In appropriate circumstances the council, through the Personnel (Appeals) Sub-committee, may reinstate an employee notwithstanding that they had earlier been dismissed for committing an act or acts amounting to gross misconduct.

The following acts and similar offences are regarded as gross misconduct and have in the past led to local authority employees being dismissed:

   (i) Theft, or attempted theft, from the authority, its employees, on the authority's premises or from premises, malicious damage to, or any other unlawful act which involves, the property being visited during the course of employment.
   (ii) Unauthorised removal of the authority's property of the authority.
   (iii) Offences of a dishonest or fraudulent character, examples of which would be falsification of expense claim forms, drivers' record books, etc.
   (iv) Wilful disregard of instructions concerning the collection, transfer, security and paying in of monies, the issue and receipt of tickets and the completion and submission of associated documents.
   (v) Wilful action or serious negligence which endangers life or limb, including deliberate damage to, or neglect of, or serious misappropriation of safety equipment and any significant breach of safety rules or codes of practice, and safe working procedures.
   (vi) Fighting, acts of violence and physical intimidation.
   (vii) Sexual offences or sexual misconduct at work.
   (viii) Being under the influence of alcohol or non-prescribed drugs in circumstances where it could constitute a health and safety hazard or where it would be in breach of a position of responsibility and trust.
   (ix) Unauthorised disclosure or use of confidential information.
   (x) Criminal offences and/or conduct of such a nature (whether on or off duty) that the employee would be unsuitable to carry out their duties.
   (xi) Without prior management agreement, taking other paid employment

whilst receiving pay or other benefits from the authority during a period of sickness or unauthorised absence.
(xii) Unlawful discrimination against a fellow employee or member of the public on grounds of sex, marital status, disability, colour, race, nationality or ethnic or national origin.

This list is neither exclusive nor exhaustive, and in addition there may be other offences of similar gravity which would constitute gross misconduct.

(b) Misconduct is conduct of such a kind as to warrant disciplinary action rather than dismissal for the first offence. The local disciplinary procedure will be followed with the warning being related to the severity of the offence. The following list does not contain every possible offence and other actions of a similar nature may also be classed as misconduct:

(i) *General conduct.* An employee is expected to conduct themselves at all times in a manner which will maintain public confidence in both their integrity and the service provided by the authority.

Whilst carrying out their duties or acting as a representative of the authority, an employee shall not:

(A) Act in an oppressive or abusive manner towards a fellow employee or member of the public.
(B) Without authorisation, accept any fees, gifts, hospitality, favours or other reward on their own behalf, or on behalf of a third party, beyond that which is authorised as their proper remuneration.
(B) Conduct themselves in a way which offends decency.

(ii) *Working arrangements.* Employees are expected to comply with the agreed arrangements relating to conditions of appointment such as hours of work, meal breaks, requests for leave, sickness absence, absence from duty, etc.

(iii) *Working procedures.* Employees are expected to observe agreed working procedures and safety rules, regulations and codes of practice.

(iv) *Documentation.* Employees are expected to take all reasonable steps to ensure that records such as flexitime cards, expense claim forms, overtime claims, car mileage claims, etc., are accurate and available at the correct time.

(v) *Care of tools, materials, etc.* Employees are required to take due care of all stores, materials, tools, plant, equipment and vehicles and any other property of, or under the control of, the City Council, and must report to their senior officer any loss, defect or damage to any such property which has been issued to or used by them, entrusted to their care.

(vi) *Miscellaneous.* Examples of other general matters which will be classed as misconduct are:

- Failure, by wilful neglect, to undertake the assigned duties of the employment.

- Being under the influence of drink or non-prescribed drugs or sleeping whilst on duty, without medical reason.
- Being an accessory to a disciplinary offence by another employee.
- Unauthorised use of council vehicles.

Appendix 2
Sample disciplinary procedures

Brighton Borough Council

1 *Introduction*

1.1 *Objective of the procedure*

This disciplinary procedure is designed to clarify the rights and responsibilities of management, unions and employees in respect of disciplinary action. The aim is to ensure consistency in the application of disciplinary measures and fairness for the individual who becomes subject to them.

1.2 *Scope*

The procedure applies to all employees of the council with the exception of those covered by the separate arrangement contained in the National Conditions of Service of the Joint Negotiating Committee for Chief Officers.

Short-term contracts. For those employees on contracts of less than six months the procedure will be shortened by the exclusion of Stages 1 and 2 below, although the general principles will apply in all cases.

Casuals. Casual employees are not covered by the procedure. The term 'casual' applies to those who are engaged as required for occasional or irregular work or to meet an emergency.

1.3 *Trade union officials*

The term 'union official' throughout this document means either a member of the NALGO Branch Executive Committee or a steward of the GMBATU or NUPE or a full-time officer of one of these three recognised unions.

No action under this procedure except suspension with full pay in cases of alleged gross misconduct should be taken against a trade union official until all the circumstances of the case have been discussed with the branch secretary or full-time official of the particular union. In respect of NUPE this will always be the full-time official.

1.4 *Representation*

The employee has the right to be represented at any formal disciplinary interview. Before every interview, therefore, the employee must be informed that he/she has the right to be accompanied by his/her union official or a fellow employee of the borough council. In an interview which may result in a final warning or in a dismissal the employee should be strongly advised that he/she should be accompanied by his/her union official.

Brighton Borough Council

1.5 *Appropriate manager*

Chief Officers will clearly identify the manager responsible for handling disciplinary matters for each group of employees and at each stage of the procedure. In the absence of the designated manager the Chief Officer may delegate to another manager of the department the responsibility for hearing a case or appeal.

1.6 *Appeals*

At every stage of the procedure the employee has the right of appeal in accordance with Section 3.

1.7 *Time limits*

The time limits applicable at each stage of the procedure are clearly laid down. The parties to a disciplinary matter may, on occasions and by mutual consent, modify the time limits.

2 *Procedure*

The following agreed procedure should be adhered to in all cases in accordance with the management guidance notes.

2.1 *Stage 1. First written warning*

(a) Offences other than alleged serious and gross misconduct will, on the first occasion, be dealt with at this stage.
(b) The employee will be interviewed by his/her immediate superior accompanied by the departmental Personnel Officer within five working days of the alleged offence or notification of it to the department.
(c) At the end of the interview the supervisor will decide whether a written warning is warranted. If so it will be given to the employee on the prescribed form as soon as possible and within three working days of the interview.
(d) Any warning given will remain in effect for twelve months and a copy of the warning form will be placed on the employee's personal file.

2.2 *Stage 2. Second written warning*

(a) Further alleged misconduct, other than alleged serious and gross misconduct, committed within twelve months of a first written warning being issued will be dealt with at this stage.
(b) The employee will be interviewed by his/her supervisor/assistant section head accompanied by the departmental Personnel Officer within five working days of the alleged offence or notification of it to the department.
(c) At the end of the interview the supervisor will decide whether a written warning is warranted. If so it will be given to the employee on the prescribed form as soon as possible and within three working days of the interview.
(d) Any warning given will remain in effect for twelve months and a copy of the warning form will be placed on the employee's personal file.

2.3 *Stage 3. Final written warning*

(a) This stage will apply in either of the following circumstances:

    (i) A further alleged misconduct within twelve months of a Stage 2 written warning being issued.
    (ii) Alleged *serious misconduct*, which will be dealt with in the first instance at this stage.

(b) Where serious misconduct is alleged the Industrial Relations Officer will be consulted and an interview arranged within five working days of the alleged offence or notification of it to the department. The departmental Personnel Officer will attend the interview which will be conducted by the appropriate section head.

(c) At the end of the interview the section head will decide whether a final warning is warranted. If so it will be issued on the prescribed form, which will be given to the employee as soon as possible and within three working days of the interview.

(d) Any warning will remain in effect for twelve months and a copy of the warning form will be placed on the employee's personal file.

2.4 *Stage 4. Dismissal*

(a) This stage will apply in either of the following circumstances:

    (i) Further alleged misconduct within twelve months of a warning being issued at Stage 3 of this procedure.
    (ii) Alleged gross misconduct, which will be dealt with in the first instance at this stage.

(b) In most cases of alleged gross misconduct it will be inappropriate for the employee concerned to work on after the alleged offence. The employee's immediate superior has the authority to suspend him/her from duty with full pay pending the disciplinary interview.

(c) The Industrial Relations Officer will be consulted and an interview arranged within five working days of the alleged offence or notification of it to the department. The departmental Personnel Officer will attend the interview, which will be conducted by the Chief Officer.

(d) Cases dealt with at this stage of the procedure will, if proven to be gross misconduct, result in dismissal. However, a Chief Officer hearing a case of alleged gross misconduct may decide, upon considering the facts, that the alleged offence, although proven, is not gross misconduct but nevertheless constitutes misconduct or serious misconduct and may issue an appropriate written warning in accordance with Stages 1, 2 or 3 of this procedure.

(e) The Chief Officer will inform the employee of his/her decision at the conclusion of the interview. The decision will be confirmed in writing within three working days of the interview and a copy will be sent to the employee's trade union representative. A further copy will be placed on the employee's personal file.

Brighton Borough Council

3 *Appeals*

3.1 *Officer hearing appeal for Stages 1–3.* Office hearing appeal for Stages 1-3. An employee may appeal against the decision at any stage of the procedure. Appeals at the first, second and third Stages will be heard by an officer who is senior to the officer who gave the warning.

(a) *Time limit.* The appeal is to be made on the prescribed form, which should be sent to the Chief Officer within five working days of receipt of confirmation of the decision.

(b) *Appeal against warning given at Stage 4.* If the appeal is against a warning given by the Chief Officer at Stage 4 of the procedure the form will be passed to the Industrial Relations Officer, who will arrange for the case to be heard by the Chief Officer of another department.

(c) *Appeal hearing arrangements.* Within five working days of receipt of an appeal against a warning, the appropriate officer will hold a meeting with the employee and his/her union official or a friend who is an employee of the borough council (if the employee has decided to be accompanied). The departmental Personnel Officer will attend appeal hearings.

(d) *Confirmation of decision.* The officer hearing the case may uphold or reject the appeal and will give his/her decision orally at the meeting. The decision will be confirmed in writing within three working days of the meeting.

(e) There will be no further right of appeal against the warning.

(f) *Successful appeals.* If the appeal is upheld, the warning form will be removed from the employee's personal file and destroyed along with any other correspondence relating to the matter.

3.2 Appeals against dismissal will be heard by the Council's Disciplinary Appeals Committee.

(a) *Appeal against dismissal.* The appeal is to be made on the prescribed form, which should be sent to the borough Personnel Manager within ten working days of the interview at which the dismissal was decided.

(b) *Arrangements for hearing appeals against dismissal.* Upon receipt of the appeal the borough Personnel Manager will convene a meeting of the council's Disciplinary Committee within ten working days.

(c) The procedure to be followed at meetings of the council's Disciplinary Appeals Committee is given at Appendix 2 to this procedure.

(d) *Confirmation of decision.* The committee may allow or reject the appeal and the decision will be given orally to the employee and his/her union official at the conclusion of the meeting. The decision will be confirmed by the borough Secretary in writing within three working days of the meeting.

(e) *Successful appeals against dismissal.* If the appeal is allowed, the employee will be reinstated in his/her employment and all correspondence related to the case will be removed from his/her personal file and destroyed.

(f) The Disciplinary Appeals Committee is the final level of appeal within the council.

(g) (i) This right of appeal is not prejudiced by any action the employee or his/her union may take towards placing a complaint before an industrial tribunal or the provincial council; nor

(ii) Are his/her or his/her union's rights before the provincial council (in the event of a difference over this procedure) prejudiced by his/her failure to exercise this right to appeal.

Brush Electrical Systems

Section 1. Introduction

1.1. The purpose of this procedure is to provide guidance for and regulate arrangements between management, trade unions and employees, so that all concerned are aware of their responsibilities, rights and obligations.

The objective is to maintain a procedure which not only specifies rules of conduct, but aims always to reconcile justice for the individual with the need for disciplined operations within the company and for the well-being of its other employees.

This procedure assists employees whose conduct is in question, and protects others from the effects of such conduct.

It also allows employees involved in minor misdemeanours the opportunity to improve their standards of conduct, although it has to be recognised that in cases of persistent or gross misconduct, the continued employment of an employee will not always be possible.

1.2. Whilst on company premises or engaged on company business, employees must conduct themselves according to the rules and standards of conduct laid down in the company rules.

1.3. In the event of an employee not adhering to the general standards of behaviour on the company site, there are four levels of formal action within the terms of the disciplinary procedure to which he would be subject.

	Action	**Management authority***
(i)	Formal verbal warning	Immediate Supervisor
(ii)	Written warning	Immediate Supervisor
(iii)	Final written warning – including, where appropriate, suspension without pay	Immediate Supervisor/ Manager
(iv)	Dismissal	Departmental Manager

*These levels of management authority are indications only and in practice will be dependent upon the management organisation in the area concerned.

1.4 The procedure outlined in section 3 is designed to ensure that a fair and consistent approach is adopted to all disciplinary problems and that no disciplinary decisions are taken without full investigation of all the facts, including the employee's previous record.

1.5. In the interests of fairness and consistency, there is a formal appeals procedure against written warnings, suspension or dismissal.

1.6. Although normal disciplinary standards apply to trade union officials, where disciplinary action is necessary beyond a formal verbal warning, the circumstances of the case will be discussed with the Personnel Manager, who may wish to involve the senior trade union representative or full-time official before the appropriate disciplinary action is implemented.

1.7. For certain actions, the procedure will operate progressively from verbal warning to dismissal, but for more serious breaches of discipline it may be necessary to suspend or dismiss an employee on the first occasion and therefore dispense with one or more of the earlier stages.

The procedure provides for these alternatives.

1.8. It is possible to make a broad distinction between those actions where, if disciplinary action is considered necessary, its effect should be progressive and those actions for which dismissal would be appropriate as the initial penalty. The first group may conveniently be termed 'misdemeanours', the second 'gross misconduct'.

1.9. Misdemeanours are actions which are relatively minor, and, taken in isolation, have little effect on the work situations or the well-being of other employees.

Isolated misdemeanours by employees, which may be the result of ignorance or misunderstanding, will normally be dealt with in an informal manner without involving the formal procedure.

1.10. Persistence, either in one particular type of action or in a mixture of actions, which is sufficient to constitute an identifiable pattern of unsatisfactory behaviour will be dealt with by a progressive response under the formal terms of the disciplinary procedure.

This would involve a formal verbal warning for a first recorded breach, a written warning for a second breach with ultimate liability in cases of continued indiscipline to dismissal.

1.11. Generally, breaches of discipline amounting to gross misconduct are those which are of such a nature that they may be actionable at law or have an immediate adverse effect on other employees or the working environment.

They could include, for example (although this is by no means an exhaustive list), stealing, assault, fraud, wilful damage, sleeping during working hours, drunkenness, clocking offences, sexual harassment and offences which infringe such laws as the Factories Act and the Health and Safety at Work Act.

Acts of gross misconduct would normally warrant summary dismissal; the offending employee forfeiting all rights of contractual notice.

1.12. It should be noted that the existence of a recognised laid down discipline procedure in no way restricts the normal informal relationship between an employee and his supervisor, which may involve the supervisor giving an employee in his charge an informal unrecorded verbal warning for an isolated misdemeanour and informally advising the appropriate representative of the issue.

Section 2. Investigate suspension

2.1. If the circumstances surrounding an alleged incident of gross misconduct appear such that management considers it inappropriate to allow an employee to finish the shift, he will be placed on investigative suspension.

Investigative suspension may also be extended beyond the end of the shift into subsequent shifts whilst a full investigation is carried out. However, it is not anticipated that an employee would remain suspended for investigative purposes for more than three consecutive shifts.

2.2. The employee concerned will be advised when he is required to return to work to assist the investigation.

During the period of investigative suspension the employee will be in receipt of normal basic pay.

2.3. It will be made clear to the employee that investigative suspension is *not* part of the formal disciplinary procedure and is not in any way intended to deal with the alleged misconduct.

2.4. The employee's shop steward/representative will be informed of any action to be taken.

Section 3. Operation of the procedure

3.1. When any form of misconduct is alleged to have taken place the employee's immediate supervisor/manager will consider the allegation. The employee will in all circumstances be given the opportunity to present his case. Taking into consideration the seriousness of the alleged misconduct the supervisor/manager will then decide upon the appropriate level of disciplinary action. If an employee has a clear record for two years preceding the alleged offence, only in exceptional circumstances will disciplinary action prior to that two-year period be referred to.

3.2. If the misconduct is of a minor nature the supervisor/manager may decide that the misdemeanour would only warrant informal counselling in which case he will talk with the employee on his own and, if the allegation is confirmed, warn the employee informally.

The supervisor/manager will always make a clear distinction between informal counselling and formal use of the disciplinary procedure. Where the formal disciplinary procedure is invoked, the employee will be given a disciplinary action form, and where the stage of procedure exceeds a formal verbal warning, will be advised of his right to appeal.

3.3. Disciplinary action other than Stage 1 (formal verbal warning) will be recorded on the employee's record Whilst no limit is set as to the amount of time a formal warning will remain on an employee's record, full account will be taken of the length of time elapsed since a formal warning was last given, if and when the employee concerned is the subject of another disciplinary offence.

3.4. In the event of alleged gross misconduct the supervisor/manager will advise the individual and the appropriate representative of the seriousness of the alleged misconduct. The supervisor/manager will immediately instigate an investigation and involve a higher level of management. In most instances of alleged gross misconduct the employee will immediately be placed on investigative suspension.

3.5. In all cases involving the formal procedure, where the employee is a member of a recognised trade union, the appropriate representative will be given the opportunity to be present.

An employee who is not a member of a trade union can be accompanied by another employee of his choice.

The company will not accept the presence of any external third party at a disciplinary meeting with the exception, in certain circumstances, of a trade union official.

Night shift

Where the appropriate levels of management and trade union representatives are not available, no employee should be dismissed outside day shift working hours. Investigative suspension, however, will if necessary be implemented on any shift.

Section 4. Stages of the procedure

4.1. When it has been decided that formal disciplinary action is necessary, one of the following stages of the procedure will be invoked. The employee will be advised, usually in the presence of his representative, and given a copy of the company disciplinary action form.

Continued misconduct

4.2. If an employee does not heed the warnings given, the next level of the procedure will be brought into operation. Further incidents will be dealt with in the same manner, involving the next higher level of action until eventually the employee behaves responsibly or is dismissed.

Formal verbal warning

4.3. The appropriate action for relatively minor misdemeanours which in isolation are not of serious consequence, particularly relevant when the employee has not taken heed of informal counselling. Administered by immediate supervision usually in the presence of the employee's representative. Although a disciplinary action form is used to confirm that the reprimand is the first stage of the procedure, the facts are not entered on the employee's record.

Written warning

4.4. For more serious misdemeanours or continued transgression of the company rules, the employee will be advised of his liability to further disciplinary action in the event of further breaches of discipline, and will also be advised of his right of appeal to a higher level of management. Administered by immediate supervision, confirmed by disciplinary action form and facts entered on employee's record card.

Final written warning (including, where appropriate, suspension)

4.5. Where an employee is issued with a final written warning he will be advised of his liability to be dismissed in the event of a future breach of discipline. He will also be advised of his right to appeal. Administered by supervision, although the next line of management will become involved. A disciplinary action form will be issued and the facts recorded on the employee's record.

Suspension will be without pay.

Dismissal

4.6. Dismissal will be confined to cases of gross misconduct or persistent indiscipline where the conduct of the individual is not acceptable to the company and warrants dismissal. This final stage of the procedure will normally be administered by the departmental manager after consultation with a member of the Personnel Department. The employee will be advised of his right of appeal and the Personnel Manager will be informed of the dismissal.

Section 5. Appeals procedure

5.1. The appeals procedure is intended to safeguard the interests of employees and demonstrate that justice has been done.

5.2. With the exception of Stage 1 of the disciplinary procedure (formal verbal warning), employees have a right of appeal against all other stages of disciplinary action.

Where the employee wishes to appeal, disciplinary action will not be implemented until the appeals procedure has been completed, except in the case of dismissal for gross misconduct.

5.3. In any case of undisputed gross misconduct, although the individual concerned has the right to contest that dismissal, the disciplinary action will take place with immediate effect prior to any appeal. Where the circumstances are disputed by the employee, investigative suspension will normally be implemented.

The domestic appeals procedure

5.4. Notice of appeal must be lodged by the employee or his representative with the supervisor/manager or with the Personnel Manager within one full working shift, where this is practicably possible.

5.5. Initially an appeal will be heard by the next level of management above that which issued the discipline notice (normally the department manager). It is essential that the person who gave the notice of the disciplinary action is present at this appeal.

A further stage of appeal is available to the employee whereby the circumstances are considered by a member of the company's executive. The Personnel Manager or a delegated member of the Personnel Department must be present at this final stage of the company's domestic appeals procedure.

5.6. When making an appeal an employee will normally be accompanied by his representative or colleague, unless he waives this right, in which case this must be recorded.

5.7. Whenever possible the appeal will be heard and decision made within two full working shifts of the notice of appeal being lodged.

5.8. If the appeal is found to be completely justified, management will rescind the disciplinary decision. If it is felt that the appeal is not fully justified, but has some merit, management may reduce the original penalty imposed.

5.9. The result of the appeal will be given to the employee and his representative and to the members of the management concerned. Where the appeal proceedings have involved a company executive (second stage) the decision will normally be in writing.

Cases involving dismissal only

5.10. Where an employee under notice of dismissal is not satisfied with the result of the domestic appeal it is open to him in accordance with the terms of the procedure agreement to call through the trade union for an External Works Conference. In such cases the person will remain an employee of the company until such time as either agreement is reached or this procedure is exhausted.

5.11. Employees dismissed for gross misconduct may also have their case considered at an External Works Conference but their employment will have been terminated at the original disciplinary hearing.

Section 6. Supplementary guidelines – attendance

Introduction

6.1. Employees whose work attendance record is unsatisfactory through habitual lateness, unauthorised absence or persistent absence are liable to have disciplinary action taken against them.

6.2. Disciplinary action will generally be progressive in the event of continuing unsatisfactory attendance relating to any one or any combination of the above categories.

Where an unsatisfactory attendance record is identified within the first year of employment, the employee will be formally reprimanded; however, unsatisfactory attendance is likely to result in dismissal without the disciplinary procedure being adhered to in its entirety.

Lateness

6.3. Every employee is expected, as a condition of his employment, to be available for work at the stipulated starting time. Disciplinary action will be taken against employees who are habitually late. Informal counselling may be sufficient for isolated instances of lateness.

6.4. The disciplinary procedure should be applied where an employee is late on five occasions within a period of four consecutive working weeks

6.5. Further disciplinary action should be taken if the employee is subsequently late on four occasions within a period of four consecutive working weeks.

6.6. Employees who are habitually late over a period in excess of four weeks but who are within the above guidelines will be subject to individual examination and discipline.

Unauthorised absence

6.7. Absence will be regarded as unauthorised if an employee:

- Fails to comply with company sickness absence notification and certificaiton requirements.

- In cases other than sickness absence, fails to obtain prior authorisiation from his supervisor/manager, or in exceptional circumstances, where advance authorisation cannot be sought, fails to subsequently supply a satisfactory explanation for the absence.

Disciplinary action will be taken at an appropriate level, depending upon the nature of the unauthorised absence.

Unauthorised early leaving

6.8. Employees are required to remain at work until the normal finishing time. Unauthorised early leaving is regarded as a serious offence and will result in disciplinary action, which may be at the written warning level for a first occurrence.

6.9. If it is necessary for an employee to leave the site before the normal end of shift or half-shift he should obtain permission from his supervisor/manager in advance.

Persistent absence

6.10. Unacceptable periods of recurring absence, even where there has been full compliance with company sickness absence notification and certification requirements, is viewed by the company as a serious matter. Whilst each case will be carefully investigated, where it is considered appropriate disciplinary action will be taken.

6.11. Patterns of absence may occur for the same or different reasons and may involve frequent short periods or a smaller number of longer periods of absence away from work. Each individual case will be examined in detail to determine if any formal action needs to be taken.

Cadbury, Bournville

The objective of this procedure is to maintain a good standard of conduct and performance at work. It has been developed in line with the ACAS Code of Practice on such matters. The full procedure, 'Bournville Code of Practice – Non-Management,' which is held by your Manager and in your Personnel Department, contains three categories of offence. Details of these and the methods for dealing with disciplinary offences are set out below:

1 *Misconduct – examples:*
- Poor time keeping/attendance.
- Poor work performance.
- Refusal to work.
- Breach of site safety rule.
- Prolonged absence from place of work e.g. unauthorised visits to other departments.
- Hygiene offences – e.g. untidy or dirty appearance, wearing prohibited jewellery.
- Damage to property e.g. writing on walls, intentional damage to overalls.
- Horseplay.
- Gambling.

Cadbury, Bournville

2. *Serious Misconduct – examples:*

There may be occasions when misconduct is considered to be insufficiently serious to justify dismissal, but sufficiently serious to warrant only one written warning, which in effect will be both first and final.

- Hygiene, e.g. failure to notify contact with a notifiable disease.
- Fighting, e.g. intentionally causing minor physical injury.
- Clocking offence.
- Smoking.
- Serious breach of site safety rule or breach of statutory regulations.
- Prolonged absence from place of work e.g. unauthorised absence from site or, whilst in a position of responsibility.
- Drunkenness – incapable of work.
- Falsification of information for Fringe Benefit purposes.

3. *Gross Misconduct – examples:*

- Theft.
- Drunkenness, whilst in a position of responsibility.
- Fighting e.g. attack on an employee, one which causes serious injury.
- Fraud e.g. serious clocking offence or falsification of work record.
- Damage e.g. sabotage.
- Use of an offensive weapon.
- Serious breach of safety rule or statutory regulations, which may result in injury or gross damage.
- Hygiene e.g. continuing to attend work whilst knowingly having a notifiable disease.

If an employee breaks the Company Rules, then the following disciplinary procedure will be adhered to. Any subsequent offence will result in the next stage of the procedure being implemented.

Category of Offence	First Stage	Second Stage	Third Stage	Fourth Stage
Misconduct	(1) Formal Verbal Warning	(2) First Written Warning	(3) Final Written Warning	(4) Dismissal
Serious Misconduct	(3) Final Written Warning	(4) Dismissal		
Gross Misconduct	(4) Dismissal			

NB. Informal warnings are not part of the formal procedure
The number key refers to the person responsible for taking disciplinary action:

(1) Line Manager. (2) Appropriate Area Manager. (3) Personnel Officer. (4) Personnel Department.

Verbal Warning

i. A formal verbal warning will be confirmed in writing.
ii. This warning will remain effective for 3 months

First Written Warning

This warning will remain effective for 6 months.

Final Written Warning

In normal circumstances this will remain effective for 12 months.

NB. For offences of I.D.C. there should not be a time limit on the warning and employees should be informed that failure to report contact with I.D.C. again would result in dismissal.

Dismissal

Where offences of Gross Misconduct are committed and proven the employee will normally be summarily dismissed without notice or payment in lieu of notice.

Representation

At any formal stage of the Discipline Procedure, an employee has the right to be accompanied by a trade union representative or a fellow employee of his choice.

Appeals

An employee has the right to appeal against any formal disciplinary action taken against him.

Probationary and Temporary Employees

All disciplinary offences under the misconduct procedure by probationary/temporary employees may result in dismissal even for a first offence, as will serious or gross misconduct.

Security of Employment

It is our belief that a prosperous and expanding company coupled with our existing practice of the forward planning of labour requirements are the surest guarantees of security of employment. Nevertheless, we recognise there may be circumstances beyond our control, which could result in redundancies. Employees will not be declared redundant until every effort has been made to find suitable alternative employment both within the Site and Cadbury Schweppes PLC.

Our redundancy policy is set out in full in the Security of Employment Agreement which is available for inspection in your Personnel Department.

Termination of Employment

The period of notice an employee is required to give to terminate employment is

1 week for factory employees and 4 weeks for administrative staff. The length of notice given to terminate any non-management employment on Site by the Company is:

- one week for employees with between four weeks and two years continuous employment.
- one week for each year of continuous employment for employees with more than two years service, up to a maximum of twelve weeks.

Notice in writing must be given to your Personnel Department through your manager.

Where sickness or industrial injury occurs during notice including absence of three days or less, doctor's statements are required. Otherwise such time will be treated as absence without permission.

Holiday entitlements which are due may be taken during the notice period by mutual agreement between management and employee.

The Company reserves the right of immediate dismissal for gross misconduct. In certain circumstances the Company reserves the right to give the equivalent wages in lieu of the required period of notice (see Disciplinary Procedure).

Inventions

If during your employment any invention occurs to you, you must promptly raise the matter with your Manager, so it can be determined whether the invention belongs to the Company or yourself. If the invention belongs to the Company, you must do everything necessary to enable the Company to make full use of the invention.

Co-operative Insurance Society

1 *Objective*

This procedure applies to all the society's employees employed at Chief Office, Regional and Claims Offices, Central London Fire and Accident Office, Solicitor's London Office and Administration Officers at Divisional Offices and has been agreed with the Manufacturing, Science and Finance Union on behalf of its members.

The society's disciplinary procedure has been compiled in accordance with the principles and standards set out in the ACAS Code of Practice on Disciplinary Rules and Procedures and in the ACAS advisory handbook *Discipline at Work*. It is designed to help maintain good standards of conduct and working practices which are essential for the handling of the society's affairs and for the safety and well-being of all its employees. By setting out clear stages the procedure should ensure fairness and consistency in the treatment of employees who fail to observe the expected standards. The procedure should not be viewed primarily as a means of imposing sanctions but be seen instead to emphasise and encourage improvements in individual conduct.

Employees are required to observe all the society's rules concerning conduct and working practices. These include rules concerning health and safety at work, those referred to in the Conditions of Employment handbook, those which employees are required to observe in a personal or professional capacity and those rules which apply collectively, including 'local' rules which apply to particular departments or offices. Disciplinary action will be considered where an employee is in breach of these rules or has failed to meet required standards in relation to conduct, attendance, timekeeping, job performance, health and safety or any other relevant matter.

Where, because of incapability, an employee has difficulties in performing the duties required the circumstances should first be discussed by the appropriate department manager with a member of Remuneration and Employee Relations Section, Personnel and Management Services Department. The case will then be dealt with in accordance with the guidance notes in Appendix 1. It is recognised that because of the nature of such cases it might not always be appropriate to issue warnings in accordance with the full disciplinary procedure.

2 *Counselling*

In certain circumstances, where it is considered by a manager or supervisor that an employee is failing to achieve the required standards, or when a minor breach of discipline has occurred, the manager or supervisor should provide informal counselling to the employee. This will take place before any formal action is taken. The employee should be informed of the standards required and will be given help or training to ensure that he or she achieves those standards. In such cases the supervisor should keep a record of the counselling. If informal counselling is considered to be inappropriate, for example when the offence is of a more serious nature, or when following informal counselling an employee fails to improve or maintain an improvement, then the formal disciplinary procedure will be invoked.

3 *Basic principles*

The following principles will be observed at all stages of the procedure.

(i) Disciplinary action beyond an oral warning will not be taken without prior approval from the Remuneration and Employee Relations Section, Personnel and Management Services Department.

(ii) No disciplinary action will be taken until the case has been fully investigated and every effort will be made to complete the investigation as quickly as possible.

(iii) An employee will be notified prior to a formal disciplinary interview of the nature of the complaint(s) against him or her.

(iv) An employee will have the right to be accompanied by a trade union representative or work colleague at all stages of the formal procedure and to call witnesses where appropriate.

(v) An employee will be given the opportunity to state his or her case before any decision is made.

(vi) At each stage of the formal procedure, an employee will be informed of the standard(s) required, the need to improve and will be given reasonable time to achieve the required improvement.

(vii) An employee will have the right to appeal against any disciplinary measure taken under the formal disciplinary procedure.

(viii) The decision to dismiss an employee may be taken only by the Manager, Personnel and Management Services, or an authorised official.

(ix) Where gross misconduct is considered to have occurred, an employee will, where necessary, be suspended immediately on full pay pending a detailed investigation of the incident. The period of suspension will be as brief as circumstances permit.

(x) With the exception of gross misconduct, an employee will not be dismissed for a first breach of discipline.

(xi) In the case of a trade union representative, no disciplinary action beyond an oral warning will be taken until the circumstances of the case have been discussed with a more senior trade union representative or full-time official.

4 *The formal procedure*

Where an employee's conduct or performance is such as to warrant disciplinary action, the stages outlined below will apply. Before any disciplinary action is taken, other than in Stage 1, the matter should be discussed by the appropriate department manager with a member of Remuneration and Employee Relations Section, Personnel and Management Services Department. Examples of behaviour which can result in disciplinary action are cited in Appendix 2.

The procedure can be initiated at any stage outlined below, depending upon the seriousness of the alleged misconduct.

Stage 1. Oral warning. An oral warning may be issued if an employee does not meet acceptable standards of conduct or performance. He or she will be advised of:

- The reason for the warning.
- The standard required and the consequence of failing to meet it.
- The time scale.
- That it is the first stage of the disciplinary procedure.
- Any other disciplinary action taken and the reasons therefore.
- The right of appeal.

An oral warning will normally be given by a senior supervisor, following discussion of the case with an appropriate official of the department concerned. The incident will be recorded and written advice of the warning sent to the Remuneration and Employee Relations Manager, Personnel and Management Services Department. A copy will also be provided to the employee.

Stage 2. Written warning. A written warning, together with any other disciplinary action as outlined in section 5, will be given when an official within the employee's department or office, or other authorised official, is satisfied that:

(i) The offence is sufficiently serious to justify a written warning without the previous stage being followed, or

(ii) There is a continuing failure to meet the standards required in the previous stage, or

(iii) A further offence has occurred which need not necessarily be related in nature to an earlier breach of standards or performance.

Stage 3. Final written warning. A final written warning, together with any other disciplinary action as outlined in section 5, will be given when the manager of the employee's department or office, or other authorised official, is satisfied that:

(i) The offence is sufficiently serious to justify a final written warning without the previous stages being followed, or

(ii) There is a continuing failure to meet the standards required as specified in the previous stages, or

(iii) A further offence has occurred which need not necessarily be related in nature to an earlier breach of standards or performance.

Stage 4. Dismissal. An employee may be dismissed if he or she fails to achieve the required improvement stipulated in the final written warning. This will follow a disciplinary interview conducted by the Manager, Personnel and Management Services Department, or an authorised official. An employee may be dismissed summarily in accordance with section 6 of this procedure.

A warning given to an employee under section 4 of this procedure will cease to have affect in any subsequent disciplinary action arising from any further complaint after the expiry of the following periods of time provided that there has been no cause for further disciplinary action during that period.

- Oral warning: six months.
- Written warning: twelve months.
- Final written warning: twenty-four months.

A letter confirming a written or final written warning will be sent to the employee by Personnel and Management Services Department, setting out details of:

- The reason for the warning.
- The standard required and the consequence of failing to meet it.
- The time scale.
- Any other disciplinary action to be taken, and the reasons therefore.
- The right of appeal.

The employee will be required to acknowledge in writing receipt of a written or final written warning.

A letter confirming the dismissal under sections 4 or 6 of this procedure will be sent to the individual concerned from Personnel and Management Services Department. The letter will outline the reason(s) for dismissal, the date of termination of employment, the right of appeal and the manager who will hear the appeal.

5 *Other forms of disciplinary action*

Other disciplinary action will be taken where it is considered appropriate and will include:

(i) Withholding of service and/or annual increments.

(ii) Withholding of sickness payments. (These payments will normally be withheld only in cases where an employee's absence record is not satisfactory.)

(iii) Withholding of half-yearly lump-sum payments. (These payments will normally be withheld only in cases where an employee is unco-operative in an administrative change or in any subsequent adjustment of establishment levels.)

(iv) Withdrawal of flexitime facilities. (These facilities will normally be withheld only in cases where an employee is in breach of the flexi-time regulations.)

(v) Deductions from wages. (Deductions will normally be made only in cases where the society has suffered a financial detriment as a consequence of misconduct or negligence by an employee, for example, breach of flexitime regulations, unauthorised leave, fraudulent wage claims.)

(vi) Demotion to a lower grade.

Such action will be notified to an employee following a disciplinary interview and where appropriate will be confirmed in writing at the same time as any written notification of the warning. Where appropriate, a time limit for the action will also be stipulated.

6 *Summary dismissal*

Certain types of action may be considered by the society to constitute gross misconduct and to be grounds for summary dismissal. Examples of behaviour which can constitute gross misconduct are cited in Appendix 3.

In a case where gross misconduct is considered to have occurred the employee(s) will, if necessary, be suspended immediately on full pay pending an investigation of the incident. The period of suspension will be as brief as circumstances allow. The penalty for cases of gross misconduct will be summary dismissal, unless there are mitigating circumstances which the society finds acceptable and in such cases alternative disciplinary action will be taken.

Where it is decided to issue a final warning in lieu of summary dismissal, the warning will remain in force and will not expire after a period of time. After twenty-four months, however, it can only be reactivated in relation to a further case of gross misconduct.

7 *Appeals*

An employee wishing to exercise his or her right to appeal against disciplinary action should notify the Deputy General Manager (Administration) in writing, stating the grounds on which the appeal is based. The appeal must be made within a period of seven days of the date of the oral warning being issued, or of the date on which a letter is received confirming the disciplinary action.

An appeal against an oral warning given under section 4, Stage 1, of this procedure will be heard by the Remuneration and Employee Relations Manager.

An appeal against other disciplinary action given under section 4 of this procedure will be heard by one of the following officials:

- Manager, Personnel and Management Services.
- Deputy General Manager (Administration).

An employee will be notified of the manager hearing the appeal in the written notification of the warning or dismissal. The decision made by the official hearing the appeal will be final and the employee will not have recourse for a rehearing of his or her case under any other of the society's procedures.

8 *Short-term employees*

The society reserves the right not to follow the full warning procedure for an employee with less than 52 weeks' service whose employment is considered to be unsatisfactory. Except in cases of gross misconduct, the society would normally issue an oral warning where appropriate and at least one written warning prior to dismissal.

Appendix 1. Incapability guidelines

The following guidelines supplement the society's disciplinary procedure. Where a manager or supervisor is satisfied that an employee has difficulties in performing adequately the duties required because of incapability (by reference to skill, aptitude, health or any other physical or mental quality), and the society is satisfied that the incapability is genuine, it will be appropriate to follow the following guidelines.

In dealing with such cases, the society will seek to treat each employee fairly and compassionately, whilst attempting to minimise disruption to the work of the employee's section or department.

Job performance. It is the society's aim at all times to obtain an improvement in an employee's performance.

The society will take action which will include:

- Informing the employee as to where there is a shortfall in standards.
- Giving the employee an opportunity to provide an explanation.
- Giving the employee time to achieve the required standard(s) and warning of the likely consequences of failing to improve. Wherever practicable, the employee will be offered assistance in the form of training and/or closer supervision.

If, despite these measures, there is a failure to improve or to maintain the improvement at a level which the society finds acceptable, the employee will:

- Be informed of the nature of his or her continued unsatisfactory performance and given an opportunity to provide an explanation.
- Be warned of the consequences of a continued failure to improve and the likelihood of dismissal.
- Wherever practicable, be considered for suitable alternative work.

An employee will not normally be dismissed because of unsatisfactory job performance unless warnings and an opportunity to improve have been given.

Ill health. The society will take action which will include:

- Undertaking a thorough investigation to establish an employee's medical condition and the effect of his or her absence(s) on the section or department, including seeking to obtain a medical report on the employee's condition in accordance with the Access to Medical Reports Act 1988.
- Consulting the employee and discussing the matter with him or her, in order to ascertain the true medical position and the likelihood of the employee's ability to undertake his or her duties to a level which the society finds acceptable.
- Where a full and prolonged return to work is not anticipated, consideration will be given to other appropriate options, for example, an application for early retirement on the grounds of ill health, suitable alternative work, or

return on a part-time basis.

The contract of employment will not be terminated on the grounds of ill health until this procedure has been exhausted.

Appendix 2

Examples of behaviour which, depending on the circumstances, can lead to the disciplinary procedure being invoked:

- Foul, abusive or threatening language.
- Poor timekeeping.
- Poor attendance.
- Failure to adhere to smoking rules.
- Failure to maintain acceptable personal hygiene standards.
- Misuse of company property.
- Negligence.
- Poor standards of work/and or performance.
- Disruption of the work of others.
- Refusal to carry out a reasonable and properly authorised instruction.
- Failure to maintain an acceptable standard of dress and appearance.

The above are examples of breaches of discipline and are neither exhaustive nor exclusive.

Appendix 3

Examples of behaviour which, depending on the circumstances, can constitute gross misconduct:

- Foul, abusive or threatening language.
- Poor timekeeping.
- Poor attendance.
- Failure to adhere to smoking rules.
- Failure to maintain acceptable personal hygiene standards.
- Misuse of company property.
- Negligence.
- Poor standards of work/and or performance.
- Disruption of the work of others.
- Refusal to carry out a reasonable and properly authorised instruction.
- Failure to maintain an acceptable standard of dress and appearance.

The above are examples of breaches of discipline and are neither exhaustive nor exclusive.

Appendix 3

Examples of behaviour which, depending on the circumstances, can constitute gross misconduct:

- Racial/sexual harassment or discrimination against an employee or policyholder.
- Gross negligence in failing to carry out work responsibilities.
- Threatening an employee or other person during the course of employment.

- Flexitime and self-certification offences with the intention to defraud.
- Refusal to carry out a reasonable and properly authorised instruction, after the employee concerned has been warned of the consequences of continuing to refuse.
- Fighting or assault on another person during the course of employment.
- Act of sabotage or malicious damage concerning the society's assets.
- Conduct or negligent work likely to endanger people or property (for example, smoking in high-risk fire areas).
- Criminal offences related to the work situation.
- Incapability through alcohol or drugs or possession of illegal drugs.
- Theft, fraud or deliberate falsification of records with intent to obtain money, property or benefit from the society or one of its employees or policyholders.
- Breach of any Code of Conduct rules or regulations issued by LAUTRO or IMRO or any disqualification under the Financial Services Act (or other similar legislation).
- Failure to protect computerised information by non-compliance with statutory obligations or society policy and procedures.

The above are examples of offences constituting gross misconduct and are neither exhaustive or exclusive.

County Nat West

8.1 *Introduction*

The disciplinary procedure is designed to safeguard and protect the interests of the individual, other employees and the company's reputation by providing a framework for management and employees to ensure that the required high standards of job performance and conduct are met and maintained. This procedure applies to all employees and the aim is to ensure consistent and fair treatment for all.

8.2 *Principles*

Disciplinary action may be necessary where expected standards of performance or behaviour are not met, and the company accepts its responsibility for ensuring that disciplinary action will not be taken until the case has been fully investigated.

Disciplinary matters will be dealt with in a fair and efficient manner in accordance with the Advisory, Conciliation and Arbitration Service (ACAS), Code of Practice on Disciplinary Procedures.

At each stage in the procedure employees will be advised of the nature of the complaint against them and will be given the opportunity to state their case before any decision is made. No employee will be dismissed for a first breach of discipline except in the case of gross misconduct, when the penalty will normally be dismissal without notice or payment in lieu of notice.

At disciplinary interviews held under the procedure, employees may be accompanied by a colleague or manager of their choice from their particular business/cost area. The person accompanying the employee may contribute at the interview with the prior agreement of the individual and the line manager involved in the interview.

An employee will have the right of appeal against any disciplinary penalty imposed. The disciplinary procedure may be implemented at any stage if the individual's alleged misconduct or performance warrants such action.

The company will review the disciplinary procedure in the light of any legislative changes or variation in appropriate codes of practice. Any changes will be notified to employees.

8.3 *Responsibilities*

Line managers are responsible for explaining the company's standards of discipline for job performance and conduct to their employees and for ensuring that they observe them.

Employees are required to familiarise themselves with their Terms and Conditions of Employment Statement, together with the staff handbook, both of which establish the conditions of service and the high standards of conduct expected within the company. Copies of both are distributed on commencing employment.

8.4 *Disciplinary action*

The key points for line managers to remember when handling a disciplinary situation are that:

- The intention is to encourage improvement.
- The matter should be dealt with promptly and all relevant facts gathered.
- Managers should exercise firmness in order to maintain satisfactory standards, while applying the rules in a fair and consistent manner.
- Each case should be considered on its merits.
- The disciplinary procedure is there to be followed.

Three separate situations where disciplinary action may be required have been established and these relate to:

(i) Unsatisfactory job performance.
(ii) Misconduct.
(iii) Gross Misconduct.

(i) *Unsatisfactory job performance.* It is important that employees have a clear understanding of what is required of them when completing specific tasks. Line managers will have given direction and advice to employees at the start of their employment. Training and development will also be available to ensure that the required standards of performance can be satisfactorily reached and maintained.

The annual performance appraisal provides a formal opportunity to assess job performance against specific objectives which have been established, and general attributes.

Line managers are expected to resolve any performance-related problems through informal discussions in the normal course of work and also on a formal basis at appraisal interviews.

Unsatisfactory performance in the job may relate to specific tasks or to the general level of competence as a whole. The disciplinary procedure will be initiated if a line manager is satisfied that an employee clearly understands what is expected and has been given sufficient training and guidance in the duties involved yet is still not performing to the required standard.

(ii) *Misconduct.* The majority of cases of misconduct will concern a breach of one of the company's procedures. When procedures are not followed or an act of misconduct is committed there is a recognised system to deal with the situation which ensures that the individual concerned has a fair hearing and that the facts and the outcome are properly recorded.

Where an offence (other than one which constitutes gross misconduct) has been committed, or an employee's conduct or behaviour is in question, the line manager concerned will investigate the facts. When these are established, the line manager will endeavour to discover the reason for the committal of the offence or the behaviour in question. If the reason is outside the employee's control, appropriate action to resolve the problem will be taken or due allowance made. Should the cause involve a non-work-related problem, the Personnel Department will normally be consulted and the appropriate action taken in conjunction with the employee's line manager.

If the reason is within the employee's control, the line manager will decide whether an informal talk with the employee is sufficient or whether Stage 1 of the disciplinary procedure should be initiated.

The following are examples of acts of misconduct, some of which do not directly involve an established company procedure:

- Failure to adhere to the company's working practice or procedures as set out in the terms and conditions of employment.
- Habitual lateness.
- Failure to comply with the company's absence reporting procedures (see section 1.9 of the staff handbook).

(iii) *Gross misconduct.* Behaviour constituting gross misconduct will render an employee liable for immediate suspension on full pay, normally for no more than five working days, while the company investigates the alleged offence. The decision to suspend will be made by the head of the appropriate business/cost area. A senior member of the Personnel Department will notify the employee of his/her suspension and co-ordinate the investigation. A full investigation of the incident(s) will be undertaken by the relevant line manager, Operational Audit Group/Compliance and a senior member of the Personnel Department. A meeting will be held at which the employee will have the opportunity to state his/her case and any mitigating circumstances will be taken into consideration. A record of this meeting, signed by the employer, will be made.

Gross misconduct will normally lead to summary dismissal (i.e. without notice) but only after a full investigation of the case. Examples of gross misconduct include:

- Insider dealing.
- Theft.
- Fraud.
- Assault.

- Bankruptcy.
- Falsifying records.
- Committing a criminal offence such as to adversely affect the company's standing and reputation. (The right is reserved where an individual has been charged with committing a criminal offence to implement disciplinary action, where it is deemed by the company to be fair and reasonable.)
- Breach of compliance procedures as set out in the compliance manuals and technical guidance notes.
- Violation of personal share-dealing account rules.
- Breach of company or client confidentiality.
- Refusal to work contractual arrangements.
- Loans to colleagues.
- Being under the severe influence of drink whilst at work.
- Being under the influence of non-medically prescribed drugs whilst at work.
- Conduct of any kind such as to endanger the health or safety of others.
- Gross insubordination to superiors in the company.
- Gross negligence in the performance of duties.
- Unacceptable behaviour to clients.
- Deliberate damage to the company's property.
- Breach of security or action resulting in damage to the company's computer systems.
- Breach of any professional or institutional rules, codes of conduct or business ethics which might adversely affect the interest of the company.

The above list is not exhaustive, and any other serious offence likely to reflect upon or discredit the company or cause loss of trust by the company in the employee may be considered to justify summary dismissal.

In such circumstances, summary dismissal of an employee or such other disciplinary action as may be appropriate will be decided by the appropriate head of the business/cost area and the head of Personnel.

A senior member of the Personnel Department must always be consulted immediately an instance of gross misconduct has occurred or comes to light and thereafter at all stages throughout any subsequent proceedings to ensure that all legal obligations to the individual are properly fulfilled.

8.5 *Disciplinary procedure*

It is important that the Personnel Department be notified in advance when any stage of the disciplinary procedure is to be initiated. Admonishments of a minor nature should not be considered part of the formal disciplinary procedure and need not be notified.

A three-stage procedure will normally be followed before dismissal is considered. However, in certain circumstances, depending on the seriousness of the misconduct, it may be appropriate to enter the procedure at Stage 2, first written warning, or Stage 3, second written warning (final).

(i) *Stage 1. Oral warning.* If the failure is thought to be within the employee's own control, then the individual will be interviewed by the line manager concerned, offered the opportunity of explaining the alleged shortcomings and subsequently given whatever advice, help or reprimand may be considered necessary in the circumstances. The individual will then be given an agreed and specified time (not normally less than four weeks) in which to improve. The employee will be advised of the reason for the warning, and informed that it is the first stage of the disciplinary procedure. A brief note of the oral warning will be made by the line manager and kept on the departmental files for twelve weeks. After that time the note will be removed, subject to satisfactory conduct and performance, and will not be used or taken into account if disciplinary action is taken in the future.

(ii) *Stage 2. First written warning.* If the performance or conduct of an employee falls significantly short of the required standard, during the period set at Stage 1 above, then a first written warning will be issued. This will follow a full discussion with the relevant line manager, personnel manager and the individual concerned. A record of that interview must be made. The written warning in the form of a letter from the Personnel Department will detail specific areas for improvement with defined objectives to be met, if appropriate, within a period not exceeding eight weeks.

Employees will be asked to acknowledge receipt of the first written warning. A copy of this will be placed on the personal file of the employee for a period of twelve months from the date of issue. If the required improvement is achieved, the warning will be removed from the file after this period and will not be used or taken into account if disciplinary action is taken in the future.

(iii) *Stage 3. Second written warning (final).* A full investigation will be held. If there is no improvement in performance or conduct within the period previously set then a second written warning (final) will follow.

The serious nature of this stage of the disciplinary procedure will be outlined in a full discussion with the relevant line manager, personnel manager and the individual concerned in order to encourage an immediate and sustained improvement in the standard of performance. It will be made clear that any further disciplinary action will result in dismissal. A record of that interview must be made. The individual will then be given an agreed and specific time (not normally less than eight weeks) in which to improve.

Employees will be asked to acknowledge receipt of the second written warning (final) in the form of a letter from the Personnel Department. A copy of this will be placed on the personal file of the employee for a period of eighteen months from the date of issue. If the required improvement is achieved and sustained, the warning will be removed from the file after this period and will not be used or taken into account if disciplinary action is taken in the future.

(iv) *Stage 4. Dismissal.* Dismissal may result in the following instances:

(a) If the required improvement in performance or conduct previously defined has not been met.
(b) If the level of performance or conduct indicates that the employee is incapable of reaching the required standards.
(c) If there are specific instances of serious negligence, lack of judgement or any other action which in the company's view represent a performance level significantly lower than that which is expected.

Dismissal will be authorised by the head of the business/cost area after full consultation with the line manager and personnel manager. A formal letter of termination of employment from the personnel manager will record the reasons for dismissal and detail, where applicable, previous warnings administered.

A summary of the stages of the disciplinary procedure follows in Appendix A.

8.6 *Appeals procedure*

Employees have a right of appeal at all stages of the company's disciplinary procedure. It is intended, however, that formal procedures will be conducted in such a way that such appeals should be infrequent.

Appeals must be made in writing, and include a written submission of the grounds for appeal, within three working days of any disciplinary action being taken. This provides the employee with the opportunity to restate their case. An individual will be able to comment on any new evidence arising during the appeal before any decision is taken. The members of the appeal committee follow in Appendix B. A decision will be conveyed to the employee within three working days for oral and first written warnings; five working days for all other appeals. The decision at this stage is final.

Appendix A. *Disciplinary procedure*

Disciplinary stage	*Nature*	*Type*	*Conducted by*
Stage 1 Oral warning	Unsatisfactory job performance or conduct	Investigation and verbal	Line manager
Stage 2 First written warning	Significantly short of required standard or failure to improve	Investigation and written	Line manager and personnel manager
Stage 3 Second written warning (final)	Serious misconduct or sustained poor performance	Investigation and written	Line manager and personnel manager
Stage 4 Dismissal	Sustained poor performance and/or misconduct	Investigation and written	Line manager and personnel manager
	Gross misconduct	Investigation Written	Line manager and senior member of Personnel Department, head of business/cost area and head of Personnel

Appendix B. *Appeals procedure*

Disciplinary stage	Line of appeal	Time to Appeal	Result of Appeal within
Stage 1 Oral warning	Personnel manager	Three working days	Three working days
Stage 2 First written warning	Senior member of business/cost area and independent personnel manager	Three working days	Three working days
Stage 3 Second written warning (final)	Senior member of business/cost area and independent personnel manager	Three working days	Five working days
Stage 4 Dismissal	Head of Personnel and head of business/cost area	Three working days	Five working days
Dismissal for gross misconduct	Chief executive and head of independent business/cost area	Three working days	Five working days

9 *Grievance procedure*

It is recognised that employees may have grievances relating to work, or conditions of employment.

In most instances these problems should be resolved quickly and efficiently on an informal basis with line management. However, there may be occasions when a more formal approach will be required, and in such instances the following procedure should apply:

(i) *Stage 1*. The employee should in the first instance discuss the grievance with his/her immediate line manager or, if the grievance concerns him/her, with the line manager's superior.

If the problem is not satisfactorily resolved Stage 2 may be invoked.

(ii) *Stage 2*. Should the grievance remain unresolved the employee may refer the matter to the head of the relevant business/cost area who will advise the Personnel Department.

If the grievance has not been resolved within a period of ten working days the employee may invoke Stage 3.

(iii) *Stage 3*. At this stage the employees has the right to make a written statement to the head of Personnel, who will investigate the grievance and, where appropriate refer to the chief executive. A decision will be conveyed to the employee within a period of fifteen working days. This decision will be final.

GEC Measurements

1 *Purpose*

The purpose of this procedure is to ensure that, except in cases of gross industrial misconduct, where an employee's conduct falls below that expected, then the employee should be given the opportunity to improve and therefore reduce the possibility of being dismissed.

Built into this procedure is the right of the individual to appeal against the disciplinary action proposed.

It is recognised and expected that, for any minor or isolated infringement of company rules or procedures, supervisors or managers may give employees informal verbal warnings as part of their day-to-day supervisory duties.

Where any employee's conduct fails to improve as a result of these informal warnings, or where the breaches of company regulations are more serious, it will be necessary to use the formal domestic disciplinary procedure, as outlined below.

This procedure does not affect existing agreements with the recognised unions relating to the handling of disciplinary matters or dismissals, nor does it affect the statutory rights of employees to complain to an industrial tribunal of unfair dismissal.

2 *Stages of the disciplinary procedure*

2.1 *Stage 1.* At the earliest opportunity, and normally within forty-eight hours of the alleged misconduct, the employee will be interviewed by the immediate supervisor to be advised of the alleged misconduct and be given the opportunity to reply.

The employee will have the right to be accompanied by a union representative or a person of the employee's own choice at this meeting.

If following the interview and any subsequent investigation, the supervisor is satisfied that an act of misconduct has taken place, then the employee will be given a formal verbal warning and, if appropriate, a time limit for improvement will be specified. This verbal warning will be confirmed, in writing, to the employee, the employee's representative, where applicable, and the Personnel Department.

The employee has the right of appeal against this decision which will be to take the matter up at Stage 2 of the grievance procedure. The employee must give the immediate supervisor notice of intention to appeal normally within five working days of receiving the written confirmation.

2.2 *Stage 2.* If the employee's conduct fails to improve in the specified time, or if there is further misconduct before the verbal warning is discounted, a further disciplinary interview will be held. This interview will normally be held within five working days of the end of the specified time, or the further misconduct.

The immediate supervisor's manager or supervisor will conduct the interview with the employee.

The employee will have the right to be accompanied by a union representative or a person of the employee's own choice at this meeting.

A personnel officer will be involved at this stage.

If, following the interview and any other subsequent investigation, the manager is satisfied that a further act of misconduct has taken place, then the employee will be given a formal first written warning. This will contain details of the misconduct and previous misconduct and will specify, where appropriate, a time limit within which an improvement will be expected to be forthcoming from the employee. It will also specify the nature of further disciplinary action that would be implemented in the event of continued or future misconduct, i.e. Stages 3 and 4.

A copy of the first written warning will be given to the employee, a copy will be placed in the employee's personal file, and, where applicable, a copy will be given to the employee's representative.

The employee has the right of appeal against this decision, which will be to take the matter up at Stage 3 of the grievance procedure. The employee must give the immediate supervisor's manager or supervisor notice of intention to appeal normally within five working days of receiving the first written warning.

2.3 *Stage 3.* If the employee's conduct fails to improve in the specified time, or if there is further serious misconduct of a different nature before the first written warning is discounted, a further disciplinary interview will be held. This interview will normally be held within five working days of the end of the specified time, or the further misconduct.

The departmental manager will conduct the interview with the employee.

The employee will have the right to be accompanied by a union representative or a person of the employee's own choice at this meeting.

A personnel officer will be involved at this stage.

If, following the interview and any subsequent investigation, the departmental manager is satisfied that a further act of misconduct has taken place, then the employee will be given a final written warning. This will contain details of the misconduct and previous misconduct and will specify, where appropriate, a time limit within which an improvement will be expected to be forthcoming from the employee. It will also specify the nature of further disciplinary action that would be implemented in the event of continued or future misconduct, i.e. Stage 4.

A copy of the final written warning will be given to the employee, a copy will be placed in the employee's personal file, and, where applicable, a copy will be given to the employee's representative.

The employee has the right to take the matter up through the appeals procedure contained in the grievance procedure. The employee must give the departmental manager notice of intention to appeal normally within five working days of receiving the final written warning.

2.4 *Stage 4.* If the employee's conduct fails to improve in the specified time, or if there is further serious misconduct of a different nature before the final written warning is discounted, a further disciplinary interview will be held. This interview will normally be held within five working days of the end of the specified time, or the further misconduct.

The senior manager/director of the function will conduct the interview with the employee.

The employee will have the right to be accompanied by a union representative or a person of the employee's own choice at this meeting.

The Personnel Manager will be involved at this stage.

If, following the interview and any subsequent investigation, the management are satisfied that a further act of misconduct has taken place, then the employee will be issued with notice of dismissal.

The employee will be given written details of the reason for the dismissal. A copy of the dismissal letter will be sent to the Personnel Department to action the leavers procedure and, where applicable, a copy will be given to the employee's representative(s).

The employee has the right of appeal against dismissal, which will be to take the matter up with the Personnel Manager. The employee must give the senior manager/director notice of intention to appeal normally within three working days of receiving the notice of dismissal.

The Personnel Manager will hear the appeal in the presence of the individual's senior manager/director, the employee and the negotiating committee of the appropriate union or a person of the dismissed employee's own choice.

The decision of the Personnel Manager will be communicated to all parties in writing.

2.5 *Acts of misconduct.* The following list is not intended to be comprehensive and merely serves to provide examples of misconduct which through the application of the above disciplinary procedure could lead to dismissal:

- Persistent absence.
- Persistent lateness.
- Wilful or persistent bad workmanship or failure to meet company standards.
- Refusal to obey reasonable and lawful management instructions.
- Intentionally breaking company rules.
- Discriminatory action against other employees.
- Intentionally wasting or misusing time or materials.
- Unauthorised absence.
- Wilful or premeditated insubordination.
- Horseplay.
- On duty knowingly under the influence of drink or non-prescribed drugs.
- Offensive language and/or behaviour.
- Sexual harassment.
- Intentionally endangering the health and safety of employees.

2.6 Discounting of warnings. The purpose of the above procedure is to regulate the conduct of employees and to offer the opportunity of improvement. Where employees who have received warnings conduct themselves satisfactorily during the period after receiving the warning then it is the intention of this procedure that such warnings be discounted and not used thereafter to the detriment of the employees.

For Stages 1 and 2, warnings will be discounted after a period of six months' satisfactory conduct. For Stage 3, warnings will be discounted after a period of twelve months' satisfactory conduct.

Except in the case of gross industrial misconduct, the disciplinary procedure will reopen at Stage 1 when previous warnings have been discounted.

3 *Gross industrial misconduct*

3.1 Procedure. In the case of suspected gross industrial misconduct, the employee may be immediately suspended on full pay by a senior manager/director pending an investigation and a subsequent disciplinary hearing.

The employee will have the right to be accompanied by a union representative or a person of the employee's own choice at this hearing.

If, following the investigation and subsequent disciplinary hearing, the management are satisfied that an act of gross industrial misconduct has occurred, then the employee will be dismissed without notice, regardless of whether or not the employee has received previous warnings.

If an employee is dismissed for gross industrial misconduct then the right of appeal is as contained in 2.4 above. However, in cases of gross industrial misconduct, the employee must give the senior manger/director concerned notice of intention to appeal within one working day of receiving the notice of dismissal. In this event the employee will be deemed to be suspended without pay until the outcome of the appeal is known.

3.2 *Acts of gross industrial misconduct.* The following list is not intended to be comprehensive and merely serves to provide examples of acts considered to be gross industrial misconduct:

- Fighting.
- Theft of company property.
- Theft of another employee's property.
- Submitting false claims for expenses, hours worked or for work done.
- Flagrant breach of safety regulations, including smoking in hazardous areas.
- Malicious damage to property of the company or of that belonging to any employee of the company.
- Wilful disclosure of the company's confidential information to the detriment of the company.
- Serious acts of discrimination or sexual harassment.

IBC Vehicles

13.1 *Introduction*

The unions accept that it is the responsibility of management to maintain discipline on the basis of reasonable standards of conduct and a procedure for fair and consistent disciplinary action.

13.2 *Dealing with disciplinary issues*

In dealing with disciplinary issues the following principles will apply:

(i) In the instance of an alleged disciplinary offence the employee and his representative concerned will be so informed.

(ii) Where appropriate, supervision/management will conduct preliminary investigations to establish the facts before memories fade. This may include questioning witnesses and taking statements.

(iii) In the event of an allegation of gross misconduct the employee will be suspended on annual salary pending the holding of any preliminary investigation and pending the completion of the disciplinary hearing. Such suspension is not a penalty. *Note.* In circumstances requiring prolonged enquiry the company reserves the right to suspend employees without pay.

(iv) Employees have the right to be accompanied by a representative from within the company at all disciplinary hearings. In the case of an appeal against dismissal, their accredited in-plant senior representative will also be present.

(v) The employee, with the assistance of his accredited in-plant representative will be given full opportunity to state his case.

(vi) Following the hearing and full consideration of the evidence, disciplinary action, if any, will be determined. Written confirmation of all disciplinary actions, except verbal warnings, will be provided to the employee and to his in-plant representative.

(vii) In determining the disciplinary action to be taken against an employee who has been found to have committed an offence management will take account of all relevant extenuating circumstances.

(viii) Warning will be disregarded if twelve months have elapsed without further disciplinary action.

(ix) Union representatives are subject to the same standards as all other employees but will, if the subject of a disciplinary hearing, be represented by their accredited in-plant senior union representative, and in the case of dismissal, representation by his full-time union official. The accredited in-plant senior union representative has the right to be represented by his full-time union official.

13.3 *Progressive disciplinary action*

13.3.1. The following disciplinary procedure applies to all employees except those who are within their probationary period.

13.3.2. It is recognised that in the course of his day-to-day responsibilities a supervisor may have occasion to comment informally upon an employee's conduct or performance, and often this will be the best way of handling issues. Where, however, the matter is more serious or where there has been a lack of improvement following informal comment, then application of the following formal procedure will be advised to the employee and his representative.

13.3.3. In the case of offences such as poor workmanship, leaving early without permission and poor timekeeping and attendance, disciplinary action will normally be progressive and will take one of the following recorded forms.

- Stage 1. Formal verbal warning.
- Stage 2. First written warning.
- Stage 3. Final written warning.
- Stage 4. Dismissal.

Note 1. The authority to decide on the issue of final written warnings and on dismissal will lie with the management, and for the majority of employees this will be at company executive level.

Note 2. It must be emphasised that some offences may be sufficiently serious to require a penalty that omits a stage or stages of progressive action.

Note 3. The penalty of suspension without pay will not normally be used, the final written warning stage being regarded as the equivalent stage. In some instances, however, suspension without pay is an appropriate penalty and can be imposed.

13.4 *Gross misconduct*

13.4.1. No employee will be dismissed for a first offence except for gross misconduct. The following list, which is not exhaustive, gives examples of gross misconduct:

(i) Pilfering or the unauthorised possession of company property or the property of other employees.

(ii) The wilful or grossly negligent damage or destruction of company property or the property of other employees.

(iii) Fighting, assault, using physical violence on another person.

(iv) Indecent or grossly offensive conduct.

(v) Defrauding the company.

(vi) The falsification of company documents.

(vii) Gross insubordination, or persistent refusal to carry out a proper instruction.

(viii) Sleeping during working hours.

(ix) Prolonged and unauthorised absence from the workplace.

(x) Being intoxicated by alcohol or drugs while at work.

(xi) Bringing any drugs for non-medical purposes on to, or being in possession of them, on company premises.

(xii) A wilful or grossly negligent breach of safety regulations likely to endanger himself or others.

(xiii) Prolonged unauthorised absence.

(xiv) Criminal offences arising from the employee's job.

(xv) Criminal offences not arising from employment but which clearly demonstrate the employee to be unsuitable to the company or fellow employees.

13.4.2. Dismissal for gross misconduct will be without the normal period of notice and without pay in lieu.

13.5 *Court cases*

13.5.1. If any disciplinary matter would be the subject of a prosecution before a court of law, the company is not precluded from investigating the matter and from taking disciplinary action prior to the court hearing.

13.5.2. Employees on remand in custody will normally be suspended without pay. Since remand in custody can be prolonged, the company does not undertake to hold employment open indefinitely.

13.6 *Appeals*

13.6.1. An employee has the right to appeal against disciplinary action and to be accompanied by his union representative. If he does, then the appeal will be heard by a member of management above the level of the supervisor/manager who took the disciplinary hearing, together with a senior member of the Personnel Department. They will be responsible, after hearing all the available evidence, for making a decision that will be final.

13.6.2. All appeals must be registered with the supervisor/manager who took the disciplinary hearing within twenty-four hours (one working day) of the decision being made.

13.6.3. A decision to summarily dismiss an employee following a disciplinary hearing will not be implemented until twenty-four hours following that decision. If an appeal is made within that period then the decision will not be implemented prior to the appeal being held, subject to the appeal being heard within five working days of the original decision. The employee will be suspended on annual salary during the period between the time of the decision to dismiss and the time when that decision is implemented.

13.7 *Young trainees*

Young trainees must observe the standards of conduct in Appendix 6 in the same way as other employees. They are also subject, should the necessity arise, to the same corrective and disciplinary measures, but with the inclusion of the following provisions that take some account of the special character of the training relationship that exists with them:

(i) While departmental supervision and fellow employees will exercise day-to-day responsibility for the conduct and performance of trainees undergoing training in their areas, the application of formal corrective or disciplinary measures will be the responsibility of the Personnel Department.

(ii) Trainees have the same right to representation as other employees.

(iii) At the discretion of a senior member of the Personnel Department, there may be discussion or correspondence with the parents or guardian of a trainee involved in a disciplinary matter.

(iv) Disciplinary offences on college premises will be considered in the same way as if they had been committed on company premises.

Peradin

1 *Purpose*

The purpose of this disciplinary procedure is to protect the interests and safety of the employee and the company in a just and reasonable manner. It is essential that employees should be aware of the rules and required standards of work and conduct and of the procedure to be followed.

2 *Procedure*

In the normal course of their duties, supervisors are required to make employees aware of any shortcomings in performance or conduct.

It is recommended that written warnings of Stages 1 and II below will follow the issue of formal verbal warnings where appropriate. If the employee wishes, his/her trade union representative or a colleague of his/her choice may be present when this verbal warning is given. It is stressed, however, that verbal warnings do not have to be issued prior to the application of the written procedure.

Thus where persistently poor performance at work occurs or an employee is failing to maintain proper standards of attendance and timekeeping or certain types of misconduct or malpractice are committed then the procedure set out below will be followed:

Stage I. The employee's supervisor will inform the employee that he/she is dissatisfied with a particular aspect, giving reasons. If the employee wishes, his/her trade union representative or a colleague of his/her choice may be present when the warning is given. The supervisor will warn him/her that there must be an improvement in the specific aspect, within an appropriate time scale. Detail of this warning will be entered on a warning card. A copy of this card will then be issued to the employee, his/her representative and the supervisor concerned.

Stage II. Should there be a continuing case for complaint after two warnings given at any step of the procedure (taking into account totting up) the supervisor will report the matter to the departmental manager, who will interview the employee concerned in the presence of the supervisor. If the employee requests it, his/her representative or some other person of his/her choice may also be in attendance. Further to this interview, if the departmental manager is satisfied that further action is warranted a final warning will be issued to the employee, stating clearly the possible penalty for failure to improve within a defined time scale. This warning will be reported on the appropriate card and a copy issued to the employee, representative and supervisor concerned.

Stage III. If no improvement occurs after the final warning (taking into account totting up and certain serious offences outlined in Clause 3 below) the facts will be reported to the senior functional manager concerned. After appropriate consultations with the Personnel Manager and the appropriate senior trade union representative on site (if applicable) and having listened to all the circumstances of the offence(s), including mitigation, the senior functional manager will decide what action should be taken, bearing in mind particularly, but not exclusively, the possible penalty defined in the warning issued at Stage II. The decision, and reasons for it, will be communicated to the employee in the presence of his/her supervisor and representative if applicable.

3 *Serious breaches of discipline/misconduct*

3.1 Under certain circumstances (listed below) the conduct of an employee will constitute a hazard to himself or other employees of the company. These circumstances may be:

(i) Tampering with safety devices with the deliberate intent to render them inoperable.
(ii) Drunkenness.
(iii) Smoking in a prohibited area.
(iv) Fighting or attacks on personnel.
(v) Wilful damage.
(vi) Arson.
(vii) Other mutually agreed serious offences which may occur from time to time.

Depending on the circumstances, the employee may be suspended immediately without pay pending an investigation of the matter which will be undertaken at the earliest possible moment. Stage III of the procedure will be followed without recourse to Stages I and II.

In the event that the disciplinary hearing finds the alleged offence not proven, then compensation for the period of suspension imposed will be applied.

3.2. In those cases (listed below) where the offence does not constitute a hazard, the supervisor will report the matter to the departmental manager. An inquiry will follow under Stage III of the general procedure without recourse to Stages I and II. The circumstances where this action may apply are:

(i) Theft of property.
(ii) Falsifying documents (including clocking offences).
(iii) Sleeping on duty.
(iv) Leaving work without permission.
(v) Refusal to obey a reasonable instruction.
(vi) Any offence that contravenes criminal law.
(vii) Other mutually agreed serious offences which may arise from time to time.

Depending on the circumstances the employee may be suspended immediately without pay pending an investigation of the matter which will be undertaken at the earliest possible moment. Stage III of the procedure will be followed without recourse to Stages I and II.

In the event that the disciplinary hearing finds the alleged offence not proven, then compensation for the period of suspension imposed will be applied.

3.3. Damage to moulds, tools, machinery and equipment which is caused by reason of culpable negligence by an employee or by failure to observe procedures or instructions will result in the convening of a Stage III inquiry. Provided that the mould(s), tool(s), machinery and equipment have previously been maintained in good condition and that the employee concerned is known to be suitably qualified by experience and/or training, then the penalty will be suspension for up to three shifts.

A second offence within six months will again be dealt with using Stage III. The penalty following investigation will normally be suspension for *three* shifts, although dismissal may result should circumstances warrant this.

A third offence within six months of the second will attract dismissal using Stage III of the procedure. In all cases of this kind the Personnel Manager will be informed by report of the department manager, and the matter will be recorded on the employee's personal file. The employee and shop representative will be requested to sign the report and, if a refusal is given, a note to that effect will be attached to the report.

Suspension

Any employee suspended for any proven disciplinary offence will not be paid during the period of suspension. Where previous suspension has not effected an improvement, dismissal may follow. Full details of suspension(s) will be entered on the employee's personal record and will be notified in writing to the employee and his representative and foreman.

5 *Dismissal*

In the event of dismissal a full report of the case will be prepared by the Personnel Manager which will be jointly signed by him and the senior functional Manager concerned.

6 *Right to appeal*

At all stages of the procedure an employee is entitled to appeal through the grievance procedure. Any employee dismissed under Stage III is entitled to make an appeal direct to the appropriate functional director of the company, if he wishes to do so. Request for an appeal hearing should be registered with the Personnel Manager within three days of the decision to dismiss being given.

7 *Totting up*

In all cases in which warnings have been given, subsequent completion by the employee of each period of six months' satisfactory service or service without further offence will result in the deletion of one warning from the employee's record. (*Note.* Warnings given at any stage of the procedure are not counted by the type of offence but by occasion.)

Royal Ordnance

1 *Purpose and scope*

1.1. The following procedure is established to ensure fair and consistent handling of alleged failures to observe rules and standards of conduct. The parties to this agreement recognise that (other than for gross misconduct) disciplinary action should not be viewed solely as a means of imposing sanctions, but rather as a means of encouraging improvement in unacceptable conduct and attendance.

1.2. No disciplinary action will be taken against an employee until the case has been fully investigated.

1.3. At every stage in the procedure the employee will be advised in writing of the nature of the complaint against him/her and will be given the opportunity to state his/her case before any decision is made.

1.4. At all stages of the disciplinary process, an employee will have the right to be accompanied by a trade union representative or colleague.

1.5. No employee will be dismissed for a first breach of discipline except in the case of gross misconduct.

1.7. The procedure may be introduced at any stage if the employee's misconduct warrants such action.

1.8. This revised procedure together with an illustrative list of offences will be brought to the attention of all employees. Line managers with disciplinary responsibilities and all trade union representatives will be issued with a copy of the procedure and the attached notes.

1.9. This procedure and attached notes for guidance supersede the codes, procedures and practices which previously applied within Royal Ordnance. The parties to this agreement reserve the right to seek agreed revisions to the procedure and attached notes in the light of operating experience, case law, etc.

2 *Informal counselling*

Informal counselling by the line manager may be a more appropriate response to a minor offence than formal disciplinary action. Counselling should take the form of a discussion with the objective of determining and agreeing the improvements required.

3 *Procedure*

3.1. *Investigation of alleged offences.* Immediately an offence is reported, the background is to be investigated by the line manager with a view to deciding whether formal disciplinary action should be taken. The advice and assistance of the Personnel Department should be sought in conducting the investigation. Statements, as necessary, should be obtained from the alleged offender and witnesses.

3.2. *Formal disciplinary reports.* If it is decided to take formal disciplinary action a disciplinary report is to be raised by the Personnel Department.

3.3. Notification to the employee. The employee will be informed in writing of the nature of the offence and the decision to take formal disciplinary action. The letter will indicate that a disciplinary hearing will be convened normally within ten working days and that the employee may have the assistance of a trade union representative or colleague in framing his/her response at the hearing.

3.4. *Disciplinary hearing.* The purpose of a disciplinary hearing is to seek to resolve any doubts about the facts of the case and to allow the employee concerned to fully state his/her case.

At Stages 1 and 2 the disciplinary hearing will be conducted by the immediate line manager. In Stage 3 and 4 cases it will be conducted at an appropriate more senior level of management.

A member of the Personnel Department will be present at all formal disciplinary hearings.

The employee and any representative are to be given the opportunity to consider official evidence, introduce evidence and call witnesses.

A record of the hearing will be produced and a copy given to the employee.

3.5. Disciplinary action. For offences other than those involving gross misconduct there will be four stages of formal disciplinary action:

1 Recorded verbal warning.
2 Written warning.
3 Final written warning.
4 Dismissal with notice or payment in lieu of notice.

Stage 1. *Recorded verbal warning.* Following the disciplinary hearing, it may be decided that a first offence warrants a recorded verbal warning from the immediate line manager. Such warnings lapse after six months.

Stage 2. *Written warning.* Following the disciplinary hearing, it may be decided that a serious first offence or repetition of a previous unlapsed offence warrants a written warning. Such warnings lapse after six months.

Stage 3. *Final written warning.* Following the disciplinary hearing, it may be decided that a very serious first offence or repetition of a previous unlapsed offence warrants a final written warning. Such warnings lapse after twelve months.

Stage 4. *Dismissal with notice or payment in lieu of notice.* Following the disciplinary hearing, it may be decided to take discharge action for repetition of an offence which has previously resulted in the issue of an unlapsed final written warning.

If, after due consideration, it is decided that the employee should be dismissed the line manager will pass the disciplinary papers to the Personnel Manager. The Personnel Manager will ensure that proper procedures have been observed and, if satisfied, ratify the decision. He/she will then issue a discharge letter, briefly detailing the offence, the appeal procedure and indicating the effective date of discharge.

3.6. *Gross misconduct.* Certain offences may lead to dismissal without recourse to the progressive disciplinary procedures outlined at 3.5 above. Gross misconduct is defined as misconduct so serious in its nature that the essential trust required between employer and employee is permanently destroyed, e.g. physical violence, theft, fraud or breach of rules which are specific to the nature of the business.

If, after due consideration, it is decided that the employee should be dismissed the line manager will pass the disciplinary papers to the Personnel Manager. The Personnel Manager will ensure that proper procedures have been observed and, if satisfied, ratify the decision. He/she will then issue a discharge letter, briefly detailing the offence, the appeal procedure and indicating that discharge is effective from the date the letter is issued.

3.7. *Suspension from work with pay.* In certain cases it may be necessary to suspend alleged offenders from work in order to conduct the necessary disciplinary investigations. In the case of gross misconduct offences such suspension will normally continue until a disciplinary decision is made.

4 *Appeals*

4.1. If an employee wishes to appeal against a formal disciplinary decision or penalty he/she must do so, in writing, to the Personnel Manager within five working days of the decision being communicated. The appeal letter must clearly indicate the grounds for the appeal, e.g. new evidence, improper hearing, severity of punishment.

4.2. Appeals will be arranged without undue delay.

4.3. If the appeal is against a decision other than dismissal, the Personnel Manager will arrange an appeal hearing chaired by a senior line manager who has not previously been involved in the case and has no personal interest in it.

4.4. If an appeal is against a decision to dismiss, the Personnel Manager will arrange an independent appeal hearing conducted, as appropriate, by the site operations manager or the function director in the case of divisional or company head office employees.

If, after due consideration, it is decided that dismissal represents a harsh penalty for the offence, a period of unpaid suspension of up to ten working days, transfer to other work or downgrading may be determined to be more appropriate penalties.

4.5. After due consideration of an appeal, it must be decided whether or not the original decision and penalty should stand, be withdrawn or the penalty be reduced. Appeal decisions will normally be notified within three days.

Weidmuller (Kipton Products)

1 *Policy*

The company recognises that the best form of discipline is self-discipline. All employees are therefore encouraged to perform their work in a responsible and conscientious manner, adhering to the rules and regulations of the company and its accepted code of conduct.

Weidmuller (Kipton Products)

However, for those occasions when discipline falls below the expected level, it is essential to have clear and simple procedures which can be applied in a fair and consistent manner.

The type of disciplinary action to be taken will depend upon the gravity of the offence, and in all cases a corrective approach will be adopted to encourage improvement in an individual's conduct. The exception to this rule will be gross misconduct, when normally summary dismissal will apply.

In the majority of cases of misconduct the desired corrective action will be achieved by issuing the employee with an informal warning without recourse to the formal discipline procedure.

The following rules and procedures have been compiled to assist both employees and management in dealing with those cases where *formal* disciplinary action is considered necessary.

2 *Company rules*

Offences committed by employees may vary in severity and for this reason the following examples of misconduct have been grouped under two headings, namely Gross Misconduct and Other Misconduct.

2.1. Gross misconduct. Examples of offences (not exhaustive) which *will normally result in summary dismissal* are:

- Gross neglect of duty.
- Grossly offensive behaviour.
- Gross neglect of safety rules.
- Deliberate damage to company assets.
- Incitement or use of physical violence towards anyone at all on company premises or whilst on company business.
- Fraudulent timekeeping.
- False, and misleading statements, e.g.:

    (i) On application for employment or at medical examination.
    (ii) At accident investigation.
    (iii) During employment designed to harm the company and/or other employees.

- Failure to obey instructions given by the company (provided these are in accordance with accepted practices).
- Theft, incitement to steal or deliberately damaging property on the company premises.
- Bringing of firearms and/or misuse of offensive weapons on the company premises.
- Drunkenness during working hours.
- Accepting secret profit or bribe.
- Divulging confidential information.
- Allowing private interest and duty to conflict.
- Misuse of drugs.
- Clocking in or out for another person.
- Sleeping on duty.

2.2. *Other misconduct.* Examples of offences (not exhaustive) which will result in disciplinary action other than summary dismissal are:

- Disregard of hygiene/safety rules of the company.
- Poor timekeeping/attendance.
- Unauthorised absence/non-notification of absence.
- Abuse of company/statutory sick pay schemes.
- Unsatisfactory work performance.
- Offensive behaviour.
- Unauthorised absence from place of work.
- Abuse of flexitime rules.
- General neglect of duties.
- Gambling other than in approved places, i.e. Sports and Social Club.

3 *Procedure for handling disciplinary investigation*

3.1. Employees must understand and conform to both the general standards of behaviour required at work and those specifically relating to their job.

On the occasion when performance falls below the expected level the employee's supervisor/manager must deal with the disciplinary issue promptly, fairly and in a professional manner.

3.2. The type of disciplinary action (informal or formal) will depend upon the gravity of the offence committed and the employee's previous disciplinary conduct. Where possible, a corrective approach should be adopted, to encourage improvement. The only exception being in the case of gross misconduct, when a dismissal without notice will normally apply, following a disciplinary hearing.

3.3. Details of any alleged misconduct should be passed via the immediate senior person on duty (e.g. chargehand) to the supervisor/manager who is responsible for implementing the initial stages of the discipline procedure.

3.4. If the offence warrants more than an informal verbal warning, a formal investigation will be carried out *promptly to establish the facts* before recollections fade. At this stage the Personnel Department must be informed of the alleged offence. The employee concerned will then be advised of the date, time and place of the disciplinary hearing.

3.5. Where the offence cannot be dealt with owing to the absence of the supervisor (i.e. outside normal day work hours) the chargehand should attempt to contact the employee's supervisor or manager. The chargehand will then instruct the employee to report to the supervisor at the earliest convenient time. In the case of alleged gross misconduct the employee will also be instructed to clock off and leave the company premises. Should the final decision be in the employee's favour, he or she will be recompensed for the earnings lost.

3.6. Before any disciplinary hearing, the employee concerned must be given reasonable opportunity to consult his or her employee representative or a fellow employee.

3.7. In the event of suspected gross misconduct or in the absence of a key witness it may be necessary to delay the disciplinary hearing for a short period. In this situation the employee may be suspended for a period of up to three working days, during which time he/she should be available to attend work if required, subject to reasonable notice.

3.8. No formal disciplinary action should be taken without full investigation of the facts and the employee's attendance at a disciplinary hearing. The procedure for conducting disciplinary hearings is as follows:

(a) The meeting should be chaired by the employee's supervisor or manager who possesses the appropriate level of authority in relation to the alleged offence (see section 4.3). A member of the Personnel Department will attend all hearings and will document all further actions.
(b) If it has been impractical for the employee to consult an employee representative or fellow employee prior to the hearing, an employee representative will automatically be requested to attend. The representative will be asked to remain if so desired. Alternatively, if requested, a fellow employee may attend as a witness.
(c) At the start of the hearing the employee must be informed of the complaint and the possible consequences.
(d) The employee should be given the opportunity to explain his or her account of the incident. When new information is presented which is relevant to the case, an adjournment should be considered to allow for consultation or verification of facts.
(e) Except in very straightforward cases, a short adjournment should be held before the employee is informed of the decision. The penalty should be based on the known facts, previous penalties applied in similar cases, the employee's disciplinary record and general conduct, any mitigating circumstances and whether the proposed penalty is reasonable in all circumstances.
(f) After imposing a disciplinary penalty, the employee will be reminded of the right to appeal and the procedure to be followed (see section 5).
(g) Details and duration of any disciplinary action, corrective action required and consequences of further offences or failure to improve will be subsequently given in writing to the employee and a copy placed on the employee's file.
(h) If an employee is dismissed he or she will receive notice or if considered desirable payment in lieu of notice in accordance with the statutory requirements or contract of employment.

An employee dismissed on the grounds of gross misconduct will lose the right to notice or payment in lieu of notice.

4 Penalties

Where the facts of the case, established at a formal disciplinary hearing, appear to call for disciplinary action, the following procedures should be observed according to the type of offence:

4.1. *Penalties:*

Type of offence	Occasion	Penalty
Minor misconduct	First	Formal verbal warning
	Second	Written warning
	Third	Final written warning
	Fourth	Dismissal with notice or pay in lieu of notice
Serious misconduct	First	Final written warning or any lesser penalty as appropriate
Gross misconduct	First	Summary dismissal

Note:

Minor misconduct. Offences of minor nature which should be dealt with under the full disciplinary hearing procedure before dismissal.

Serious misconduct. Offences of a serious nature which require more severe penalties than associated with a minor offence but are not considered to warrant summary dismissal.

Gross misconduct. Offences which require summary dismissal following a disciplinary hearing.

Repeated minor misconduct. Where a disciplinary penalty has recently expired, and the original offence is repeated, it may be considered fair to impose a written or final written warning instead of a verbal warning.

Examples of penalties which may also be added to the above at the discretion of management are:

- Transfer to other work.
- Loss of privilege.
- Loss of company sick pay up to three days per occasion of sickness absence.
- Suspension without pay for up to three working days.
- Reaffirm a previous penalty.
- Demotion in job status and pay.

4.2. *Duration of warnings.* Disciplinary warnings will remain in force for a period of twelve months from the date of the disciplinary decision. The only exception being a final written warning, which will remain in force for two years.

A current disciplinary warning will remain in force irrespective of a previous warning expiring.

4.3. *Authority levels for imposing penalties.* Line supervision and management within the employee's department structure will have the authority to impose penalties outlined in section 4.1 as follows:

(a) Directors have the authority to impose all penalties.
(b) Managers have the authority to impose all penalties, with the exception of dismissing or demoting an immediate subordinate.
(c) Supervisors (including foremen) have the authority to impose verbal and written warnings.

In the absence of an authorised person an agreed deputy will be appointed or, if impractical, the hearing will be delayed until the person returns to work.

5 *Appeals procedure.*

5.1. An employee may appeal against a disciplinary decision at the end of the hearing or within three working days. In the case of suspension, or dismissal, the appeal should be made as soon as possible.

An appeal requested after the disciplinary hearing should be notified to the Personnel Department.

5.2. Appeal hearings will normally be arranged within three working days of the request or at some other time which is mutually agreed. In the case of suspension, or dismissal the appeal hearing will be arranged as soon as possible.

5.3. The appeal hearing will normally be chaired by an executive or company director and every opportunity will be given for the person making the appeal to present his or her case. The employee may be accompanied by an employee representative or fellow employee. A member of the Personnel Department will also be present.

5.4. When an appeal has been requested no action to implement disciplinary penalties will be taken until the appeals procedure is complete. In the event that the penalty is upheld the action indicated will apply from the date originally imposed. The decision will be binding and final.

6 *Special notes*

6.1. Disciplinary action against an employee representative can lead to a serious dispute if it is seen as an attack on the Employee Representative Committee's function. Although normal disciplinary standards will apply to their conduct as employees, no disciplinary action beyond a verbal warning will be taken until the circumstances of the case have been discussed with the chairman of the Employee Representative Committee.

6.2. The disciplinary rules and procedures apply to all permanent full and part-time employees. People undertaking student training, casual holiday work or short-term temporary work will not be covered by these procedures and may be dismissed without formal hearings, subject to legislation, following consultation with the Personnel Department.

6.3. New employees working within a recognised trial period who fail to meet the required standards of work or conduct within that period will have their employment terminated with notice. Wherever possible the employee should be given the opportunity to improve following the receipt of a written warning prior to dismissal.

6.4. Disciplinary action is the responsibility of the management and supervision, and whilst chargehands conduct many supervisory tasks they do not have the authority to impose disciplinary action other than an informal warning.

6.5. When a department manager or director is not available to conduct a disciplinary hearing or appeal the Personnel Executive may nominate a replacement from the same or higher authority level.

Wiggins Teape

1 *Introduction*

It is sometimes necessary for management to discipline employees for contravention of the company's rules or failure to conform to the accepted standards of conduct or job performance. For standards of lateness see para. 8, section 2, Employee Handbook.

In drawing up this agreement the parties recognise that when these occasions arise it is an advantage to all concerned to have a jointly agreed disciplinary procedure which ensures:

1.1. That employees are aware of the standard required and the disciplinary action which may follow if they are ignored.

1.2. The level of management authorised to deal with disciplinary matters and award punishment is fully understood.

1.3. That all formal disciplinary actions are recorded and the employee is given a copy of this record.

1.4. There is a right of appeal against disciplinary action taken and the procedure is understood.

1.5. The employee has the right to be represented at any formal interview or hearing on a disciplinary issue and the employee's representative should be present unless specifically requested otherwise by the employee. (See notes for guidance, para. 2.)

2 Informal warnings/counselling

2.1. The purpose of the disciplinary procedure is to encourage improvement in individual behaviour and work performance and is not to be viewed as merely a means of imposing sanctions. As part of the everyday work relationship the immediate supervisor will counsel employees regarding all aspects of their behaviour and work performance, pointing out when they are not meeting the expected standards, offering guidance for improvement and taking action to assist in this, which may include retraining.

2.2. In such cases, after establishing the facts, the supervisor may feel there is no need to resort to the formal procedure and it is sufficient to talk the matter over with the employee. Such discussion should normally take place out of the hearing of other employees unless it is operationally necessary to take immediate action. There is a clear distinction between an informal oral warning of this kind issued in the context of counselling and a verbal warning issued under Stage 1 of the formal procedure, and the recipient must be left in no doubt as to which type of warning has been issued. Informal oral warnings will not be documented in the employee's personal record, but the supervisor should make a file note (copied to departmental manager) of this for reference purposes.

2.3. Occasions in which informal oral warnings are given must not be allowed to escalate into disciplinary interviews, as this may mean the employee is denied trade union representation. If the informal oral warning fails to resolve the matter, the discussion should be adjourned and the issue pursued under the formal disciplinary procedure. Where the supervisor comes to the conclusion that disciplinary action is not appropriate it should be made quite clear to the employee that no action is to be taken.

3 Formal disciplinary procedure relating to offences not warranting summary dismissal

3.1. *Stage 1. Formal verbal warning.* (a) Where an employee is not meeting an acceptable standard, e.g. on timekeeping, absence or job performance, he/she should be issued with a verbal warning by the employee's immediate superior.

The employee's trade union representative should attend unless specifically requested otherwise by the employee.

(b) They should be told the reason for this warning and the length of time it will remain active, namely three months. This warning should be confirmed in writing and copied to the Personnel Department and the employee's representative.

(c) Failure to achieve and maintain the required standard in the time specified will result in action being taken under Stage 2 of the procedure.

3.2. *Stage 2. First written warning.* (a) This stage will be invoked in cases of failure by an employee to maintain the recognised standard after being issued with a verbal warning. The employee's trade union representative should attend unless specifically requested otherwise by the employee.

(b) The employee will be interviewed by his supervisor/shift manager, who should be accompanied by the employee's foreman or another supervisor/member of management. As a result of this interview, if the supervisor considers it necessary, the employee will be informed that he or she will be receiving a formal first written warning.

(c) This warning will state the nature of the offence, whether they have been previously warned, and the length of time the warning will remain in effect, which should be six months, and the consequences of a further repetition of the offence during this time.

(d) A copy of this warning will be given to the employee's departmental manager, his trade union representative and the Personnel Department.

3.3. *Stage 3. Final written warning.* (a) This stage will be invoked in the following circumstances:

(i) Where there is insufficient improvement following the issue of a first written warning in accordance with Stage 2 of the procedure.
(ii) Where the issue involves serious misconduct it will be dealt with in the first instance at this level.

(b) The employee will be interviewed by the departmental manager, together with the employee's supervisor/shift manager, and a member of the Personnel Department, who will record the meeting.

The employee's trade union representative should attend unless specifically requested otherwise by the employee.

(c) Any warning issued at this stage will remain in effect for twelve months. He must also be advised that failure to meet and maintain the required improvement will result in dismissal.

3.4. *Final stage. Termination of employment.* (a) This stage will be invoked in the following circumstances:

(i) Where there is insufficient improvement following the issue of a final warning.
(ii) Where there is further misconduct following the issue of a final warning

(b) The employee will be called to the disciplinary hearing, which will be held by the departmental manager, together with the employee's supervisor and the Personnel Services Manager. The employee's trade union representative should attend unless specifically requested otherwise by the employee.

(c) Should an employee reach this stage in the procedure he will normally be liable for dismissal, dependent upon the facts of the issue.

4 *Summary dismissal for gross misconduct*

Offences which fall into categories 1-3 in para. 12 are of such a serious nature that they cannot be condoned by allowing the employee to continue his/her normal work and will justify summary dismissal of the employee(s) concerned. Once management has been notified of the offence the following will apply.

(i) The employee(s) concerned will be suspended. This means he will be asked to leave the premises and told to report back at a definite time and date, which should normally be within twenty-four hours of the incident occurring or if the incident occurs at a weekend on the Monday following. This will provide management with an opportunity to investigate the case and ascertain the facts.

(ii) If management finds there is substance in the case the employee(s) will be asked to attend a disciplinary interview.

(iii) If management find against the employee(s) their contract of employment will be terminated by dismissal, summarily without notice. Their pay will cease as of that time and no pay in lieu of notice or holiday pay will be paid.

(iv) If, following the disciplinary interview, it is decided not to proceed, arrangements should be made for the employee to start back at work as soon as is reasonably practicable.

5 *Right of appeal*

An employee may appeal against the decision at any stage of the procedure provided:

5.1. Appeals must be made in writing to the departmental manager within three working days of the decision.

5.2. Appeals at all stages will be heard by the level of management immediately above that previously involved. In the case of dismissals, appeals will be held at an appeal hearing, chaired by the mill manager, who will give his decision within a maximum of five working days of the appeal hearing.

5.3. There shall only be one appeal under this procedure. However, before the issue is referred to the external industry grievance procedure, provision may be made for the matter to be referred to the General Manager.

6 *Flexibility of procedure*

It is recognised that the above procedure is not to be regarded as a dogmatic statement of the steps that must be completed before any disciplinary action can be taken against an individual. The more serious offences will be dealt with by the final steps in the procedure without regard to the preliminary verbal or formal warning.

7 *Suspension without pay*

7.1. It is not normally part of the disciplinary procedure to suspend a person without pay. However, in very exceptional circumstances, and at management discretion, an employee may be suspended without pay following a disciplinary interview, as an alternative to dismissal.

7.2. At the time of suspension, the departmental manager will state the period of suspension, and this will be confirmed in writing. Concurrent with suspension without pay will be a final warning, which will remain in effect for not less than twelve months.

7.3. Where in a particular case the employee was suspended with pay prior to the disciplinary hearing, it shall be open to the parties to agree that this period will be unpaid and will be taken as part, or all, of any period of unpaid suspension. In some cases retrospective payment arrangements will have to be made to effect this agreement.

7.4. The maximum period for suspension without pay is five working days/shifts.

8 Time period for warnings

8.1. Warnings will remain active on an employee's record for the time periods detailed below, these being considered reasonable times for an employee to make and maintain the required standards:

Verbal warning: three months.
First written warning: six months.
Final written warning: twelve months.

8.2. There may be occasions where an employee's conduct is satisfactory throughout the period the warning is in force, only for this to lapse thereafter. Where a pattern emerges, and there is evidence of continual abuse, the employee's overall disciplinary record will be considered in deciding the stage of procedure appropriate and the length of time any warning will remain active. Where this pattern indicates excessive absenteeism, the individual will be withdrawn from the company sick pay scheme.

9 Authority to take disciplinary action

9.1. Foremen are authorised to issue verbal warnings and suspend an employee with pay pending a disciplinary interview.

9.2 Supervisors/shift managers can issue first written warnings and verbal warnings.

9.3. The following are authorised to take all forms of disciplinary action, including dismissal:

General Manager	Mill Accountant
Mill Manager	Production Manager
Deputy Mill Manager	Commercial Manager
Chief Engineer	Personnel Manager
Technical Manager	Quality and Technical Services Manager
Purchasing Manager	

10 Consistency of disciplinary action

The responsibility for discipline is line management's. However, the Personnel Department will be responsible for keeping disciplinary records and for advising line management on the need to maintain a consistent and fair approach. Managers should, therefore, consult the Personnel Department at the earliest stage in all cases relating to possible disciplinary action.

11 Criminal offence

11.1. Where an employee is charged with a criminal offence outside of their employment this will not be treated as an automatic reason for dismissal. The main considerations should be whether the offence is one that makes the individual unsuitable for their type of work or unacceptable to other employees.

11.2. Where a criminal offence is committed during the course of an individual's employment, the matter will firstly be reviewed within the terms of the procedure at a disciplinary hearing.

Management will decide, depending upon the circumstances, whether to involve the legal authorities.

12 *Possible disciplinary actions with regard to certain offences*

Offence

1. Removing or helping another person remove mill property from the mill without authorisation. Removing or helping to remove another employee's or contractor's property.
2. The deliberate damage or destruction of mill property, a fellow employee's property or a contractor's property.
3. The deliberate falsification of documents or records with an intent to defraud the company. This includes the clocking of a fellow employee's clock card where this is done to misrepresent the payment entitlement of that employee.
4. Unauthorised absence from mill grounds during working hours without being clocked out, without authority.
5. Violence or fighting on mill premises, including aggressive behaviour that contributes towards a physical confrontation.
6. Arrival for work or being discovered at work under the influence of alcohol or non-prescribed or illegal drugs.
7. The continued refusal to carry out the legitimate instructions of supervision. Legitimate in this context is defined as instructions that do not contravene mill rules, mill or group health and safety policies, or the customary and formal agreements with trade unions.
8. Disclosure to a third party of confidential company information.
9 Sleeping at work.
10. A deliberate breach of mill/group safety policy.
11. To act in a dangerous manner or carry out a dangerous practice such that the safety of yourself or a fellow employee is put at risk.
12 Smoking outside designated areas.
13 Habitual lateness.
14 Excessive absenteeism.
15 Failure to meet the required standards of performance.
16 Unauthorised distribution of notices.
17 Absence from place of work without permission.
18 Failure to wear protective clothing, safety equipment (e.g. goggles, face mask) or hearing protection.

Guidelines for operating the disciplinary procedure

1 *Establish the facts*

Before considering a matter within the disciplinary procedure it is the responsibility of the management/supervision to establish the facts clearly and have available any documentary evidence that may be relevant. Any witnesses to the incident should be interviewed quickly, before their recollections fade, and statements taken. The manager has to be clear precisely what the complaint/issue is, and he should obtain personal details such as age, length of service, past disciplinary history and current warnings.

Wiggins Teape

Disciplinary procedure – action

Groups	First occasion	Second occasion	Third occasion
1 2 3	Summary dismissal		
4 5 6 7	*Minimum* One day/shift suspension without pay *Maximum* Summary dismissal	Summary dismissal	
8	*Minimum* One day/shift suspension without pay *Maximum* Up to five days' suspension without pay	Termination of employment	
9 10 11	*Minimum* Final written warning *Maximum* Up to five day's suspension without pay.	*Minimum* Up to five days' suspension without pay *Maximum* Termination of employment	
12 13 14 15 16 17 18	*Minimum* Verbal warning *Maximum* Final written warning	*Minimum* First written warning *Maximum* Up to five days' suspension without pay	*Minimum* Final warning *Maximum* Termination of employment

2 *Operating the procedure*

2.1. When the investigations have been completed and if it is decided that the matter should be pursued under the procedure the employee should be asked to attend a disciplinary interview and informed of the complaint. He/she should be told the time, date and place and informed of his right to representation. The manager/supervisor/foreman should arrange for his/her representative to attend, unless specifically requested otherwise by the employee.

2.2. At the disciplinary interview/hearing the facts of the case should be outlined and considered and the employee and his representative should be given the opportunity to give their version of the incident. Each party may question the persons concerned and examine the evidence.

It is important that no disciplinary action is decided until the employee has had this opportunity.

2.3. After general questioning and discussion, summarise the main points concerning the offence, the points raised by the employee and refer to any documents, evidence, etc. Before making the decision an adjournment should be taken so that consideration can be given to the points raised. If, during the interview, facts emerge which require further investigation, adjourn the meeting until another date in order to investigate these. Under normal circumstances the disciplinary interview should be reconvened within forty-eight hours.

2.4. Should, on the facts of the case, it be decided that the individual be issued with a warning under the procedure it is essential that the following be made absolutely clear and communicated to the employee:

- The offence, and where he went wrong.
- The period during which his record will remain under review.
- Any necessary retraining.
- Any subsequent action that will follow if the standards are not met on the misconduct reported.

Warnings should be given in private with the persons identified in the various stages of the procedure present.

2.5. Details of any disciplinary decision should be communicated in writing to the employee, with copies sent to the Personnel Department and their representative.

2.6. Employees with six months' service or more have the right to request a written statement of the reason for dismissal. This statement must be provided by the Personnel Department.

Appendix 3
Sources of information and further reading

General textbooks

ANDERMAN, STEVEN. 1992. *Labour Law*. London: Butterworths.
LEWIS, DAVID. 1990. *Essentials of Employment law*, third edition. London: IPM.
OSMAN, CHRISTOPHER (ed.). 1990. *Butterworths Employment Law Guide*. London: Butterworths.
PITT, GWYNETH. 1992. *Employment Law*. London: Sweet & Maxwell.

Specialist Books

AITKIN, OLGA. 1992. *Contracts*. London: IPM.
DICKENS, LINDA, et al. 1985. *Dismissed*. Oxford: Blackwell.
DRUMMOND, HELGA. 1991. *Managing Difficult Staff*. London: Kogan Page.
EDWARDS, MARTIN. 1991. *Dismissal Law*, second edition. London: Kogan Page.
GREENHAIGH, ROGER. 1992. *Industrial Tribunals*. London: IPM.
INCOMES DATA SERVICES. 1988. *Unfair Dismissal*. London: IDS.

Reference Books

The following works are updated periodically:

Encyclopedia of Labour Relations Law. London: Sweet & Maxwell.
Harvey on Industrial Relations and Employment Law. London: Butterworths.

Journals

Industrial Relations Services publish *Industrial Relations Review and Report and Industrial Relations Legal Information Bulletin*. Incomes Data Services produce *Incomes Data Brief*. These publications are issued twice monthly, focus on current developments in the field and provide explanations and comment.

Bibliography

ADVISORY, CONCILIATION AND ARBITRATION SERVICE, 1990. *Discipline at Work: the ACAS advisory handbook.*
— *Personnel Records.* ACAS Advisory Booklet 3.
— *Absence.* ACAS Advisory Booklet 5.
— *Employee Appraisal.* ACAS Advisory Booklet 11.
— 1990. *Health and Employment.* ACAS Advisory Booklet 15.
BREWSTER, C., and CONNOCK, S. 1980. *Industrial Relations Training for Managers.* London: Kogan Page.
CAMPBELL, D. N., FLEMMING, R. L., and GROTE, R. C. 1985. 'Discipline without punishment at last'. *Harvard Business Review*, July-August, 162-78.
DANIEL, W. W., and MILLWARD, N. 1983. *Workplace Industrial Relations in Britain.* London: Heinemann.
DICKENSON, F. 1988. *Drink and Drugs at Work: the consuming problem.* London: IPM.
EDWARDS, P. K., and SCULLION, H. 1982. *The Social Organisation of Industrial Conflict: control and resistance in the workplace.* Oxford: Blackwell.
EDWARDS, R. K., and WHITSON, C. 1989. *'Industrial discipline, the control of attendance and the subordination of labour: towards integrated theorising'*, Work, Employment and Society, 3 (1), 1-28.
EMPLOYMENT DEPARTMENT. 1989a. *Alcohol in the Workplace: a guide for employers.* ED 1989 (PL880).
— 1992. *Sexual Harassment in the Workplace: a guide for employers.*
EMPLOYMENT DEPARTMENT/HEALTH AND SAFETY EXECUTIVE. 1990. *Aids and the Workplace: a guide for employers.* ED 1990 (PL893).
EVANS, S., GOODMAN, J. F. B., and HARGREAVES, L. 1985. *Unfair Dismissal Law and Employment Practice in the 1980s.* Department of Employment Research Paper 53. London: HMSO.
FLETCHER, C., and WILLIAMS, R. *Performance Appraisal and Career Development.* London: Hutchinson.
GOULDNER, A. 1954. *Wildcat Strike.* New York: Harper.
HEALTH AND SAFETY EXECUTIVE. 1981. *The Problem Drinker at Work: guidance on joint management and trade union co-operation to assist the problem drinker.* London: HMSO.
— 1990. *Drug Abuse at Work: a guide for employers.* HSE (IND(G)91L).
HENRY, S. 1982. *Private Justice: towards integrated theorising in the sociology of law.* London: Routledge.
INDUSTRIAL RELATIONS REVIEW AND REPORT. 1991. 'Discipline at work', 2 August, 7-14.

INSTITUTE OF PERSONNEL MANAGEMENT. 1979. *Disciplinary Procedures and Practice*. London: IPM.
— 1992. *Sexual Harassment in the Workplace: a review of the literatue and current developments*. London: IPM.
JENKIN, M. 1987. *Smoking Policies at Work*. London: Health Education Authority.
MARCHINGTON, M., and PARKER, P. 1990. *Changing Patterns of Employee Relations*. Brighton: Harvester.
MILLWARD, N., and STEVENS, M. 1986. *British Workplace Industrial Relations, 1980-84*. Aldershot: Gower.
RUBENSTEIN, M. 1990. *Preventing and Remedying Sexual Harassment: a resource manual*. London: Industrial Relations Services.
SALAMON, M. 1987. *Industrial Relations Theory and Practice*. Hemel Hempstead: Prentice-Hall.
TERRY, M. 1977. '*The inevitable growth of informality*'. British Journal of Industrial Relations, 15, 76-90.
UPTON, R. 1987. 'What makes a disciplinary procedure appealing?'. *Personnel Management*, December, 46-9.

List of cases

Abernethy v. *Mott Hay & Anderson* [1974] IRLR 213   123
Alidair v. *Taylor* [1978] IRLR 445   89, 90
Auguste Noel v. *Curtis* [1990] IRLR 326   71
Bliss v. *South East Thames Regional Health Authority* [1985] IRLR 308   107, 123
Boots v. *Lees* [1986] IRLR 485   118
Bouchaala v. *Trust House Forte* [1980] IRLR 382   109
Boychuk v. *Symons* [1977] IRLR 395   109
Bracebridge Engineering v. *Darby* [1990] IRLR 3   108
Braund v. *Murray* [1991] IRLR 100   124
British Home Stores v. *Burchell* [1978] IRLR 379   79
British Leyland v. *Swift* [1981] IRLR 91   123
W. Brooks & Son v. *Skinner* [1984] IRLR 379   21
Clark v. *Civil Aviation Authority* [1991] 412   66
Colwyn Borough Council v. *Dutton* [1980] IRLR 420   124
Courage v. *Keys* [1986] IRLR 427   124
Coward v. *John Menzies* [1977] IRLR 428   91, 108
Dairy Products v. *Beverstock* [1981] IRLR 265   97, 108
Dietman v. *London Borough of Brent* [1988] IRLR 299   111, 123
Dobie v. *Burns* [1984] IRLR 329   109
East Lindsey District Council v. *Daubney* [1977] ICR 566   82
Fitzpatrick v. *British Rail* [1991] IRLR 376   123
Freemans v. *Flynn* [1984] IRLR 486   124
Fyfe v. *Scientific Furnishings* [1989] IRLR 331   124
Gardner v. *Beresford* [1978] IRLR 63   80
Glitz v. *Watford Electrical Company* [1979] IRLR 89   91, 108
Hardwick v. *Leeds Area Health Authority* [1975] IRLR 319   107
Harris v. *Courage* [1982] IRLR 509   79
Hobson v. *GEC* [1985] IRLR ICR 777   107
Hollister v. *National Farmers Union* [1979] IRLR 238   108, 109
Hutchinson v. *Enfield Rolling Mills* [1981] IRLR 318   108
Igbo v. *Johnson Matthey* [1986] IRLR 215   108, 114
Kraft Foods v. *Fox* [1979] IRLR 431   124
Laughton v. *Bapp* [1986] IRLR 245   102
Laws Stores v. *Oliphant* [1978] IRLR 251   92, 108
Leonard v. *Fergus & Haynes* [1979] IRLR 235   107
Charles Letts v. *Howard* [1976] IRLR 248   108
Ladbroke Racing v. *Arnott* [1983] IRLR 154   25
Linfood Cash and Carry v. *Thomson* [1989] IRLR 235   79
London Transport Executive v. *Clarke* [1981] IRLR 166   108, 123
Lucas Services v. *Carey* (EAT 917/83)   79

List of cases 197

Lynock v. *Cereal Packaging* [1988] IRLR 510   84
Marley Homecare v. *Dutton* [1981] IRLR 380   65
Marshall v. *Sloan & Co.* [1981] IRLR 264   108
Meyer Dunmore International v. *Rogers* [1978] 167   17
Millbrook Furnishing v. *McIntosh* [1981] IRLR 309   91
Moore v. *C & A Modes* [1981] IRLR 71   105
Monie v. *Coral Racing* [1980] IRLR 464   76
Moyes v. *Hylton Castle Working Men's Club* [1986] IRLR 482   67
Murco Petroleum v. *Forge* [1987] IRLR 50   80
Murphy v. *Epson College* [1984] IRLR 271   109
Nelson v. *BBC* (No. 2) [1979] IRLR 304   124
Norfolk County Council v. *Bernard* [1979] IRLR 220   108
Nova Plastics v. *Froggatt* [1982] IRLR 146   109
P. v. *Nottinghamshire County Council* [1992] IRLR 362   123
Parr v. *Whitbread* [1990] IRLR 34   80
C. A. Parsons & Co. v. *McLoughlin* [1978] IRLR 65   16, 98
Piggott v. *Jackson* [1991] IRLR 309   108
Polkey v. *Dayton Services* [1987] IRLR 503   61, 123
Proctor v. *British Gypsum* [1992] IRLR 7   79
R. v. *Secretary of State* ex parts Equal Opportunities Commission [1991] IRLR 493   123
Richmond Precision v. *Pearce* [1985] IRLR 179   109
Robb v. *London Borough of Hammersmith and Fulham* [1991] IRLR 72   111
Rowe v. *Radio Rentals* [1982] IRLR 187   60
RS Components v. *Irwin* [1973] IRLR 239   101
Savage v. *Sainsbury* [1980] IRLR 119   80
Scottish Special Housing v. *Cooke* [1979] IRLR 264   79
Securicor v. *Smith* [1989] IRLR 356   80
Showboat Entertainments v. *Owens* [1984] IRLR 7   23
Slaughter v. *Brewer* [1990] IRLR 420   124
Sovereign House v. *Savage* [1989] IRLR 115   123
Spencer v. *Paragon* [1976] IRLR 373   107
Spink v. *Express Foods* [1990] IRLR 320   65
Staffordshire County Council v. *Donovan* [1981] IRLR 108   123
Sutcliffe v. *Pinney* [1977] IRLR 349   109
Sutton & Gates v. *Boxall* [1976] IRLR 486   108
Taylor v. *Parsons Peebles* {1981] IRLR 119   18, 98
Tele-trading v. *Jenkins* [1990] IRLR 430   124
Torr v. *British Rail* [1977] IRLR 185   93
Tower Hamlets Health Authority v. *Anthony* [1989] IRLR 394   72
Trico-Folberth v. *Devonshire* [1989] IRLR 397   120
Turner v. *Vestric* [1981] IRLR 23   109
UCATT v. *Brain* [1980] IRLR 357   92
Ulsterbus v. *Henderson* [1989] IRLR 251   79
Walton v. *TAC* [1981] IRLR 357   79, 108
Weddell v. *Tepper* [1980] IRLR 96   79
West Midlands Co-operative Society v. *Tipton* [1986] IRLR 112   60, 77
Whitbread v. *Mills* [1988] IRLR 501   80
White v. *London Transport Executive* [1981] IRLR 261   88

List of statutes and regulations

Access to Medical Reports Act 1988   82
Construction (Head Protection) Regulations 1989   5
Continental Shelf Act 1964   113
Courts and Legal Services Act 1990   123
Employers' Health and Safety Policy (Exception) Regulations 1985   25
Employment Protection (Consolidation) Act 1978   19, 20, 24, 56, 73, 80, 87, 91, 106, 108, 109, 112, 113, 123, 124
Fair Employment Act 1976   117
Health and Safety at Work, etc., Act 1974   20, 24, 94, 95
Misuse of Drugs Act 1971   97
Race Relations Act 1976   5, 23, 99, 117
Rehabilitation of Offenders Act 1974   93
Safety Representatives and Safety Committee Regulations 1977   95
Sex Discrimination Act 1975   5, 99, 117
Trade Union and Labour Relations (Consolidation) Act 1992   116
Wages Act 1986   16, 72

Index

Absenteeism
   extended leave and 86–7
   long-term through ill health 81–3
   medical investigation of 82
   persistent short-term 83–4
   unauthorised 86
Alcohol, *see* Drinking
Appeals
   generally 48–9
   grounds for 75
   hearings 76
   unfair dismissal and 77
   warnings and 71
Appearance, personal 107
Arbitration 49–52

Brighton Borough Council
   disciplinary procedure 142–6
Brush Electrical Systems
   disciplinary procedure 146–52
   disciplinary rules 125–30

Cadbury Bourneville
   disciplinary procedure 152–5
   disciplinary rules 130–36
   procedure extract 38–9
Compensation, unfair dismissal and 119–21
Competition, with the employer 101–2
Conciliation 49–52
   unfair dismissal claims and 121–3
Confidence, breach of 102
Consultation, with workforce 10–13, 54–6

Convictions 93
Co-operative Insurance Society
   disciplinary procedure 155–62
   incapability guidelines 31
County Nat West
   disciplinary procedure 162–8
   procedure extracts 45, 50

Damages, for breach of contract 110–12
Deductions, from wages 72
Demotion 73
Disabled persons 83
Disciplinary decisions, communication of 78
Disciplinary hearings
   adjournment of 68–9
   attendance at 69
   criminal offences and 62, 68
   delay in holding 65
   fairness of 67
   investigatory suspensions and 63
   notification of 64
   preparation for 64
   representation at 65
   timing of 66
   witnesses at 64
   witness statements and 67
Disciplinary penalties 69
Disciplinary procedures
   ACAS model 35–7
   communication of 18–22, 56–8
   counselling and 42–3
   coverage of 27–9
   drafting 54–6

employee representation in 52–4
implementation of 56–8
management responsibilities under 43–8
organisational level and 27–8
penalties and offences under 34–42
right of appeal in 48–9
subject matter of 29–34
third-party intervention in 49–52
workers covered by 28–9
Disciplinary rules
communication of 19–22
drafting 10–13
implementation of 18–23
lawfulness of 5
monitoring 23
offences and penalties 13–18
subject matter 6–10
Discrimination, in rules and procedures 5, 21, 23, 29, 32–4
Dishonesty 92–4
Disloyalty 100–102
Dismissal
date of 77
group 75
meaning of 114–5
reasons for 115–7
unfair, *see* Unfair dismissal
with notice 73
without notice 74
Disobedience 90–92
Drinking, problems with 7, 29–30, 96–7
Drugs, abuse of 29–30, 97–8

Employee representation 52–4

Fidelity, duty of 100
Fighting 98–9
Fines 15–16, 40–41
Frustration, of contract 83

GEC Measurements
disciplinary procedure 169–72
procedure extract 14
Grievance procedures 51–2

Handbooks 21–22, 56
Harassment sexual and racial 29–34, 56, 99–100
Health and safety policies 20
HIV/AIDS 84–6
Hygiene, personal 107

IBC Vehicles
disciplinary procedure 172–5
procedure extract 11–12
Ill-health 29–31
absenteeism and 81–4
Imprisonment 106
Injunctions 110–11
Investigations, preliminary 62

Job descriptions 8–11
Joint disciplinary bodies 53–4
Joint working parties 10, 55

Language
abusive 94
requirements 5
Leicester City Council: extract from harassment and discrimination procedure 32

Management responsibilities 23, 43–8
Media activity 105
Mediation 49–52
Misconduct
gross 16–18, 38, 74
outside employment 104–5
Mobility clauses 5
Monitoring disciplinary practices 23, 44, 56

Non-punitive discipline 43

Index

Offences, outside employment 105
Oxford City Council
 disciplinary rules 139–41

Pay, withholding of 72
Penalties, *see* Disciplinary rules, Disciplinary procedures
Peradin
 disciplinary procedure 175–8
Performance, poor 29–31, 87–90
Personnel departments, role of 44
Pressure
 from third parties 104
 from colleagues 104
Probationary periods 40, 88

Re-engagement 118
Reinstatement 118
Reorganisation
 of business 103
Restraint clauses 100
Royal Ordnance
 disciplinary procedure 178–80
Records, importance of 78

Shift workers 45–8
Short-service employees 39–40, 112
Smoking 94–6
Statement of particulars of employment 20–21, 56
Suspension
 investigatory 41, 63
 with and without pay 14–16, 41, 72–3

Third-party intervention 49–52
Timekeeping 90
Trade union activities, dismissal for 116
Trade union officials, action against 53
Trade unions, discipline and 10–11, 21, 52–4, 58
Training 23, 57–8
Transfers 15, 73

Unfair dismissal
 exclusions and qualifications 112–14
 meaning of dismissal 114–15
 remedies 117–21
 statistics 2

Violence, *see* Fighting

Warnings 14, 34–8, 70–72, 89–90
Weidmuller (Kipton Products) Ltd
 disciplinary procedure 180–85
 procedure extract 17
Wiggins Teape
 disciplinary procedure 185–92
 procedure extract 18
William Grant and Sons
 disciplinary rules 136–9

Young workers 21, 40